Harvard Studies in Business History XXIX

Edited by Alfred D. Chandler, Jr.
Isidor Straus Professor of Business History
Graduate School of Business Administration
George F. Baker Foundation
Harvard University

British Mercantile Houses in Buenos Aires • 1810-1880

VERA BLINN REBER

Harvard University Press
Cambridge, Massachusetts
and London, England   1979

Library of Congress Cataloging in Publication Data

Reber, Vera Blinn, 1941-
British mercantile houses in Buenos Aires, 1810-1880.

(Harvard studies in business history; 29)
Bibliography: p.
Includes index.
1. Great Britain—Commerce—Argentine Republic—History.
2. Argentine Republic—Commerce—Great Britain—History.
3. Mercantile system—Argentine Republic—History.
4. Merchants—Argentine Republic—History.   5. Merchants
—Great Britain—History.   I. Title.   II. Series.
HF3508.A66R4   382'.0941'082   78-15743
ISBN 0-674-08245-1

For those who taught me

Editor's Introduction

PROFESSOR REBER's study provides the first detailed analysis of the operations, activities, and economic functions of the private (nonchartered) mercantile house. One of the most significant instruments of commercial and early industrial capitalism, it was most widely used by the British, and most effectively by them in less industrially advanced areas such as Latin America. Professor Reber tells the collective story of these enterprises at one major commercial center during the period of their greatest influence, and she does so with greater accuracy and more careful analysis than one finds in other existing histories. Unlike other writers on the general role of merchants in underdeveloped areas, Professor Reber describes and explains precisely how these enterprises carried on their business and how their activities changed over time. In addition, she places these firms solidly in their larger economic, political, and social environment. Finally, she explains their impact on the economic development of the region in which they operated.

In describing the operations of the British mercantile houses, Reber carefully delineates their basic business methods—the use of the partnership form, the nature of contracts, their internal organization, their accounting practices, types of services rendered, methods of buying and selling, relations with shippers, and their role as correspondents for other enterprises. She provides valuable new materials on financing and on the sources of short- and long-term credit. Particularly useful is her discussion of how goods were obtained in Britain and then sold and distributed in Argentina and nearby regions, and how local goods—hides, foodstuffs, and other materials—were obtained in Argentina, shipped, and sold in Britain. Professor Reber also analyzes the nature of competition and cooperation: competition not only among the British houses but among the houses of Great Britain and those of other nations, and cooperation in the form of associations, information-gathering agencies, and social contacts. Such analyses permit her to evaluate the factors that brought success or failure to these businessmen. Most important of all, the author shows how these business practices and procedures changed as the steamship, cable, and railroad transformed transportation and communication.

Before describing and analyzing the policies and methods of the import-export houses, Reber outlines carefully the changing political and business milieu in which they operated. She shows how immigration and improved transportation altered markets. She reviews the risks and difficulties raised by political instability, internal domestic conflict, external wars and blockades, and droughts, epidemics, and other acts of nature. The impact of business cycles and shifting governmental fiscal and monetary policies including taxation and tariffs are well presented.

The final chapters provide, first, a balanced evaluation of the role of the British mercantile house in the growth of the economy of Argentina and on its structural transformation from a colonial subsistence to a commercial exporting one. Reber is particularly effective explaining the role of the houses in capital formation. Second, these chapters analyze the British houses as entrepreneurial innovators, comparing their achievements and activities with those of local merchants and merchants of other nations.

All this makes for first-rate business history. The study looks at a business institution from the inside, focuses on the changing ways in which it operated, indicates how the external environment affected the evolution of practices and procedures, and evaluates its performance in terms of its impact on the larger economy and society.

Acknowledgments

I DEEPLY appreciate the assistance of the Henry L. and Grace Doherty Charitable Foundation, which financed the year's travel in Argentina that encouraged research for this book. A Fulbright-Hays Grant permitted me to study in the United Kingdom for five months, and a Ford Foundation Grant through the University of Wisconsin generously supported the writing of the first drafts of the manuscript as well as travel to Ottawa to examine the Baring Brothers papers at the Canadian Public Archives.

Without the generous cooperation of the staffs of libraries and archives in Argentina, the United Kingdom, Canada, and the United States, it would have been impossible to understand the operation of British mercantile houses in Buenos Aires. My appreciation is extended to the following Argentine institutions: the Archivo General de la Nación, Archivo Histórico de la Provincia de Buenos Aires, Archivo Histórico de la Municipalidad de Buenos Aires, Archivo Público de Geodesía de la Provincia de Buenos Aires, Archivo de Tribunales de la Plata, Archivo y Museo Histórico del Banco de la Provincia de Buenos Aires, Biblioteca del Congreso, Biblioteca de Instituto Torcuato di Tella, Museo y Archivo de General Mitre, and the archives of St. John's Pro-Cathedral. I gratefully acknowledge the assistance of the following United Kingdom libraries and archives: the Public Record Office; University College, London, which generously allowed access to the Frederick Huth and Company papers and the London and River Plate Bank papers; the John Rylands University Library of Manchester, which holds the Hodgson papers; the Baring Brothers archives; the Bank of England Record Office; the H.M. Customs and Excise Library; the Dorset Record Office; the Guild Hall Library; the Kleinwort and Benson Ltd. archives; the Manchester Central Reference Library; the John Rylands Library; the General

Post Office archives; the Probate Registry; and the Sun Alliance and London Insurance Group archives. The Canadian Public Archives and the Library of Congress both provided useful facilities. My thanks are also due to the staffs of libraries at the University of Wisconsin and Shippensburg State College.

The Centro de Investigaciones Sociales of the Institute Trocuato di Tella provided me with an affiliation in 1968. Pedro D. Conno and Alberto S. J. de Paula of the Archivo y Museo Histórico del Banco de la Provincia de Buenos Aires kindly compiled for me a list of shareholders of the Western Railroad. T. L. Ingram, Archivist of Baring Brothers, encouraged my research. Scott Bruntjen, Signe Kelker, and Barbara Taylor of Shippensburg State College Library offered invaluable assistance in the verification of facts.

I am also indebted to many people who allowed me to examine private papers in their possession. In Argentina Señora Avela Grondoña permitted access to the Gowland papers, Señora Justa Dose de Zemborain allowed me to use the Armstrong collection, Clement Gibson made available the Gibson papers, Alberto Casares Lumb shared his family papers, and John Lough lent me the Krabbé and Williamson papers. In the United Kingdom I am indebted to Hugh MacIntyre, who allowed examination of the Wright papers, and particularly to Mr. and Mrs. A. D. MacIntyre, who brought the papers from Scotland and kindly entertained me in their home in Birkenhead.

I owe a special word of thanks to Señora Fritz Laufer, who made sure that I saw all sides of Buenos Aires life and accompanied me on many interesting outings. Ernest C. Warr, Secretary of the British Chamber of Commerce, gave me the necessary introductions to the British community and showed a lively interest in my research. Horacio Juan Cuccorese of the University of La Plata advised me on research concerning railroads. José María Mariluz Urquijo and his wife, serving as my unofficial advisers in Buenos Aires, lent me needed books, asked penetrating questions, continually emphasized the importance of archival research, and graciously read and criticized a draft of the manuscript.

My time in the United Kingdom was made convenient and enjoyable by a bedsitter in the flat of the late Pat Simpson. Colin Lewis shared his research on British railways in Argentina. D. C. M. Platt discussed his perspective of the British in Argentina and introduced me to Cambridge. Ezequiel Gallo, an Argentine lecturer at Oxford who now is with the Di Tella Institute of Argentina, shared his research, and R. A. Humphreys showed me various British archives. A. B. Smith taught me much about British business practices and behavior overseas, saw that I had a proper introduction to British pubs, and aided me through many drafts of the manuscript.

I am deeply indebted to William P. Glade, who encouraged the choice of my research topic and read early drafts of the manuscript; to Thomas Skidmore, who taught me much about economic history; to James Scobie, who made constructive criticism; and to John L. Phelan, who supervised my original dissertation, protected me from my critics, and advocated experimentation. I gratefully acknowledge the help of my colleagues and friends Phyllis Erwin, Allen Howard, Mary Karasch, Jay Lehnertz, Charles Loucks, and John Offner, who read the roughest drafts, listened to half-formed ideas, challenged my interpretations, and were my harshest critics and strongest supporters. My appreciation is also extended to Nancy M. Werner, Susan C. Brown, and Shirley Mellinger for conscientiously reading and typing drafts of the manuscript. To my parents I am grateful for understanding all the trials of teaching and research and for being my most devoted teachers and persistent supporters.

V. B. R.

Shippensburg, Pennsylvania
May 1978

Contents

TABLES

FIGURES

British Mercantile Houses
in Buenos Aires • 1810-1880

1.

A Perspective

As PRIVATELY financed commercial enterprises dealing in the import and export of goods, British mercantile houses helped to shape the pattern of nineteenth-century international trade. Seeking their own profits in competition with Latin American, North American, French, Spanish, and other European entrepreneurs, British merchants in areas such as Argentina packed, shipped, financed, and marketed goods and produce in response to both European demand for raw materials and the competitive production of British industry. The rapidly expanding demand for raw materials gave primary producing countries a competitive trading advantage that increased their real income; at the same time, the British import-export houses encouraged growth in peripheral areas of the world such as Argentina by enlarging the market for Argentine produce and encouraging the investment of idle domestic resources in the creation of basic services. Thus, British mercantile houses in Buenos Aires served the interests of individual entrepreneurs, those of Argentina, and the needs of Europe, creating new opportunities for capital and labor and integrating the nation into the world economy.

Even before the nineteenth century, British merchants operated successfully in South America as merchant adventurers. Although Spain sought to exclude foreigners from South America and to regulate trade at Seville and Cádiz through merchant guilds under the supervision of the Casa de Contratación, a government agency established in 1503, Spain's dependence upon British goods made control difficult, and a small volume of legitimate direct foreign trade was permitted. As early as the sixteenth century, British merchants familiarized themselves with the South American environment while evading Spanish law, participating in contraband trade, and exploiting loopholes in Anglo-Spanish treaties. Foreign merchants who resided in Seville and Cádiz arranged the reex-

1

port of their goods to the New World. English, French, and Dutch traders formed house partnerships with Spanish merchants who could then buy goods directly and more cheaply from foreign manufacturers. At other times Spanish mercantile firms became fronts for foreign firms. By the seventeenth century foreigners controlled as much as five-sixths of the total commerce of South America.[1]

Even in the core areas of Peru and Mexico, Spain experienced severe difficulties in enforcing its commercial control. In peripheral regions such as the Río de la Plata, restriction never proved effective. As early as the 1620s Buenos Aires depended upon the contraband imports and the export of the products from an expanding livestock industry. British evasion of the Spanish monopoly became systematized when the commercial treaties between Great Britain and Portugal in 1654 and 1661 allowed Brazil to import British goods through Lisbon. Informally, Brazil became the entrepôt for the Río de la Plata region and made a mockery of Spanish regulations.

In 1713 the governments of England and Spain recognized British commercial interest in the Río de la Plata in the Treaty of Utrecht, which ended the War of Spanish Succession. This treaty granted British merchants the privilege of operating the slave trade for thirty years in South America, and it gave them an opportunity to place agents in many ports under the pretext of regulating the slave traffic. Later the British merchants received permission to import clothes for the slaves and saw the chance for further infringement upon the Spanish monopoly. By 1778 the Spanish government recognized commercial reality by authorizing the Río de la Plata area to trade directly with Spain and her American colonies. Although foreigners were still excluded from trade and consignments had to be shipped in Spanish vessels officered and largely manned by Spaniards, the domination of British goods in the Spanish market opened up further opportunities for British merchants. Even these restrictions collapsed in 1797 when a Royal Order authorized trade between neutrals and ports in Latin America, because the Spanish merchant navy, faced by a war with Great Britain, could not operate securely. British merchants who resided in Spain and had developed a market for their goods in South America were thus well prepared to transfer their business houses to the New World when opportunities became available.

The British naval invasion of the Río de la Plata region on June 8, 1806, under Commodore Sir Home Popham and a disastrous second assault on Buenos Aires, July 5, 1807, under Major General Whitelocke marked a new relationship between Argentina and the United Kingdom. However, neither invasion represented the beginning of British mercantile opportunities in Argentina nor the dawn of Anglo-Argentine relations. Popham's invasion was based on commercial interests that led him to take the initiative without official instructions from the British government. In Buenos Aires, situated sixty to seventy sailing days from the important trading countries, Popham saw an excellent market for British goods as well as a source of hides, tallow, bullion, flour, meat, wood, and hemp. The London merchants encouraged the invasion by leading Popham to believe that he could easily take and hold Buenos Aires. During the short time Popham occupied the city he promoted a trade policy that benefited British commerce, and on his return to London the merchants presented him with a jeweled sword for his efforts.[2]

The surrender of the British forces in Buenos Aires on August 12, 1806, encouraged a second British invasion the next year which brought the death, capture, or injury of over one-fourth of the 12,000 British troops. This disaster quickly led to a treaty between Major General Whitelocke and Viceroy Santiago de Liniers on July 7, 1807, in which the British evacuated the Río de la Plata region in return for the release of British prisoners. Thereafter, with the possible exception of the Anglo-French blockade of 1845-1848, the United Kingdom sought to extend influence in South America through trade and investment rather than by conquest. For the Argentines, British control in the area did not offer Buenos Aires commercial freedom but merely a larger market and closer connections with London. After the expulsion of the invaders a local government formed under Liniers adopted a liberal commercial policy that permitted the British and other foreign vessels to trade in Buenos Aires. However, when Baltasar Hidalgo de Cisneros, the new viceroy, arrived from Spain, he reinforced Spanish power, at first with leniency and then with toughness. The authorities adopted a resolution in November 1809 supporting free trade, although they disallowed the commercial activities of British merchants. Britons were forbidden to acquire property, to establish business enterprises, and to sell their cargoes in the open market because internal trade was reserved for Spaniards. In December 1809 Viceroy Cisneros ordered the British to leave Buenos Aires, to the delight of the old Spanish merchants, who loaned one million Spanish gold pesos to the government as an inducement for the continued closure of the port.[3]

Although the British were unsuccessful in their efforts to conquer and control the Río de la Plata, the Popham invasion represented the end of an era. The Spanish trade monopoly was completely broken and Spanish authority shattered. The successful expulsion of the British troops in 1807 gave the necessary faith and political strength to the Argentines to dismiss Cisneros in 1810 when he reimposed the tight trade restrictions of the Spanish Empire. Once the Spanish monopoly was broken and independence was firmly established, trade restrictions could no longer be enforced because Britain provided one of the principal channels by which the produce of Argentina flowed onto the world market. Taxes on British trade provided the chief source of revenue for the state, and loans from British merchants helped finance the operations of the government.

WITH THE independence of Argentina, British import-export houses became the means of organizing the trade of Buenos Aires. Discernible as early as the fourteenth century in Europe and the sixteenth century in Latin America, mercantile houses obtained worldwide influence in the nineteenth century at the expense of merchant adventurers, chartered companies, and merchant banks. Under the stimuli of increasing industrial production, rising demand for raw materials, and an absence of heavily capitalized institutions willing to risk their future in remote overseas territories, the multifunctional and flexible organization of mercantile houses served merchant interests well. Functioning as banking institutions, import-export houses elaborated the financial infrastructure by extending credit to governments and investing in agriculture, mining, railroads, shipping, and industrial enterprises while continuing to finance the marketing of goods and produce.

Although merchant adventurers operated in Buenos Aires in the early part of the century, they soon faced difficulty in competing with merchant houses. Trading on a free-lance basis, merchant adventurers failed to establish formal business premises, which left them vulnerable to economic instability and political pressures. Investing in a cargo of goods, they freighted wares to other parts of the world for sale or barter. Rather than establish a house of trade, merchant adventurers would simply risk profits in another cargo, possibly for another destination.[4] In contrast, import-export businesses maintained premises in such places as Buenos Aires, where British merchants participated in the interior, coastal, and overseas trades, not as transients seeking a quick profit but as solid members of the commercial community able to evaluate the political and economic environment.

Import-export houses also differed from chartered companies, which were monopolistic trading enterprises with political obligations. Chartered companies were developed so that a nation might control a certain area and regulate its external trade. Because of the close relationship with the government provided in their charters, these monopolistic companies represented a government's political interests and served the cause of national economic expansion until the United Kingdom initiated a worldwide pattern of free trade. The imperialistic base of chartered companies made them an outdated institution in independent Argentina.[5]

In the nineteenth century, in Argentina as in Europe, merchant banks represented an alternative organization of trade. They carried on many of the same functions as mercantile houses, although they were more heavily capitalized and offered larger and more extensive financial services. Since mercantile houses also dealt in bills of exchange, a draft could be signed by a drawer requesting a drawee to make a payment according to specific terms and occasionally in securities. Neither the acceptance business nor the marketing of bonds was a distinguishing mark of the merchant banker. However, the greater financial resources of merchant banks permitted them to extend larger amounts of credit to mercantile houses, governments, and other businesses. Frederick Huth and Company and Baring Brothers, merchant banks in the South American trade, operated in a manner that was similar to mercantile houses throughout the nineteenth century. During the 1880s Baring Brothers, who considered themselves both financiers and merchants, even operated their own ships with captains under their instructions. But by 1880, when faced with increasing specialization in the industrialized nations, most merchant banks concentrated upon the acceptance of bills of exchange and the negotiation of bonds and securities. Mercantile houses then focused upon the import and export of goods and produce. Anglo-Argentine merchants failed to operate merchant banks extensively in Buenos Aires before 1880, probably because they did not possess the needed capital.[6]

From the perspective of British merchants in Argentina, 1810 to 1880 represented a unified and a distinct era. Political instability, denoted by frequent changes of government, foreign and civil war, and foreign blockades of the port of Buenos Aires, provided merchants with constant risks as well as opportunities. Capital investment in Argentina remained small. The basic economic infrastructure, comprising those key services which are necessary to the commodity-producing sectors of the economy such as banking and transportation, was still in its infancy. Before the extensive direct British investments in joint stock companies in the 1880s, foreign trade, conducted by import-export houses particularly with the United Kingdom, provided the essential link between government finance and government policy.

From the perspective of Argentine history, 1810 to 1880 represents an era when government was laying the foundation of internal development. May 25, 1810, traditionally denotes the date of Argentine independence from Spain and indicates the dividing line between the colonial and national periods. Although 1880 less clearly marks a major political event, it properly delineates the consolidation of the national state of Argentina and thereby signifies the profound changes in political, social, and economic development that ushered in a new era. In 1880 the dispute over the location of the federal capital ended in the agreement that Buenos Aires should become the seat of government, while the province of Buenos Aires would be administered from a center at La Plata. During the previous year the government extended its administrative control over the frontier by a series of military campaigns. In 1881 the legislature defined a central monetary system that showed the new-found self-confidence of the national government by replacing the diverse provincial currencies still circulating with a unified bimetallic standard. This change proved a stimulus to foreign investment by joint stock companies because it gave for the first time a common standard of exchange between Buenos Aires and the interior.

BETWEEN 1810 and 1880 Buenos Aires provided opportunities well suited to the simple organization and limited capital of mercantile houses. But by 1880 the chartered company, a later survivor of mercantilist organization, and the mercantile house, an early embodiment of free trade and unrestrained capitalism, were both losing their power. The Great Depression, which hit Great Britain between 1873 and 1896, led to worldwide economies of scale that ended the influence of both the chartered companies and the mercantile houses.[7] Changing political circumstances following the economic development of the United States and industrial expansion in France and Germany encouraged the United Kingdom government to usurp the political authority of its chartered companies, which thereby lost trading privileges. Mercantile houses concentrated their interests in order to cope with new forms of government restrictions, to exploit the economies of scale in the United Kingdom industries which demanded more specialized services, and to deal with more centralized markets. By 1880 railroads, large retailers, and local industries imported and exported goods directly from Europe. Although business continued to be done directly by draft on the importer, shippers or bankers increasingly financed trade by credit in Europe and the United States. As a result, some mercantile houses concentrated on their financial services and became merchant banks while others specialized in either import or export trade or else became involved in internal activities. By 1880 only a few import-export merchants still traded in all types of goods and produce, having not yet adjusted to the new internal and external conditions.

From 1810 to 1880 import-export trade promoted Argentine economic growth and development. Growth is indicated by the fact that the total values of goods and services produced within Argentina increased substantially.[8] Development took place in the sense that there was a structural transformation of the political, economic, and social systems from those of a colonial subsistence society to those of a major commercial exporting nation. This change can be observed in the employment of hidden and badly used resources, in the ability of the economy to establish self-sustained growth, in the capacity of the society to adapt, and in the application of innovations affected in a large part by the import-export trade.

The British import-export houses stimulated the kind of behavior that led to economic growth by their support of laissez-faire policies, their extension of distribution services, their awareness of and ability to capitalize on economic opportunities, and their profit-oriented attitudes. The minimal profits of the import-export trade initially financed land development, mining, railroads, and meat packing and served as a catalytic agent in attracting larger amounts of capital at the end of the nineteenth century. Trade directed by import-export merchants provided the means of transmitting economic growth from Europe to the outlying world areas. British merchants in Argentina promoted not only economic growth but also economic development through investments in banking and railroads, which aided in the transformation of the economic structures. They promoted better utilization of resources through the financing of land development, and they encouraged innovation through their adaptations to the changing nature of trade. Further, structural modifications promoted by the import-export trade went beyond economic change. The growth of agriculture, commerce, and processing, financed in part by British merchants, created new labor demands that encouraged massive immigration from Europe at the end of the nineteenth century. Government policies built upon dependence on trade led to the growth of both an urban working class and a middle class large enough to further stimulate trade by its size and demands.

The British merchants represented one of the motivating forces in the growth of Argentina. They were innovators who introduced new services and superior products at low cost. Their limited capital and technology allowed for the opening of new markets and the application of revised sales methods. The innovations of British merchants were often most apparent in the adaptation of known commercial methods to the Argentine political and economic environment. As risk takers, they anticipated the demand for future goods and services and they bore the losses of miscalculation. Risks became most apparent in banking and railroad construction and in speculation—the practice of buying commodities or foreign exchange at one time to sell at a later date in the hope of taking advantage of the price changes during the interval.

It must be stated that the economic growth in the export sector of the economy does not necessarily lead to growth in other sectors of the economy. Nor does the growth of an extractive system based on the export of primary products necessarily lead to structural changes in the system and to development. Actions taken to benefit a small minority are often detrimental to national development. Profits gained by a commercial elite rarely provide dividends for the mass of the population. The interactions among groups within a society and actions taken in response to individual interests, internal conflicts, and external stimuli all influence the degree of growth and development within the society and help to determine who benefits from the development of the nation.

Although Argentine nationalists such as Julio Irazusta have argued that the foreign role in commerce stunted the growth of a national entrepreneurial class and that foreign investments created a neocolonial situation, this conclusion seems difficult to document in the nineteenth century, when Argentine capital was limited. Indeed, D. C. M. Platt argues convincingly that before 1914 British foreign policy aimed to secure fair and equal treatment and that during this period British overseas commerce owed very little to direct government assistance and promotion.[9] Platt is less persuasive in dealing with the practical effects of this policy, for example the special privileges offered Britons by the Anglo-Argentine treaty of 1825. However, the growth of a national bourgeoisie which controlled the interior commerce during the era of the mercantile houses' domination of trade suggests the significance of the Argentine entrepreneurs in the nation's growth and development.

WITH HINDSIGHT it can be seen that the mercantile houses in Buenos Aires served both the interest of British imperialism and Argentine development. Through the medium of trade the British merchant brought Argentina within the economic influence of Great Britain, but through this same trade Argentina financed its internal development. British private capital in this period made funds available for investment before Argentine capital could finance structural changes in the economy. Before 1880 the dangers of foreign investments were more imaginary than real. Neither the amount of external capital nor the returns to the investors were large enough to concentrate crucial national industries in the hands of a small foreign minority. Although British merchants were the wholesalers of goods manufactured in the United Kingdom and the leading proponents of British culture, they had to modify their behavior in response to Argentine society. Thus, it appears that the British community was far more integrated into the total Buenos Aires community in the nineteenth century than in the twentieth. Although British merchants sought the protection of the United Kingdom authorities during civil disturbances or blockades and pressured the Argentine government for favorable commercial policy, their limited success came only at the price of many concessions to the South American environment. Argentine nationals faced disadvantages in unequal access to European capital and contacts, but they also profited from an understanding of local political and economic circumstances that few British merchants could rival.[10] The failure of the nationals to monopolize the import-export trade came from Argentine preference for the greater profits and prestige of internal activities rather than from any exceptional advantages enjoyed by foreign merchants.[11] Thus, between 1810 and 1880 the multifunctional nature of the mercantile house served merchant interests well. And through trading, banking, and investing, British merchants aided in the creation of institutions that changed Argentina from a subsistence economy to a nation which attracted immigrants, mobilized resources, and encouraged industrialization at the beginning of the twentieth century.

2.

Risk and Opportunity in Argentine Trade

TRADE in nineteenth-century Argentina offered widespread opportunities to resourceful men willing to exploit new technologies, markets, currency fluctuation, and changes in demand and cost. However, their profits were subject to risks or uncertainty, those exceptional factors influencing trade that upset the normal operations of the free market. Political instability, diverse currencies, limited banking service, and Argentina's unfavorable balance of external trade represented both potential losses and profits. Their understanding of international trade and adaptation to the local environment allowed British mercantile houses to profit.

After 1810 the national government, recognizing the risks of political instability that dissuaded merchants from trade and investment, tried to increase opportunities for foreigners. The British merchants found new opportunities because both the power structure and trading patterns had changed. The *porteños*, the residents of Buenos Aires, enthusiastically assumed control of the government and created a free and competitive market open to international commerce and finance. The political change caused Buenos Aires to turn away from the interior toward Europe. During the period of Spanish rule, Argentina had been a backwater where development was restricted to Córdoba and Mendoza, which provided the mining areas of Bolivia and Chile with food, mules, textiles, and leather. After achieving independence, Argentina saw demands for its goods and reexports diminish, since products to Chile went by sea rather than through Buenos Aires and internal disturbances paralyzed Paraguayan and Bolivian production and requirements. Unlike Buenos Aires, the inland provinces of Argentina only slowly redirected their production from interior demands toward the European economy.[1]

Favorably situated on the estuary of the Río de la Plata, Buenos Aires acted as the entrepôt between oceanic commerce and the extensive river trade that reached even as far as Paraguay. Natural advantages and the changed political structure attracted new groups of merchants, particularly from the United Kingdom, which had no connection with the previous colonial trade. Argentine merchants, who maintained their loyalty to Spain, were unfamiliar with the new forms of international trade; and, unprotected by the government's commercial policy, they could not compete successfully with the newly arrived British import-export traders. Spanish-Argentine merchants therefore confined themselves to wholesale, retail, and interior trade, leaving the import-export business to foreigners, who willingly accepted the challenges of the Argentine political environment.

Between 1810 and 1830, the formative years of Argentine national history, government efforts to encourage immigration and trade provided opportunities for British merchants. In 1816 the Congress of Tucumán, which severed Argentina's links with Spain, named Juan Martín de Pueyrredón supreme director of the nation; he was to create a financially sound government which could reduce the political chaos of the interior, finance the conflict with Spain, and liquidate past debts. His policy led to forced loans and increased tariffs in 1817; but conscious of the need for British trade and United Kingdom political support, Pueyrredón began to lower the customs duties in 1818.

Bernadino Rivadavia, who gave Argentina political leadership from 1821 to 1827, continued Pueyrredón's policies. His efforts to reform Argentina's economy, to centralize political power, and to end the war with Brazil over the Banda Oriental aroused internal opposition, although these changes met with the approval of the outside world and diminished the risks for British trade. Rivadavia's administration devoted particular attention to the encouragement of foreign immigrants. In 1824 the government sent special commissions to Europe to encourage farmers to settle in Argentina. Unfortunately, the state could not finance its promises to pay immigrant passages or to provide immigrants with land and equipment.

Rivadavia's concern with extending Argentina's influence overseas led to the signature of the Anglo-Argentine treaty in 1825. This treaty, which governed relations between the two countries for more than a century, guaranteed reciprocal freedom of commercial activities, security of property, and freedom of conscience. British merchants greatly benefited from the commercial provisions, because United Kingdom ships were free to enter Argentine ports, where Britons could occupy premises and fix prices by free negotiation with their customers. The treaty required both the United Kingdom and Argentina to admit each other's commodities under most-favored-nation privileges; thereby, the goods of both signatories gained equality under the tariffs with the lowest rate of duty applied against the produce of other states. The benefits the treaty offered were an important cause of increased British commercial power in Buenos Aires. For some twenty-five years Britons enjoyed preferential treatment, because no other group of foreign citizens had the protection of such a treaty.[2]

The climax of Rivadavia's political influence came in 1826 with the establishment of a constitution and his appointment to the presidency. However, success proved transitory. Popular discontent with Rivadavia's internal policies led to his loss of power in 1827, much to the disappointment of the British merchants, who attributed the apparent prosperity of trade in Argentina in the 1820s to the "general peace and tranquility . . . during which the most marked encouragement has been wisely extended to every branch of commerce and to the general industry of the country."[3]

A short period of political instability caused by the rivalry between the various contenders for power and the continuing war with Brazil followed the fall of the Rivadavia government. The political disorder came to an end when Juan Manuel Rosas gained power in 1829. His policies favored the merchants and landowners of the province of Buenos Aires, where, for example, the exporters of hides and salted meat and the importers of consumer goods paid minimal duties. Thus, Rosas strengthened the economy of the province of Buenos Aires and tied it closer to the international market. But in the process he contributed to the ruin of the interior's agriculture and industry.

The merchants viewed the Rosas period with mixed feelings. They initially were delighted by his assumption of power and they definitely appreciated his efforts at maintaining order. In 1835 a British merchant in Buenos Aires wrote to his correspondent in England that, with the resumption of civil peace and tranquility, public confidence was increasing in the new administration. This merchant felt that since Rosas' party was the most influential among the country people, there was every prospect of continued peace. But in the 1840s the British merchants became increasingly dissatisfied with Rosas' international policy, which encouraged currency depreciation. Particular resentment was expressed at the increasing harshness of Rosas toward foreigners. Nevertheless, Rosas' tariff policy furthered the development of Buenos Aires when it diverted the commerce of Montevideo and northern Argentina into the port by placing an extra 20 percent duty on all imports of ships that touched at Montevideo or any other Argentine port before reaching the capital. There was also a twenty percent duty on all imports shipped from the provinces abroad. This gave Buenos Aires a virtual monopoly on all seaborne trade and provoked reactions from France and the United Kingdom, who blockaded the port. The British were determined to enforce the terms of the 1825 treaty, while the French aspired to force a similar agreement.

In 1852 Rosas was thrown from power and ten years of civil war ensued, during which Argentina was divided between the province of Buenos Aires and the Confederation, consisting of the other thirteen provinces. The government of the province of Buenos Aires faced continued financial crisis during this period, while the Confederation never really succeeded in creating any political or economic unity. Civil war brought new prosperity to Buenos Aires, partly because without the encumbrance of the backward interior the city could adopt broader commercial policies. The treaty of 1825 had lost its meaning for Argentina when the United Kingdom tariffs were reorganized upon the basis of free trade in the early 1840s. Deprived of its protected market, Argentina absorbed British manufactures without trading benefits. Advantage clearly lay in negotiating similar treaties with countries like the United States that enforced protective tariffs. In 1853 the first manifestation of this new outward-looking policy came in the signing of a commercial treaty with the United States. This was followed by agreements with France, Chile, and other countries.[4]

Merchant opportunity continued to increase during the 1860s, a period of relative political stability. This trend persisted into the 1870s despite a minor depression and financial crisis in Argentina. Trade fluctuated according to the seasons, the market demand in Europe, and the general economic policy of the government. Between 1862 and 1880 Argentina was reorganized. In 1880 the political and economic disagreements between the Confederation and the province of Buenos Aires were reconciled by making Buenos Aires the capital of the Republic. The administrations of Bartolomé Mitre (1862-1868), Domingo F. Sarmiento (1868-1874), and Nicolás Avellaneda (1874-1880) dealt with occasional civil disturbances and began to reestablish the international credit standing of the country. The governments consolidated and reorganized the debts of all the provinces, made new loans, set aside funds for road construction, railroad building, and public works, and established a new bank that limited the emission of paper currency. Although the customhouse began to function normally and to bring in needed revenues, national resources became severely strained by a war with Paraguay and the government was unable to balance the budget.

IN SPITE OF government policy that sought to encourage trade and investment opportunities, British merchants faced distinct risks during periods of political disturbances. Merchants contended with privateer operations during the war for independence, Argentine internal struggles, and foreign wars with Brazil (1827-1828) and Paraguay (1864-1870). Privateers also operated during the eight years between 1810 and 1850 when Brazilian, French, and British warships blockaded the port of Buenos Aires. The consequent political problems of Argentina between 1810 and 1880 prevented the government from balancing its budget and paying its overseas debts. Merchants suffered because wars and civil disturbances caused the depreciation of currency and an increase in national expenditure. The need to finance these expenses by overissues of currency undermined popular confidence in the various governments and severely handicapped trade.

Privateering during Argentina's war for independence increased the risks of business because the confiscation of cargoes deprived merchants of capital and profits. The amount lost in a single confiscated contraband cargo in 1810 might have been as high as 100,000 pesos, equal to 5 percent of the government revenue in the period. In March of 1828 four privateers, probably with commissions from Buenos Aires, took three cargoes valued at between 30,000 and 40,000 pesos. If privateers did not harm a ship's cargo but merely took its papers, captains lost time and incurred expenses unloading in port because new manifests had to be drawn up after inspection of the goods. Since charters often stipulated the length of the time allowed for a voyage, some merchants took advantage of the opportunities given for legal privateering.[5]

Since privateering appeared necessary to defend Buenos Aires, the government issued commissions in a somewhat ineffective attempt to regulate its active sympathizers.[6] Both United States and British citizens obtained commissions from the government to fit out privateer ships and made sizable fortunes, like the American merchant David Curtis De Forest. Merchants also placed cargoes on privateer ships to avoid duty and willingly marketed the goods carried.[7]

Political disturbance affected merchant operations because the loss of interior and international markets increased the difficulty of procuring and shipping produce. As a consequence of broken communications between Buenos Aires, the interior, and Europe, import-export houses had difficulty judging the amount of merchandise needed for the market and the quantity of produce that could be exported. Political disturbances demanded that Argentine currency be reinvested quickly for fear of depreciation, although capital investments in merchandise and property could be forfeited through civil disturbance and were subject to high insurance premiums. In addition to losing international markets, merchants abandoned internal markets because the province of Buenos Aires itself limited interior trade and faced increased competition from other towns along the Río de la Plata.

Merchants suffered from the closure of the interior markets during times of civil disturbances not merely because wars were destructive but also because they diminished the price of British goods. Hodgson and Robinson wrote Owen Owens in December 1841:

> The total extinction of the Entre Ríos by the Corrientine army on the 28 ult. and the formation of an offensive and dependable alliance between the Province of Corrientes and Santa Fe to put down General Rosas—These two last events have not only knocked on the head the little business then previously was doing up the Paraná, at once, for the Entre Ríos, Santa Fe, Corrientes and even Paraguay, but they have suddenly opened out a new prospect of a protracted and destructive warfare in these Provinces, so that after getting off the whole of what we have reminded you, up to this day to ship, we beg you will suspend in toto until this storm goes over and until we again desire you to ship.[8]

Wars impoverished the middle and lower classes of the interior because country people were compelled to take up arms and could not harvest their crops, while the townspeople were subject to various military duties that decreased their income. The government paid the military so scantily that their wages did not suffice for their daily expenses and the purchase of manufactured articles was entirely beyond their means. Forced loans oppressed the wealthy individuals of the provinces, and their lack of confidence in government repayment encouraged them to avoid every appearance of prosperity so as to escape further demands.[9] Not only were markets closed but merchants often had difficulty securing produce—so much so that the arrival in Buenos Aires of a troop of carts laden with hides and other produce from the province of Córdoba in July of 1831 was seen as a happy omen that the war was almost over.[10]

If a merchant took a cargo into the interior during times of civil disturbances he risked its loss or at least the threat of confiscation by troops. Goods burnt by troops or naval squadrons were a total loss unless their value could be recovered from the government.[11] Although the city of Buenos Aires did not suffer as much destruction as did the interior provinces during civil wars, it did endure a number of sieges. During a pillage lasting for six or seven hours between the downfall of General Rosas and the establishment of the provisional government, residents suffered minor property damages.[12]

Government policy in Buenos Aires often aggravated the effects of internal disorders. During the Rosas period, for example, decrees were published which prohibited the killing of cattle throughout the province when the *saladeros* were under the control of the Unitarios, the opposition party. The prohibition of slaughtering cattle in Rosario and San Fernando increased the prices merchants paid. When the peons left the *estancias* to join the army, the stock of the country suffered. Not only was the size and condition of the animals impaired by failure to corral them at intervals but they became wild. In addition, during the war many head of cattle were killed to avoid the risk of their being stolen or seized for the use of the army, thus reducing the stock further and increasing the supply of hides.[13]

War and unrest discouraged merchants from holding capital in Argentina. The investment or export of funds quickly became crucial to success in Buenos Aires commerce, although much of the alarm came from overseas, as when Henry Miller in London asked his Buenos Aires partner, Hugh Dallas, in 1820: "Do you think it well to keep as little with you as possible of either capital or profit your having so much disturbances?"[14]

Even after political unrest had been replaced by a semblance of order, business did not always improve because United Kingdom companies found other suppliers and markets. In 1840 merchants would not do business in consignments until the government repealed the decree which rendered property of Spaniards liable to confiscation because of their alleged partiality toward the Unitarios. Wholesale and retail merchants refused to lay in goods that might be confiscated, and the popular fear of an attack on the city discouraged the purchase of goods.[15] The financial crisis following a war was occasionally disastrous for British merchants in the Río de la Plata. Facing commitments in sterling that could only be collected in depreciated Argentine currency, merchants had to liquidate land and cattle holdings at ruinous prices to pay commercial debts. Those mercantile houses that had kept away from dangerous speculations were in the strongest positions during the financial crises provoked by political circumstances.[16]

Argentine civil disturbances, however, did not create quite the chaos in the business world that might be supposed. The Paraguayan war increased the prices of hides and gave new impetus to cattle breeding, while the large government expenditures stimulated prosperity. Civil disturbances often had no detrimental effect on the city of Buenos Aires, since it was far from the battle fronts. Merchants located in the city could thus continue to operate profitably. *The Brazil and River Plate Mail* reported in 1864, "You may think that political troubles gave disquiet to foreigners, but it is only so in a mild degree. The foreigner goes quietly on enriching himself, building houses, making roads and railways, sending to Europe the products of the country and looking with placid indifference on all political agitations."[17]

The Brazilian blockade of Buenos Aires (December 21, 1825, to September 30, 1828), the French blockade (March 28, 1838, to November 1, 1840), and the Anglo-French blockade (September 24, 1845, to June

1848) made it difficult for merchants to judge the supply and demand for goods and produce.[18] Merchants were never certain when commercial transactions might be brought to a halt, and the availability of shipping became most uncertain. As a result of an impending blockade, prices of produce in Buenos Aires often increased as merchants competed to purchase large quantities. At the same time, an oversupply of Argentine produce in Europe brought the merchant decreased profits, unless the threat of a blockade seemed genuine enough to maintain high prices.

When a forewarned blockade became a reality, neutral vessels were permitted only ten to twenty days to leave the port. This period was not sufficient to allow all the ships in the port to load before departing for Europe. Ships already enroute from Europe for Buenos Aires learned of the blockade only when they touched a South American port. Such slow communications meant that ships might be leaving Europe destined for Buenos Aires up to two weeks after the blockade was declared. All ships in passage had to be redirected to another port, usually at added expenses and loss of profits. Insurance rates rose and at times merchants had difficulty insuring cargoes because they could not communicate with London to make the arrangements or because agents did not wish to bear the risk.[19]

To the chagrin of Buenos Aires merchants, blockades of Buenos Aires, particularly the French blockade, aided the rapid growth of Montevideo and loosened the hold of merchants in Buenos Aires on the Argentine market. In addition, during certain periods Uruguay did much to attract trade, primarily by opening a large number of ports. Montevideo itself allowed transhipped goods to be landed without duty and to be deposited in the customhouse for any length of time at a low storage rent. Goods could easily be reshipped to foreign ports or the interior without the payment of duties.[20]

Blockades never proved so completely detrimental to commercial interests as might be supposed because merchants quickly learned how to take advantage of situations to make sizable profits. At the threat of a blockade, British merchants liquidated as much of their produce as possible by shipments to the United Kingdom. They protected their interests further by making remittances in specie or in bills of exchange. Once a blockade began, merchants invested in hides, which could be stored, or in lands and livestock, which were generally fairly safe. During the wars of independence British ships, as neutral vessels, were accorded certain immunities from privateers. Although ships were stopped, property was rarely confiscated.

Furthermore, blockades did not always sever communications with Europe. Packets, because they were Royal Navy vessels and enjoyed some diplomatic immunity, were often permitted to land, although passengers could take only the minimum luggage. In fact, the nature of the Río de la Plata itself made it relatively easy for neutral vessels to break the blockade. During the Brazilian blockade of 1825 to 1828 one hundred and six vessels passed through the closure. Of these, seventy-three were American and eighteen were British. On November 13, 1847, during the Anglo-French blockade, twenty-six foreign vessels were loading in the port of Buenos Aires. On January 19, 1848, the blockading vessels allowed seven large merchant ships to sail for foreign ports. Not only did ocean-going vessels often avoid the blockade, but small craft continually sailed between Buenos Aires and Montevideo carrying goods or produce. During the first French blockade it was customary to transmit merchandise from the east coast of Argentina in neutral vessels to the River Paraná. At that point the goods were transferred to blockade runners who took them to Montevideo. To encourage blockade runners the government of Buenos Aires reduced the rates of duty so that during the Brazilian blockade merchants paid one-third less duty than in normal times.[21]

British merchants were at a slight disadvantage in comparison with other foreigners. The United Kingdom government generally recognized the blockades, and therefore merchants could not secure insurance on the ship's cargo. But even with this handicap, British trade was hardly affected. Those merchants who subscribed to the support of the British chapel in 1825 were the same ones who still subscribed after the war was over. The blockade of 1838-39 apparently had so little effect on British trade that in both years the level of British exports to Buenos Aires was above the average of the previous five years. In 1840 it was only 11 percent below the average.[22]

British merchants became adept at judging the influence of the blockades upon their profits and learned to quickly take advantage of any opportunity that presented itself. During a blockade hides from the interior could be bought cheaply, yet when sent to the United Kingdom after the blockade received inflated prices in a starved market. Substantial profits could be made if the arrival of goods from Europe coincided with the termination of a blockade. A merchant might order goods sent from Europe to Montevideo to be forwarded to Buenos Aires immediately upon the termination of the blockade. Goods sent to Ensenada, a port twenty-five miles south of Buenos Aires on the estuary, could be forwarded over land to Buenos Aires. During a blockade profits might be made by sending produce overland via Chile. And merchants were quite willing to sell to belligerents on both sides, when the opportunity arose.[23]

If a blockade lasted a long while, merchants suffered when goods on hand diminished to the point where business slowed and produce ready for shipment accumulated. Too large a quantity of produce on hand at the end of a blockade created an oversupplied market in the United Kingdom and hence reduced prices for Argentine produce, and at the same time raised freight rates because the demand for freights in Argentina exceeded the available shipping tonnage.[24] A long, effective blockade increased the insecurity of the political situation, further affecting the exchange market; it also encouraged Europe to develop new sources of hides and tallow. However, with the possible exception of the Anglo-French blockade, the blockades were neither long nor effective enough to seriously threaten those mercantile houses that were financially sound.

Although civil disturbances and blockades disrupted business, climate and disease more directly affected the import-export merchants, whose profits depended upon the availability of agricultural and pastoral products. James Hodgson wrote to Owen Owens and Son in 1841 to emphasize the effect of climate upon trade: "The failure of our next year's crop of wheat and the want of pasture for the cattle, cannot but have an eventually evil effect upon the import trader here as this country will have so much less to give in return for imports."[25]

The cholera epidemic of 1868-69 and the yellow fever epidemic of 1871 probably had more effect on trade than any of the civil disturbances or *coups d'etat* of the nineteenth century. The consul reports of 1868 blamed the decline in trade principally upon the interruptions caused by the prevalence of cholera.[26] In December 1867 the cholera epidemic stopped commerce in the city of Buenos Aires. The government even ordered *saladeros* to cease slaughtering cattle so that the value of exports decreased and exchange rates fell.[27] Even more detrimental to the import-export trade was the yellow fever epidemic of 1871, which killed between 21,000 and 40,000 people, or between 12 and 23 percent of the population of the city of Buenos Aires at that time. Trade in Buenos Aires was at a standstill for over two months, with all government offices, banks, and houses of business closed. The government suspended business for thirty-five days in April and May, while banks and leading commercial houses renewed all bills for sixty days. The total decline in trade caused by yellow fever was over ten and one-half million Argentine pesos. For the year 1871 the port of Buenos Aires handled but 47.5 million pesos worth of goods and produce, as against 62 million for the previous year.[28]

IT WAS the monetary and fiscal policies of the Argentine government that presented the greatest risks and opportunities to British merchants during the nineteenth century. Argentina's economic success depended upon the import of foreign capital and personnel, but to attract these foreign investments the country had to run a satisfactory balance of trade and raise sufficient revenue to finance basic services that would inspire foreign confidence. The Argentine balance of payments, capital investments, and foreign exchange—factors influenced by the international markets—

offered both potential profits and losses to British merchants. Argentina raised and lowered its tariffs in response to the state of government revenue rather than to the world economy. Government efforts to balance its budget demanded different types of taxes, which were felt by the merchants in various degrees, depending upon their ability to avoid or evade them. During the political, social, and economic changes between 1810 and 1880 one theme remained constant: foreign trade, particularly trade with Great Britain, linked government finances and policy because it provided revenue, modified government policy, and stimulated immigration.

During this period Argentina's visible balance of payments—the margin between the values of imports and exports excluding such services as shipping and capital movements—showed a surplus in only six years. The country had to attract foreign capital if it was to maintain an adequate gold reserve for its currency, because the duties and warehouse charges levied upon reexports dissuaded merchants from establishing Buenos Aires as an entrepôt for more than the interior river trade. The international balance of payments, which indicates the international standing of a country, has not been calculated for Argentina for the nineteenth century. However, it is known that the imports and exports of the country made up two-thirds or more of its international balance of payments;[29] and when Argentina had an unfavorable balance, it was more unfavorable than the trade figures themselves indicated because overseas trade required payments to foreign-owned shipping.[30]

The deficit in payments could be settled by the export of gold, but the government prohibited gold shipments during certain periods. This had a detrimental effect on trade, since merchants occasionally paid correspondents in gold rather than produce. The net result of the rising deficit in the balance of payments was both a fluctuating and falling exchange rate. Tables 1 and 2 indicate the relationship between the pound, the peso, and gold from 1810 to 1880. From the 1870s Argentina's balance of payments was significantly changed by increasing imports of British investment capital and the government's raising further foreign loans. These capital inflows contributed to Argentina's reserves and initially improved the balance of payments.[31] The government optimistically assumed that future charges of interest and profit would be successfully serviced from the enlarged trading surplus that must surely come from a more elaborate infrastructure.

Argentina's unfavorable balance of trade arose from the type of commodities produced. Exports, primarily agricultural produce, fell into four categories: raw animal produce such as wool, hides, tallow, meat; raw agricultural produce such as wheat, maize, and linseed; articles elaborated and derived from the foregoing, such as meat extracts, dairy produce, flour; and a very small quantity of minerals and manufactures. As figure 1 indicates, there was a movement from raw animal products in the 1810s to processed animal derivatives in the 1880s. The graph further illustrates an increase in the exports of hides, jerked beef, tallow, and wool from 1820 to 1850. In 1810 the major exports were those of the cattle industry: hides, tallow, jerked beef, with some specie and bullion coming from Upper Peru. Beginning in 1850, wool became increasingly important. In 1832 only 944 bales of wool were exported, but by 1865 130,532 bales were shipped from Buenos Aires, constituting Argentina's most valuable export. Jerked beef drastically decreased in importance as an export in 1880, when refrigerated meat became an important Argentine export. Hides, jerked beef, and tallow, closely related in production, decreased in importance in the 1880s when meat and wheat became Argentina's staples.

Imports increased in value, shifting from textiles and light consumer products in the early part of the nineteenth century to heavier goods for industry in the latter part of the century.[32] In 1824 Great Britain supplied Argentina with cotton and woolen manufactures and bulky items such as earthenware and furniture. The United States furnished flour, lumber, furniture, unbleached cotton cloth, reexports from India and China, pitch, and tar; Brazil furnished sugar, rum, rice, coffee, tobacco, yerba maté, lumber, and cheap cotton goods. Gibraltar, Spain, and Sicily contributed wines, brandy, oil, olives; France supplied silk goods, fine clothes, wines, and lace; Germany, Holland, Sweden, and Denmark provided glass goods, wool, lumber, iron; Havana sent silks, linens, tea from China, and coffee, molasses, sugars; Chile and Peru provided silver, gold, cocoa, cotton.[33]

Argentina's trade with the United Kingdom was the root of the balance of payments deficit, since the trade surplus with other countries did not equal the deficit with Great Britain. In 1825, 76 percent of Argentine imports came from Great Britain and 57 percent of her exports went to Great Britain; in 1880, 27.8 percent of Argentine imports came from Great Britain while 9.2 percent of Argentine exports went to Great Britain.[34] On the other hand, in 1880 Belgium provided only 5.5 percent of Argentine imports and took 24.7 percent of Argentine exports.[35] A partial explanation for the large exports to Belgium was the location of large hide and wool markets in Antwerp, which reexported much Argentine produce to other European markets, including the United Kingdom. This situation reemphasized the need of British merchants in Buenos Aires to have international contacts.

In the years 1875 to 1880, the United Kingdom supplied 24.6 to 27.8 percent of Argentine imports while buying only 7.4 to 15.1 percent of Argentine exports.[36] The shift toward heavier consumer and capital

Table 1. Price of gold per ounce in Great Britain and in Argentina, 1810-1845.

Year	Price in Great Britain (in shillings and pence)[a]		Price in Argentina (in paper pesos)[b]	
	Lowest	Highest	Lowest	Highest
1810	84/6	85/0		
1811	84/6	99/6		
1812	95/0	107/0		
1813	98/0	110/0		
1814	85/0	108/0		
1815	82/0	107/0		
1816	78/6	81/0		
1817	78/6	80/6		
1818	81/0	82/6		
1819	81/0	83/0		
1820	79/6	81/0		
1821	77/6	79/10.5		
1822	77/6	79/10.5		
1823	77/6	77/10.5		
1824		77/6		
1825		77/6		
1826		77/6	17	50
1827		77/6	40	70
1828		77/9	39	70
1829		77/9	61	102
1830		77/9	104	138
1831		77/9	100	124
1832		77/9	106	113
1833[c]		77/9	110	127
1834		77/9	117	120
1835		77/9	117	120
1836		77/9	116	121
1837		77/9	116	146
1838		77/9	129	179
1839		77/9	211	293
1840		77/9	282	514
1841		77/9	283	350
1842		77/9	268	293
1843		77/9	245	282
1844		77/9	206	244
1845		77/9	109	362

(Table 1 cont.)

[a]A. A. Feavearyear, *The Pound Sterling: A History of English Money* (London, 1931), p. 215. From 1820 the price of gold in Great Britain is the price paid by the Bank of England. The Bank continues to pay 77/6 through 1880 per ounce of standard gold in bars. During most of this period the price of gold in England was higher than in Argentina. For example, 1854-1862 gold in Argentina cost 66/6. (Great Britain, House of Commons, 1863, vol. 70, p. 12.)

[b]*Banco de La Nación Argentina en su cincuentenario: 1891-1941* (Buenos Aires, 1940), p. 115.

[c]I am indebted to N. M. Rothschild and Sons Ltd. for confirming the price of gold in Great Britain for the years 1833 to 1845.

goods caused both an increase in the total volume of trade and a decrease in the percentage dependent upon the British market. During the 1870s Argentina's major exports were tallow, wool, hides, and jerked beef. Great Britain had no demand for jerked beef and obtained large quantities of wool from Australia and South Africa, tallow from Russia and Australia, and hides from Australia, South Africa, and Brazil. Only in the 1890s when Argentina became a large exporter of wheat and meat did she develop a favorable balance of trade with Great Britain.

In this circumstance British merchants enjoyed particular opportunities because Buenos Aires profitably linked the interior with the international markets. In 1876 it seemed that "one of the peculiarities of trade of the province of Buenos Aires is that almost everything it produces is exported, and that almost everything it consumes, excepting meat, bread, and vegetables, is brought from abroad; the consequence being that the trade returns are very large compared with the small population."[37] This extreme reliance upon trade demanded institutions to deal in foreign exchange, a method for exchanging payment from one national currency to another.

In the nineteenth century the international foreign exchange market centered on London, where merchant houses and merchant banks employing foreign exchange brokers performed the necessary transactions. The main instrument for the transfer of foreign currency was the bill of exchange or bank draft, a check drawn by one bank, merchant house, or merchant bank on another. The principal factor affecting the fluctuations of the foreign exchange was the demand for imports or exports. In Argentina when imports from the United Kingdom exceeded exports, the peso declined on the foreign exchange market because the demand for pounds sterling exceeded the demand for pesos. If the balance of trade remained unfavorable the exchange rate for Argentine currency declined.

Table 2. Price of gold per ounce in Great Britain and in Argentina, 1846-1880.

| | Price in Great Britain (in shillings and pence)[a] | | Price in Argentina (in paper pesos)[b] | |
	Lowest	Highest	Lowest	Highest
1846	77/9		329	414
1847	77/9		293	397
1848	77/9		279	393
1849	77/9		243	347
1850	77/9		225	258
1851	77/9		230	380
1852	77/9		261	286
1853	77/9		296	341
1854	77/9		273	349
1855	77/9		315	356
1856	77/9		332	366
1857	77/9		328	345
1858	77/9		343	386
1859	77/9		336	367
1860	77/9		333	355
1861	77/9		347	425
1862	77/9		392	426
1863	77/9		402.(27.18)[c]	452(28.02)
1864	77/9		28.20	29.20
1865	77/9		25.42	28.70
1866	77/9		22.52	26.17
1867	77/9		24.25	25[d]
1868	77/9		25	25
1869	77/9		25	25
1870	77/9.01		25	25
1871	77/9.01		25	25
1872	77/9.24		25	25
1873	77/9.28		25	25
1874	77/9.		25	25
1875	77/9.23		25	25
1876	77/9.3		25	25
1877	77/9.42		28.12	33.55
1878	77/9.41		28.45	32.30
1879	77/9.11		31.15	32.80
1880	77/9.15		31.85	32.75

(Table 2 cont.)

[a]I am indebted to H. M. Rothschild and Sons Ltd. for information on the price of gold in Great Britain for the years 1846 to 1880.

[b]*Banco de La Nación Argentina en su cincuentenario: 1891-1941* (Buenos Aires, 1940), p. 115.

[c]From 13 November 1863 through 1880, the price of gold is quoted in pesos fuertes.

[d]From 11 January 1867 until May 1876, the Office of Exchange (Oficina de Cambios) maintained the price of one ounce of gold at 25 pesos fuertes, and pesos fuertes to paper pesos at 1 to 25.

However, foreign exchange movements were not always dominated by the normal forces of supply and demand because the suspension of gold payment, inflation, large public debts, or government instability undermined international confidence.

Import-export merchants in Argentina were primarily interested in the rate of exchange between Buenos Aires and the foreign country in which they were buying or selling goods. Fluctuations in exchange rates were exceedingly important, and merchants prudently awaited the arrival of British packets to learn the exchange rate before purchasing drafts on London. The Argentine government also regarded trade and exchange rates as matters of the utmost importance because the state derived its principal revenues from customs collections and port dues, which yielded 69.71 to 95.57 percent of the revenues between 1824 and 1870.[38] Three-quarters or more of the customs' revenues came from the port of Buenos Aires.[39]

Reliance on customs duties led to unstable government income because a reduction in trade meant decreased revenues, and this led to efforts to raise additional money by increasing the circulation of paper currency, imposing forced loans, or raising tariffs. Small fluctuations of market prices for produce in Europe drastically affected state revenue.[40] While the import and export duties varied from year to year, tariff policies during the 1820 to 1880 period (with the exception of 1835 to 1841) sought to raise revenues rather than to either discourage imports and exports or manipulate the foreign exchange market. Thus the governments kept the customs duties high enough to bring in revenues but not so prohibitive as to discourage imports or exports.

Given Argentina's dependence on tariffs to raise revenues, it is surprising that the merchants complained only rarely about excessive duties. For example, in 1812 British merchants presented a petition to the gov-

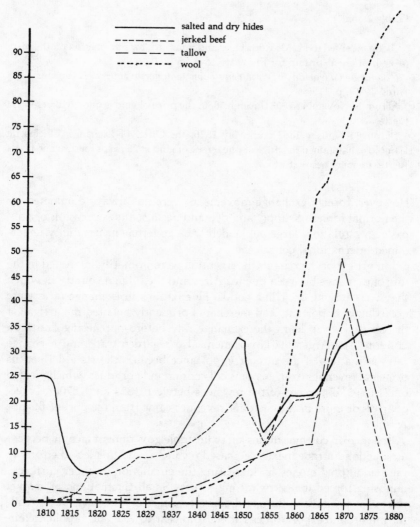

1. Argentine export of hides, jerked beef, tallow, and wool, 1810-1880 (thousands of tons).

ernment protesting that they had to pay excessive duties because customs officers overvalued many articles. In 1836 merchants resented paying increased duties on goods coming from Montevideo, which were subject to 25 percent more duty than goods coming directly from another port. Again in 1868 the government received complaints against unduly high tariffs which impeded commerce.[41]

The limited remonstrances against excessive duties can be explained by several factors. When the government kept import duties to a minimum, they could be passed on to the consumer, since Argentine industry remained unable to compete with the technology, capital, and cheap labor of Europe. When duties were raised, the contraband trade became profitable. But more importantly, British merchants dealt in both imports and exports. The government, concerned with maintaining its revenues, would raise one tariff only to decrease the other. Thus, merchants were able to balance losses on one duty against profits on another. Since the international market was far more competitive than the national market, and all merchants faced equal duty on the same goods, British merchants would prefer increased import duties to the raising of the export tariff. The fact that merchants had few complaints against the state's tariff policy and that the government succeeded in raising such a large percentage of its revenues through its customs duties suggests that the tariff policy was on the whole effective.

When customs duties and port charges were insufficient to support expenses, the government imposed other forms of taxation, often without conspicuous success. These taxes generally provided less than 20 percent of Argentina's revenues because individuals avoided or evaded their obligations under such taxes as the *contribución directa*, a levy on property and capital. Individuals only reluctantly paid license fees and stamp duties or subscribed to forced loans and voluntary bond issues.

The *contribución directa*, a potentially lucrative tax, rarely contributed more than 5 percent of the revenue. Although the tax varied during the century, it ran 1 to 2 percent on landed property, 4 to 5 percent on cattle, 8 percent on commercial establishments, and 6 percent on manufacturing.[42] By underestimating the value of their property, individuals decreased their tax liability. Merchants proved that delinquency was common, as evidenced by a comparison between their tax payments and the amount of goods they were importing and exporting. However, they experienced more difficulty in falsifying returns than landowners because the government could easily compare their returns for customhouse and tax purposes. Besides falsifying their returns, merchants avoided the tax by defining themselves as agents or commission merchants. By a single change of name they only paid half the regular tax, 4 instead of 8 percent. Some of the largest mercantile houses in the city declared that they owned no goods or capital and were simply commission merchants and agents. Thus, one house that had paid 624,307 pesos in duties upon imported and exported articles declared that it had no capital of its own. Naturally, those merchants who owned cattle falsified their number, following the example of the *estancieros*.[43]

The government also imposed a license tax (*derecho de patentes*) and a stamp duty (*papel sellado*). Commercial and industrial establishments paid the license tax, the amount depending upon the location and nature of the business. In 1870, for example, import-export houses paid between 7,000 and 12,000 pesos. Commercial travelers also had to pay for a license to cover their operations and travel within the country.[44] The stamp duty amounted to a levy upon official documents. The license and stamp duties brought in a very small percentage of revenue and the amount of revenue from these taxes varied greatly from year to year.

Although the Argentine government raised substantial revenues from customs and port dues and further revenues through such minor taxes as the capital and property tax, stamp duty, license tax, cattle tax, and the sale or rent of lands, it still generally faced a budgetary deficit between 1810 and 1880. The difference between current revenues and expenditures was financed by two other methods: forced loans and voluntary bond issues. Forced loans differed from the usual government taxes in that the state might repay the face value of the bonds or promissory notes in currency. Of the twenty-six forced loans legislated by Argentine assemblies between 1812 and 1822, all but three had repayment clauses. The government repaid approximately fifty percent of the almost three million pesos it raised in this period. During the wars with Brazil and Paraguay the government enacted further forced loans. However, newspaper coverage suggested that British commercial houses in Buenos Aires "spontaneously" subscribed to the expenses of the war with Paraguay. Merchants in fact did not really object to contributing to forced loans because the promissory notes were accepted in redemption of customs duties. Since Argentina had never had a wealthy Catholic Church like Peru and Mexico, the forced loans fell primarily upon foreign and national merchants and landowners, all of whom represented the monied classes.

The government also raised funds by floating domestic bond issues. In contrast to the forced loans, the public subscribed to these issues voluntarily but at a large discount rate—sometimes as high as 40 percent. This in effect meant that on a bond of 100 pesos, the government received only 60 pesos but had to pay interest and amortization on the 100. When the faith of investors increased, the government obviously could reduce the discount rate, but generally currency depreciation discouraged merchant investment in these issues despite the attraction of speculative opportunity.

The absence of a national monetary policy contributed to some of the greatest hazards faced by merchants in Argentina. Aldo Ferrer in *The Argentine Economy* contends that merchants and landowners supported the financing of government deficits through a policy of monetary expansion, partly by the issuing of paper currency as against the issue of domestic debts such as forced loans or bonds. He further argues that the inflation resulting from monetary expansion favored merchants and landed interests because the price of produce and goods rose faster than wages and costs. However, landowners and merchants saw their opportunities in divergent monetary policies.[45] Currency depreciation threatened the profits of import-export merchants far more than any government device to raise revenue, because their creditors in the United Kingdom demanded payment in specie or a currency exchangeable for gold, while their debtors in Argentina were bound only to repay in local currency. Losses could be avoided by investing depreciating money in produce, which had a cash value on the London market. British merchants also protected their businesses by exchanging Argentine paper pesos for gold or pounds sterling and by fixing the price of goods in sterling. However, since most imports were sold to retail merchants on three to six months' credit and because it proved difficult to fix the value of goods in sterling, merchants lost heavily during periods of rapid currency depreciation. The profits of foreign exchange often did not compensate for losses on short-term Argentine debts.[46]

Argentina's circulating media in the period 1810 to 1880 comprised bills issued on behalf of the government, paper money, and foreign or nationally minted coins. The resulting financial disorder caused by the absence of a national monetary policy heightened both the problems of currency depreciation and the slow development of a banking system. In itself, a measure of inflation benefited the growth of the Argentine economy because it reduced merchant profit margins and encouraged the purchase of goods for export or fixed assets. However, the circulation of a variety of provincial currencies and foreign coins as well as the tendency of banks to print money so that governments could pay their debts handicapped the interior trade and weakened Argentina's reserves of foreign exchange because merchants were encouraged to invest or export their profits. Monetary policy, neither effective nor enforced, the depreciation of currency, and the rudimentary banking facilities in Argentina presented British merchants with outstanding difficulties involving a large measure of uncertainty.

During the nineteenth century, Argentina did not possess a national currency. In theory several of the provinces had mints, but they never acquired any importance. The Constitutional General Assembly of April 1813 issued an order to the Casa de Moneda of Potosí to mint new money of gold and silver. The money was to bear the seal of the assembly and carry the inscription. "Provincias del Río de la Plata" and "Unión y Libertad." But the minting of money was suspended in that same year when Potosí again fell into the hands of the Spanish. In 1815 a law was passed to establish mints in La Rioja and Córdoba, but again nothing was done. In 1824 the Chamber of Deputies of Buenos Aires authorized the government to buy the necessary machines to coin money. Again the law had no effect. But about this time Córdoba and La Rioja were given the right to mint silver coins. Córdoba did mint money until 1855 and La Rioja until 1861. The coins, of irregular form and minted in small quantities, were insufficient to satisfy the needs of the country and were a factor in the merchants' complaints on the scarcity of currency. In 1863 the government recognized the foreign gold and silver that had circulated throughout the earlier period as legal tender, fixing their value in terms of pesos fuertes, which were seven-eighths silver.[47]

The monetary law of 1876, the first attempt at a comprehensive monetary law, authorized the minting of gold and silver Argentine coins and established the mint ratio between silver and gold at 16.266 to 1. (One gold peso coin equaled 4 shillings 2 pence sterling.) This law allowed the government to redefine the value of foreign gold coins, taking for its base the new Argentine peso fuerte of 1.5 grams fine gold. The London market governed the fluctuating relationship between gold and silver and determined the value of silver coins, which remained the base of all commercial transactions outside the province of Buenos Aires. The Bolivian peso, with a varying silver content, and legal tender in thirteen Argentine provinces, did not receive any legal value from the Buenos Aires government. The government hoped to substitute the peso fuerte for the foreign coins that were circulating widely in the provinces, in spite of considerable opposition to their replacement. Not until 1881 did the government delineate a central monetary system.[48]

The government attempted to regulate paper currency by legislation and the administrative influence of eight different banks during the 1810 to 1880 period. The amount of government control over the banks varied. Although the Banco de Descuentos and the Banco Nacional were private banks, the government exercised a great deal of control, even approving their directorates. For banks chartered later, the government appointed the directors, who were usually individuals with some commercial experience. Operations of all banks were subject to government regulation.

The main function of the banks through most of the nineteenth century was to issue paper currency and to make loans to the government. Therefore, they offered very few credit facilities to private individuals or at least to individuals without political connections. Before 1871 the government banks did not even deal directly in foreign exchange. When the government needed to pay bills in Europe it either shipped gold through import-export houses or bought bills of exchange on foreign houses.

Because the Argentine currency was in theory based upon gold, the banks were required to maintain a reserve of specie behind their notes. However, there was a tendency for the amount to fall below the legally required reserve. Thus, the paper currency was fiduciary money which depended on public confidence, while pesos fuertes were convertible into gold only during certain periods. As fiduciary money the value of paper currency was affected by such factors as the unfavorable balance of trade, budget deficits, overissue of currency, and unstable political situations—all of which led to the decrease in the value of the paper currency.

British merchants complained constantly about Argentine currency, lamenting the diversity, the amount in circulation, and the changing value. During the Rosas period and again when the country was facing a depression from 1874 to 1876, the increase in the money supply through government emissions of currency to provide revenue for the state exceeded the increase in goods and services. The resulting inflation worked to the disadvantage of the import-export merchants, who were generally creditors in Argentina. In 1864 approximately 150 million pesos of the 350 million in circulation were held by foreign merchants and Argentine estancieros.[49] Since the estancieros did not need currency for their transactions as much as the merchants and were inclined to be debtors, it can be assumed that foreign merchants held the largest percentage of the currency.

The disadvantages paper currency caused commerce could be partly remedied if merchants paid for imports in silver or gold, while using paper currency to purchase cattle, wool, and products of the country. The actual result was a contribution to the variation in the rates of exchange, since gold was in demand at one season and paper at another.[50] In 1852 George White summed up the damage the currency was doing to trade in a letter to Baring Brothers.

> This wretched currency is in every respect injurious to the community being based upon no tangible security and having only a fictitious and conventional value; the fluctuations are enormous and trade is thus to a considerable extent reduced to the level of a mere speculation. This is particularly the case as regards the sale of imports, which are sold commonly on long credit, six months and sometimes more. A sale may be made on apparently favorable terms, and when the time for payment arrives, the variation in the currency will not improbably be such as to give an entirely different result . . . One remedy is now obtained by making bargains in specie, or what amounts to the same thing, fixing the exchange at which the payment is to be made when due. This, however, is only a partial remedy, and in the event of any great fluctuations, the dealers and tradesmen would not be able to afford the prices stipulated, and would require extension of time, or heavy discounts.[51]

The fluctuation in the value of the paper currency encouraged extensive speculation. The government could not fix the value of the peso without alienating those strong private interests that were making profits at the expense of the general public.[52] These interests so preferred the fluctuating currency that even government efforts to fix the value encouraged speculation. A law that came into effect July 1, 1865, provided for redemption of paper money, which national capitalists held in expectation of making a 20 percent profit after the law came into operation.[53] Because of the large amount of currency in circulation, during some periods specie was scarce. In 1822 silver became so scarce that it was impossible to get ready change for a doubloon, a Spanish coin used as legal tender in Argentina. At other times the merchants issued promissory notes and *discos*, wooden disks with their seal and signature. In 1829 as in 1836 merchants complained about the scarcity of small notes in the city of Buenos Aires. In January 1865 business in Buenos Aires was considered slow not only because of a decline in prices of produce but also because of a scarcity of specie, although it was noted that Argentine paper currency was gaining in value. In 1866 commercial men expressed the opinion that because of increased mercantile operations the country required a larger amount of legal tender than was actually to be found, since the amortization of nearly one-fourth of the total issue of paper money from former years had decreased the amount in circulation.

Political factors also put pressure on the money supply. In April 1857, for example, the excitement that prevailed before the elections in the province of Buenos Aires and the large payments for that season's produce even led to the suspension of trade for want of cash. Producers in the country gave no credit and often required a large deposit in advance of delivery. These pressures on the money market might cause speculation in produce, with firms purchasing all they could at high rates before the packet came in bringing news of lower quotations on exchange rates. Firms wanting to draw on London might then have difficulty negotiating their bills of exchange.

In April 1865 paper money became so scarce that sheep were offered at very low prices while cattle sold for less than the value of the hide. To get around the shortage of funds, merchants would pay for produce with goods, send bills of exchange to London to be collected when money was more abundant, or, anticipating the season when currency was so scarce and the peso had risen in value relative to sterling, draw on their accounts some months previous to the time it was needed and employ the funds in good securities at high interest rates until they were desired.[54]

Merchant complaints on the scarcity of paper currency in circulation can be explained by two factors. First, there were periods of time when the currency was issued in relation to specie held and reserves were insufficient to support the volume of trade. Second, the seasonal nature of the trade made heavier demands on currency between August and February. Hodgson, Robinson, and Company wrote to Owens and Sons of Manchester in December of 1843:

> Such was the scarcity of paper money on the two last Saturdays that as much as 2 and 3 per cent interest per month was paid upon acceptance of a 3 month [bill] of exchange of many of the most respectable houses—foreign as well as native. The chief causes of this scarcity are attributed to the large amount of currency which at this season are sent to the country to purchase the new crop of wheat . . . Cattle for the salting establishment which concerns at this period of the year are in most active work here and the resolute hoarding of several large holdings of currency with a view of the screwing down the price of doubloons and getting up the rate of interest. [55]

A DIFFERENT series of problems for British merchants was posed by the state of the international economy. Between 1810 and 1880 advances in the technology of transportation, communication, and manufacturing, an increasing world population, the worldwide oceanic Pax Brittanica, and currency systems based on the gold standard provided British merchants with stable or expanding conditions that encouraged international trade. However, rivalry between Great Britain and the rapidly industrializing powers of France, Germany, and the United States increased competition for new suppliers of raw materials and consumers of manufactured goods.

British merchants in Argentina faced two principal risks in the world economy: the competition from other exporters of pastoral produce and the failure of the Argentine economy to absorb an increasing share of the world supply of manufactured goods. Only from the 1880s did Argentina begin to apply new technologies to the production and preservation of its produce. In 1880 Argentina had only slightly more than £20 million in British investments, 1,570 miles of railroads, and 94 percent of its exports in pastoral products. By 1908 only 30 percent of its exports were pastoral, while the agricultural sector accounted for 63 percent of production and 14,620 miles of railroad operated. In 1910 British nominal investments totaled £290.6 million rising to £357.7 million by the close of 1913. [56] The mercantile houses ultimately promoted the flow of British capital into heavy investments after 1880, when their resources proved insufficient to continue to finance the development of Argentina.

From 1810 to 1880 British mercantile houses in Argentina were a part of the broader picture of European trade expansion. The revolution of May 25, 1810, which amplified the list of duty free goods of November 1809 and opened the port of Buenos Aires to international trade, provided a new, enlarged market for European goods. Europe's search for new markets was so intense that Buenos Aires soon became saturated with goods of nearly every description. Although British merchants, confident of their skills in marketing technique, the superiority of their goods, and their preeminence in financial resources, sought a rapid turnover in sales and ready access to markets, it was the changes taking place in Europe, specifically the United Kingdom, that equipped them to exploit the new opportunities. In Britain the rapid growth of the population, the increase in acreage of land under cultivation, the accumulation of capital and its investment in productive means, and the innovations of entrepreneurs characterized the nineteenth century. All of these factors had their effect on Argentina. The rapid growth of the population meant an increased demand for both tropical and temperate agricultural products. Although Argentina did not produce tropical produce, merchants took advantage of the lucrative coastal trade with Brazil. Argentina's major exports until the 1880s—hides, skins, tallow, and wool, the mainsprings of business, trade, and government revenue—found a ready market in Europe.

The technological changes of the nineteenth century had considerable repercussions upon the operations of both business and ranching in Argentina. Merchants in Buenos Aires directly felt the effect of the new technology when, for example, improved machinery for the production of textiles progressively reduced prices and discouraged traders from holding substantial stocks. The textile market in Buenos Aires suffered from frequent crises of oversupply. The economic and industrial development of the United Kingdom depended heavily upon the manufacture of cotton goods for export. Even in 1870 the diversified structure of the British economy produced half of the total world supply of cotton textiles, and Latin America had become the largest single market for these goods by 1840.[57] The need for new markets for British goods often obscured both real demand and political instability. While the natural resources of Argentina were indeed considerable, the population in the nineteenth century was too small to consume the large amount of goods sent or to afford the high cost of foreign government loans. In 1810 the population of Argentina was only 500,000, although it reached 1,800,000 in 1869 and 4,000,000 in 1895.[58] Certainly the oversupply of textiles reduced profit margins. James Hodgson wrote Owens and Sons in 1833: "We are decided friends to prompt sales and quick returns with moderate profits convinced that in a general way no other are attainable. That such are not only the most certain, safest, enduring, but also on the aggregate the most profitable. Speaking generally, indeed compelled as you are at home to produce such immense quantity of goods, always out-turning actual consumption, not only at home, but abroad as well, it is out of the question to expect even with the best management other than my bare profits."[59]

Technological developments aggravated the problems of oversupplied markets. Although the newly developed railways, steamships, effective postal services, telegraphs, and submarine telegraph cables progressively improved the information available to merchants and manufacturers throughout the nineteenth century, the incentive to oversupply the Buenos Aires market remained strong. It was partly increased by the introduction of new techniques that made pastoral and agricultural activities seem more profitable. In the 1870s new agricultural machinery stimulated the expansion of grain production. Barbed wire fencing made it possible to combine crop raising and grazing and contributed to the expansion of both the cattle and wheat industries. The new methods of freezing meat eliminated the old salt preserving method. Immigration, which greatly accelerated after 1822, contributed new skills and attitudes to Argentina, while simultaneously leading industry and business to believe that the Republic possessed an increasing capacity to absorb both manpower and manufactures. The myth of increased opportunity rather than actual demand or purchasing power in Argentina influenced the pattern of British exports.

The demand for Argentine produce was less affected by cyclical disturbances in business conditions than was British industry. While the changes taking place in the industrial nations accentuated international specialization—a division of production between industrialized nations and nonindustrialized countries—the consumption of primary materials by the manufacturing countries continued to expand. When Wilder, Pickersgill, and Company, merchant bankers of Liverpool, wrote to the mercantile house of Hodgson, Robinson, and Company on April 5, 1837, they emphasized that the price of hides declined less than any other imported produce.[60] Similarly in the recession of 1839-1842 when business houses throughout the world curtailed their commercial operation to cut their deficits, mercantile houses in Argentina suffered relatively fewer losses from the contraction of trade. During the depression years of 1875 to 1879, when total United Kingdom exports fell, the Argentine demand for British manufactures actually increased.[61] *The Brazil and River Plate Mail* contended that domestic problems, rather than the state of the international economy, caused the abnormally high rate of failures. In effect, the crisis of 1875-1879 in Argentina affected investors in railways and public funds more than the banks and commercial enterprises dealing in Argentine imports and exports.[62] Argentina's produce in fact maintained its price level on the London market. Hides fell from the unprecedented high prices of 1872 and 1874 only back to the levels of 1870 and 1871.[63]

Argentina, like other nations in the Americas, developed during the nineteenth century under the protective shield of the Royal Navy. In the absence of oceanic wars Argentina benefited from both peace and hostilities in Europe. Peace allowed her to increase her wealth, prepare a settled policy of internal expansion, and develop new markets on the continent of Europe. War proved an even greater stimulus because British industry was then diverted from its European sources of pastoral produce to alternative suppliers such as Argentina. Once industry had secured new and reliable sources of supplies, it would be redirected to its original source only by large differentials in price. The Napoleonic Wars, for example, did much to stimulate Britain's initial interest in Argentina because the lack of Russian hides and tallow demanded alternative supplies. Even though the market demand for Argentine hides and tallow decreased under Prussian, Spanish, and Russian competition during the postwar depression, Argentina had established itself as an integral part of the international economy. Similarly, the Franco-Prussian war of 1870-71 increased the demand for Argentine hides and tallow, although it paralyzed the wool market.[64] Occasional wars also helped Argentine shipping. Because of the disturbed state of Europe in the 1850s Argentine citizens purchased merchant vessels and placed them under the flag of Buenos Aires. These ships drew some business from United Kingdom shippers and merchants but were too few to be a real threat to the position of British houses in the Buenos Aires trade.[65]

Argentina's insulation from the vagaries of European political rivalries was extended by the worldwide adoption of currencies based on a convertible gold standard, which increased trade and the scale of individual transactions by simplifying the calculations of price.[66] It was the laissez-faire policy of the United Kingdom which promoted freedom for the flow of capital from the countries of Europe to the unindustrialized countries of Latin America, Africa, and Asia. Many of the countries of Europe and the United States reduced their tariffs; when in the 1870s they raised them again, the most favored nation clause of treaties preserved for a short time the free trade nature of the earlier period. The multilateral nature of trade created interdependence in this period rather than a dependence. Great Britain demanded the raw material for its industry just as strongly as Argentina needed the manufactured goods. Low tariffs allowed both the industrialized and underdeveloped nations to benefit by trade.

Both the capital-importing and the capital-exporting nations derived substantial benefits from the freedom of capital movement. British capital financed a large part of the railroads in the United States and Latin America. The import of capital to build needed railroads promoted the development of the Argentine pampas as well as the United States' midwest. Foreign capital developed harbor facilities and such public utilities as water works and street car systems. It made possible development in countries that were capital short and promised high profit to European nationals. The export of capital was itself a stimulus to trade, as England increased trade with those countries to which her capital went. While investment of British capital in Argentina led to the increased sale of British goods there, the sale of Argentine produce in England did not increase with the same rapidity. However, by 1887 when capital and labor were moving in greater quantities into Argentina, there was a steady growth in total receipts from sale of Argentine produce in Great Britain. The outward flow of capital and the returns from it helped to accelerate trade toward the end of the 1880s and served to maintain greater trade until 1914.

With Argentina's independence, new opportunities and risks attracted British merchants, who oriented Buenos Aires and its hinterland toward the world market. The principal risks came from the repeated failures of Argentine governments to define a consistent fiscal policy and a coherent monetary system. In spite of the uncertainties imposed by fluctuating foreign exchange rates, inadequate financial infrastructure, taxation, and inflation, merchants profited. Businessmen also benefited from political disturbances because they were able to use the Anglo-Argentine community as a power base from which to press their commercial interests, which often coincided with government concerns. British merchants, acting as an essential catalyst, promoted economic growth. As imports and exports changed in nature and increased in quantity, the government gained larger revenues from greater trade. This circumstance increased national prosperity and furthered political stability.

Although the expanding world economy provided the basis for merchant opportunity in Argentina, Buenos Aires represented the local environment of British merchants. The technologies of the Industrial Revolution, which increased the demand for suppliers of raw materials and consumers of manufactured products, solidified the position of Buenos Aires as a trading center. The international gold standard and an era whose freedom from oceanic wars promoted commerce through a free trade policy also increased merchant profits in cities such as Buenos Aires. The commercial, bureaucratic nature of the city of Buenos Aires with its political power, foreign immigration, and commercial influence represented an environment that British merchants adapted to and utilized to promote their own economic interests and the power of Buenos Aires.[67]

3.

Politics and Society
in Buenos Aires

IN THE EARLY part of the nineteenth century, government officials and travelers described the physical characteristics, the ethnic structure, and the commercial significance of the city of Buenos Aires. Henry Brackenridge, a United States government official who visited Buenos Aires in 1817 and 1818, noted that

> Buenos Aires stretches along a high bank about two miles; its domes and steeples, and heavy masses of buildings give it an imposing but somewhat gloomy aspect . . . the streets are straight and regular . . . a few of them are paved, but hollow in the middle. The houses are pretty, generally two stories high, with flat roofs, and, for the most part, plastered on the outside . . . The shops, or stores, as far as I observed in my perambulation through the city, are all on a very small scale, and make no show as in our towns. There are but a few signs, and those belong chiefly to foreigners . . . The greater part of the trade which is now flourishing here, particularly hatters, blacksmiths, and many others that I might enumerate, have been established since the revolution; the journeymen, mechanics, are chiefly half indians and mulattoes.[1]

Travelers to Buenos Aires also observed Spanish influences—the public markets, religious celebrations, the cock and bull fights, dances and evening walks as well as the number of foreigners and the mixed racial population.[2] In the 1840s visitors to the city found the exteriors of houses dilapidated, the streets full of filth, but the interiors of houses contained almost as many comforts and luxuries as were found in well appointed London dwellings—an indication of the prosperity of the city and the dominance of the import-export trade.[3] Although Buenos Aires was a healthier city than most South American towns, it was not as free from disease as many European urban areas. As late as the 1870s the annual mortality, excluding deaths during epidemics, was forty-two per thousand, while in London the mortality rate was twenty-five per thousand. The average life expectancy in London was forty-one years, while in Buenos Aires it was only twenty-five. If one-fourth deduction were made for infant mortality, the average adult life totaled thirty-one years, against fifty years in London.[4]

Buenos Aires was a city in racial, cultural, and economic transition. Change showed not only in the gradual replacement of bargaining by fixed prices and the increasing ranges of European goods but in the emergence of new communities. Merchant and settler risks from the political environment of Argentina were substantially reduced because the government was determined to attract foreign capital and personnel to develop the state. Immigrants in fact provided a permanent and rapidly increasing group from whom British merchants made considerable profits. The proximity of Argentina to Europe, its temperate climate, its apparent wealth in produce demanded in Europe, and its seeming political stability in the early 1820s and especially after 1860 encouraged an inflow of immigrants and foreign capital. After the end of the Rosas era and particularly during the administration of Sarmiento between 1868 and 1874, the government made determined efforts to attract overseas money and skills.

The new naturalization law Argentina enacted in 1869 exempted individuals from the two-year residence requirement if they had served in a national or provincial government office, been in the army or navy, established a new industry in the country or introduced a new invention, promoted or constructed railroads, settled on the frontiers, married an Argentine woman, or served as a professional in any branch of industry or education.[5] In that same year 49.5 percent of the population of Buenos Aires was foreign born. In the period 1857 to 1913 forty persons left Argentina out of each one thousand entering. Three-fourths of all the immigrants had come from the rural areas of Europe and represented the lower income groups of their respective countries.[6] As table 3 indicates, the foreign population became an increasingly larger percentage of the total population of the city.

Immigrants came to Argentina intending to improve both their economic and social position. By 1871 emigration from Great Britain consisted principally of gentlemen farmers with little capital, engineers who were able to obtain unusually high wages from construction, and some opportunistic agricultural laborers. Shopmen and clerks were no longer in demand and merchants found the market competitive in their field.[7] The myth of the great future that they could make in Argentina is best illustrated by a quotation from José Salverria in a chapter entitled

Table 3. Foreign population in relation to the total population of the city of Buenos Aires, 1810-1875.

Date	Total population	Foreign-born population	Foreign-born population as percent of total population
1810[a]	46,000	1,000	2.2
1822[a]	55,460	3,749	6.8
1836	62,228[a]	30,000[b]	48.5
1852	76,000[a]	35,000[c]	46.0
1869[d]	177,787	88,121	49.5
1875[e]	236,000	125,000	54.3

[a]José Ingenieros, *Sociología Argentina* (Buenos Aires: Editorial Lasada, 1946), appendix 1.

[b]George Thomas Love, *A Five Years' Residence in Buenos Ayres during the Years 1820-1825* (London: G. Herbert, 1825), p. 52.

[c]This is an approximation based upon Woodbine Parish, *Buenos Ayres and the Provinces of the Río de la Plata* (London: John Murray, 1852), p. 177.

[d]*Brazil and River Plate Mail*, 8 March 1870, p. 6.

[e]*Brazil and River Plate Mail*, 23 October 1876, p. 6.

"The Song of the Immigrants": "Let us go to a roomy and bright country; to a country without boundaries, to a country of unawareness; to a land that does not bill, nor judge, nor collect, nor suspect; to a country where there is no fear of tomorrow, but rather loves the morrow, with the bright and happy confidence of a child. Let us go to the land of promise where there yet exists change and fortune and the unforeseen, and the crazy surprise."[8] Three conditions fostered this myth of immigrant opportunity: the writings of Argentine authors and politicians, government efforts to encourage immigration, and the general appearance of political stability and economic prosperity of Argentina after 1860.

Many Argentines were certain that immigrants would add to the prosperity of the country. Juan B. Alberdi, journalist and diplomat of the Confederation, argued that Argentina should imitate the United States. The Confederate constitution of 1853 reflects his belief in the virtues of a republican democracy and the need for industrious immigrants. Domingo F. Sarmiento, President of Argentina from 1868 to 1874, was one of the most vocal proponents of European immigration. His *Facundo* or *Civilization and Barbarism* is a condemnation of Argentine caudillism and a glorification of European culture.[9] Travelers such as Henry Brackenridge commented that Argentine nationals sought to learn the methods the United States used to stimulate immigration and expressed the belief that European immigration would bring wealth to Argentina.

Immigration buttressed Buenos Aires as the entrepôt, clearinghouse, warehouse, and distribution center for the whole Argentine Republic. The importers of the Argentine Republic were the importers of the city of Buenos Aires; the exporters of the Republic were the exporters of Buenos Aires and later of Rosario. The import-export merchants established their businesses close to both the government offices and the customhouse; in the eight block area surrounding the Plaza de la Victoria (figure 2).[10] From these conveniently situated premises, merchants lobbied Argentine government officials and foreign diplomats and consuls in their own interests. The British community, like other foreign groups of Buenos Aires, aided new arrivals in adapting to Argentina and preserved a familiar way of life. Most important, the British residents acted as a pressure group to further their own interests and protect their members.

A British community first came into existence in Buenos Aires in 1806.[11] The new commercial opportunities offered by the Popham invasion attracted individuals from England, Scotland, Wales, and Ireland. By 1824 the British community had grown to 1,355, rising to over 3,000 by 1869.[12] In the period 1876-1897, 154,554 British immigrants entered Argentina.[13] Although the census of 1869 reliably estimated the number of British residents in the city of Buenos Aires children born in Argentina of British parents were not considered British by the census takers. United Kingdom consuls repeatedly requested British subjects to register, but the new residents rarely bothered and men did not always list their wives and children.[14]

The members of the British community in Buenos Aires primarily performed commercial services as merchants, brokers, bankers, and shipping agents. A vast amount of the import-export trade passed through their hands. Through their commercial capital, experience, and connections the British established their position in Buenos Aires and influenced the broader Buenos Aires community. The British merchants' reputation for honesty gave rise to the phrase *palabra de Inglés*, still used today as a compliment denoting the highest integrity.[15]

The opening of the British commercial rooms in 1810 marked the first concrete efforts of Britons in Buenos Aires to form some type of organization for the promotion of their commercial activities and the offering of increased social contacts. The rooms offered not only social opportunities and relaxation but information of particular importance to merchants. A constant lookout was kept for vessels arriving and departing and entries made of them. The rooms contained a large collection of excellent maps, United Kingdom newspapers such as *The Courier, The*

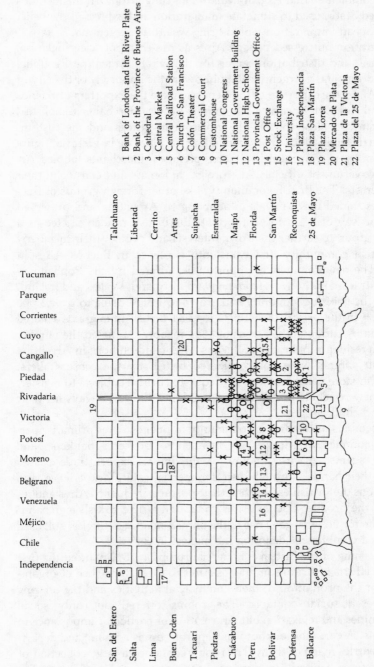

2. Map of the city of Buenos Aires, 1862.

1 Bank of London and the River Plate
2 Bank of the Province of Buenos Aires
3 Cathedral
4 Central Market
5 Central Railroad Station
6 Church of San Francisco
7 Colón Theater
8 Commercial Court
9 Customhouse
10 National Congress
11 National Government Building
12 National High School
13 Provincial Government Office
14 Post Office
15 Stock Exchange
16 University
17 Plaza Independencia
18 Plaza San Martín
19 Plaza Lorea
20 Mercado de Plata
21 Plaza de la Victoria
22 Plaza del 25 de Mayo

Times, Morning Chronicle, and *Bell's Messenger,* the Buenos Aires newspapers, and journals such as the *Shipping List, Quarterly Review,* and *Edinburgh Review.* Membership was restricted to Britons, but in 1825 the facilities of the rooms were available to any person introduced by one of the fifty-six subscribers. The most exclusive function of the rooms, the quarterly dinners where members discussed the affairs of the society, was of course restricted to the British community.[16]

The early British involvement in clubs was but one way of strengthening contacts and improving communications among themselves and other merchants. The meetings generally dealt with topics that directly affected the British community, such as welcoming a new consul, honoring a departing one, dealing with the problems of the British church or with commercial concerns. Although other British subjects were active in community affairs, merchants tended to dominate the public assemblies and committees.[17]

The British commercial rooms relocated several times during the early years and continued until 1829. In that year a new commercial room opened under the guidance of a committee of British import-export merchants. The Buenos Aires Commercial Rooms, which welcomed a wider membership, performed many of the same functions as the earlier commercial rooms. The maritime news of the day was carefully recorded, the departure of vessels noted, and a box placed to receive letters and information that was of interest to the commercial members. The diplomatic authorities of every nation resident in Buenos Aires and the officers of vessels of war, packets, and merchant vessels had free admittance. Persons of any nation were admitted as subscribers at 50 pesos currency per year in 1829, but no person who was not a member could use the rooms. The Buenos Aires Commercial Rooms continued until 1840, when Rosas imprisoned many of the merchants in the association because of their supposed political opposition.[18]

While the Argentine government suspected the intentions of commercial societies, it largely ignored the alternative opportunities for protest open to Britons, and therefore religious and educational institutions and social clubs operated as informal commercial assemblies. The Anglican Church gained recognition in Argentina under the treaty of 1825 and the British community promptly commenced the building of St. John's Cathedral. Officially classified as a consular chaplaincy of the Church of England, the cathedral received generous financial support from the United Kingdom government until 1875, when the Anglican community became self-supporting. Although the Established Church of Scotland never received such assistance, in 1833 the Presbyterian community in Buenos Aires laid the foundation stone of their own church. By 1862 the English, Scots, Americans, and Germans maintained Protestant churches in Buenos Aires. Merchants were the principal contributors to both the Anglican and Presbyterian churches. The rivalry of two established churches divided British loyalties, but Anglicans and Presbyterians alike regularly attended community and commercial meetings in the Anglican cathedral. The strength of the churches lay in the unity they gave to the British community; their weakness lay in isolating Britons from the national Catholic community of Buenos Aires.[19]

Merchants encouraged the founding of British schools in Buenos Aires and financially supported the Buenos Aires School Society. In 1827 the British community founded two schools, for boys and girls respectively, under the auspices of the Church of England. In 1838 the Presbyterians founded a school for girls and a few years later a school for boys. The schools provided basic education for the children of the British community. For higher education, wealthy Britons, like other prosperous foreigners, sent their children overseas.[20] For financial and religious reasons few nationals chose to educate their children in the Anglo-Argentine institutions, but these schools provided a badly needed service to Britons. The Argentine school system developed slowly. In 1825 only 2,526 boys and 1,788 girls, primarily in Buenos Aires, received public instruction in Argentina, while the university had 415 students. In 1860 the government of Buenos Aires allocated funds to found numerous charity schools in the capital and the province. At that time the total number enrolled in both private and public schools was 11,208.'[21]

Social activities—dinners, dances, recreation, and sports—helped to unify the British community.[22] Britons wished to make their community in Buenos Aires as much like England as possible, while making their wealth so they could return home. And in the case of import-export merchants, going back to England often became a reality. If the profits were substantial, the firm might be dissolved. Or the senior partner would return to England to run the firm there and place a junior partner in Buenos Aires. Sports clubs served as the social clubs for Britons, the place where they had the opportunity to meet each other, to discuss business, play English games, and drink British liquor. The clubs preserved the British way of life in a foreign country.

Walter Heald, who arrived in Buenos Aires in 1866 to learn the import-export trade, participated in the Football Club, rode and played cricket, and also supported the Foreign Club, the Masons, and a library society. Heald, like other Britons, enjoyed going to the races at Belgrano or to the theater and opera at the national theater, the Colón. On Sunday he might attend the Presbyterian or Anglican church in the morning and evening. He enjoyed parties, dinners, and evenings of whist. Heald aided the benefit performances for the British Hospital and helped out at the annual sport's day activities. He spent long weekends and vacations on ranches in the country hunting and riding.[23]

Although the social activities of the British community were similar to those of the Buenos Aires community, Britons displayed a preference for contact with others of their own nationality and often expressed nostalgia for England. Many merchants wrote colleagues in Great Britain requesting them to send English brewed ale, potatoes, Cheshire cheese, butter, and bacon. Others sought to maintain their way of life without such luxuries. They preserved traditions in their home by educating their children in English principles, manners, and religion. With time the British community in Buenos Aires began to acquire some roots in Buenos Aires. While some British merchants developed such social and economic interests in Argentina that they became more involved in the Argentine society than in the British colony in Buenos Aires, a few Argentine nationals sent their children to British schools and joined the British church.

THE FORMATION of commercial associations open to all foreigners proved the first stage of British assimilation into the society of Buenos Aires. In May 1841 the merchants, distressed by the disbandment of the Buenos Aires Commercial Rooms, met under the chairmanship of the Consul of the United States, Amory Edwards, to form the Sociedad de Residentes Extranjeros, the Foreign Club. This organization provided an opportunity for social and business communication and conducted a limited stock exchange for the Buenos Aires community. The association quickly grew in membership, although the entrance fee of 2000 pesos (£15 to £16) plus dues of 50 pesos per month excluded impecunious aliens.[24] Although the Foreign Club was founded and supported by immigrants, by 1880 Argentine citizens were no longer excluded and meetings were carried on in Spanish. The Foreign Club originally operated the stock exchange from 12 to 1 p.m. each day, maintained a library primarily of commercial journals, and displayed the latest maritime notices. In 1841, out of a membership of 148, over sixty percent were in commerce; the rest were involved in meatpacking, ranching, government, or industry. The Foreign Club prided itself on the contributions its members made to Argentine development and their activity in the Free Masons, the Protestant communities, and other associations.[25]

British import-export merchants were active in founding the stock exchange in July 1854 under the presidency of one of their colleagues, Daniel Gowland. Thomas Armstrong, another prominent British merchant, was president from 1857 to 1858. The stock exchange provided a locale where business, which had previously been carried on in private homes, could be transacted. In the stock exchange itself, the merchants seemed to group by nationality. Thus, the British and German brokers might be found at one location and the French and Italians at another.[26]

British merchants occasionally participated in organizations dominated by Argentines. The Rural Association, founded in 1866 with the object of protecting rural interests and improving pastoral and agricultural industry, attracted a number of Britons such as Richard Newton, a merchant and large ranch owner, who became vice president.[27] However, Argentine social clubs attracted less British support. The Progress Club, founded in 1852, and the La Plata, founded in 1860, admitted foreigners but attracted few Britons, although families like the Gowlands and the Lumbs, who had adopted Argentine citizenship, participated fully in the various activities.[28]

Britons were less inclined to take advantage of offers of citizenship than other immigrants. For example, the Spanish and Portuguese took Argentine nationality to protect themselves against accusations of disloyalty during troubles with Spain and Brazil. The British, while facing similar accusations during the blockade of 1845 to 1848, always received the protection of the Anglo-Argentine treaty of 1825 and the British Consul. Furthermore, laws which gave foreigners virtually all the rights of citizenship tended to discourage them from becoming citizens. Although foreigners could not vote, they generally were not required to perform military service. Some British merchants obtained Argentine citizenship to extend their commercial operations, protect their property, and ensure the chance of permanent residence in Argentina. Britons who married Argentine women were more likely to seek citizenship. Such men as Robert Billinghurst and Thomas Gowland, with Argentine citizenship and Argentine wives, were also active politically in Argentina. These individuals acquired both financial wealth and social status in Argentina.[29] However, it is impossible to prove that the more successful resided permanently in Argentina while the less successful returned to England, or vice versa. It can only be suggested that a larger degree of acculturation at the political and social levels aided business transactions in a society in which government contracts often went to friends or acquaintances and in which business was conducted on a personal level.

The Anglo-Argentine treaty of 1825 permitted the marriage of Protestants by religious ceremony within Argentina. Thus individuals were no longer dependent upon the British Consul or the captain of a Royal Navy vessel to perform the ceremony.[30] However, marriage between Catholics and Protestants caused more difficulty because Britons were usually obliged to conform to the rites of the Church of Rome. Before 1832 the church rarely granted a dispensation to a Catholic to marry a Protestant. In that year the marriage of Samuel Lafone to María Quevedo y Alsina on June 23, 1832, brought wide discussion of alliances between Protestants and Catholics. Samuel Lafone was a hide merchant connected with tanners in Liverpool and active in the Anglican Church. His marriage was performed by a Protestant minister and immediately denounced by the Catholic bishop of Argentina. The Ecclesiastical Court placed the mother and daughter in a convent, imprisoned and fined Lafone and his witness, and annulled the marriage. Lafone petitioned the British Consul and asked the General Assembly to rule in his favor. However, the law which nullified those marriages between persons of different religions remained in operation, and the government insisted upon ecclesiastical authorization for such marriages. When Samuel Lafone applied for a dispensation, the Catholic Church approved his marriage and on June 17, 1833, he and María Quevedo were married again, first according to the law of the Catholic Church and then in the Anglican Church.[31]

During the Rosas period, requests of dispensation were placed before the civil government, but the decision was reached according to ecclesiastical guidelines. Not until November 2, 1888, did Argentine law allow civil marriages. In effect, the laws of the Roman Catholic Church dictated that those British marrying Argentine Catholic women, while they need not become Catholic, must rear their children in the Catholic faith. Thus, in all probability, the second generation of such marriages merged into Argentine society.

The various degrees of acculturation of foreigners in Buenos Aires can be illustrated by an examination of the Foreign Club membership in 1841. Although the information on the 148 members is incomplete, there is material on the marriages of sixty-eight persons. Of these, 56 percent married Argentine women, while 25 percent married other immigrant women in Argentina. Quite often the Argentine women were members of important government or commercial families. Of the ninety-seven members on whom there is information on whether they remained in Argentina or returned to Europe or the United States, only 25 percent returned and many of these for business reasons such as to head houses in England connected with their Argentine businesses. The meager material suggests that religious acculturation of the members took place to a lesser degree than commercial acculturation, since a large percentage of members were noted as Protestants; but the baptism and marriage records of the Anglican Church yielded far fewer merchant names than would be expected if there were no religious acculturation. Argentine women clearly brought up many of their children as Catholics.[32]

The evidence concerning the acculturation of British merchants appears conflicting. On the one hand, there are the examples of merchants who took out Argentine citizenship, were active in the Argentine political scene, and married Argentine women. On the other hand, there is the evidence of a strong British community that still preserved a British way of life in Argentina. In nineteenth-century Buenos Aires, merchants provided strong leadership in an active and vibrant British community. The British educated their children in their manners and customs both in the home and in English schools in Buenos Aires and abroad. The British merchants looked toward making fortunes and returning to the United Kingdom. Many were able to do this. However, many Britons assimilated into the Argentine society. British merchants married Argentine women. Children were raised in the Catholic Church and spoke Spanish more fluently than English. Thus, by the second and third generation, many Britons had become Argentine citizens by both birth and culture and were no longer active in the British community. By June 21, 1872, for example, the British Library, which had been operating for more than forty years, ceased to exist for lack of support.[33]

The British community was a changing one—being reinvigorated by new groups of immigrants while older ones returned to England or moved into Argentine society. Those entering Buenos Aires society may be traced by the marriage and baptismal records. That the percentage of merchants in the Foreign Club marrying Argentine women is quite high and that families such as the Lumbs, the Gowlands, and the Armstrongs were by the first and second generation active in Argentine circles suggest that the movement into Buenos Aires society, even among Protestants, was significant.

THE BRITISH community in Buenos Aires served as an intermediary step between England and Argentina. It helped the immigrant adapt to life in a new environment, providing a base from which individuals could move out into the broader community. At the same time the British community sought to preserve familiar ways and to protect what was British. From this solid cohesive community, British merchants moved toward a greater participation in Buenos Aires economic, political, and social life.

The cohesion of the British community in Buenos Aires enabled Britons to exert effective pressure upon both the United Kingdom and Argentine governments. The Anglo-Argentine treaty of 1825 encouraged British businessmen to lobby for their own interests and gave the British Consul a legal basis for the defense of merchant interests. The power of British merchants in Buenos Aires politics depended in the last resort upon appeal to the international standing of the United Kingdom and the reliance of Argentina upon external trade.

British residents in Buenos Aires usually protested through committees, often under merchant leadership, which dispatched petitions to the British Consul as well as to the United Kingdom and Argentine governments. Committees prevented individual victimization and indicated widespread dissatisfaction worthy of official notice. Although ad hoc committees had been formed to deal with previous issues, on November 13, 1834, a public meeting of British merchants resident in Buenos Aires assembled to organize a permanent committee composed of seven persons chosen by ballot for a twelve month term. It was empowered to call general meetings and levy a general subscription to cover its expenses. With one exception the elected members of 1834 were all import-export merchants.[34]

The ability of British merchants to act as a body and to require certain standards among themselves made them an effective pressure group. In 1836 the committee proposed a code of ethics to govern certain aspects of business activities. Accepted by a general meeting of British merchants, this code aided their reputations as dependable men of commerce. It established procedures for the payment of foreign exchange bills under protest for nonpayment, regulated commission charges for handling cargoes in the port of Buenos Aires, and unified the fees for surveying damaged goods.[35] In 1852 the code was strengthened when the committee recommended that, in the case of vessels containing general cargoes (a large number of different goods consigned to various merchants), the merchant to whom the ship was consigned would land and take the goods through customs. Other measures adopted included the standardization of commission rates on consigned vessels; agreement that the freight charges paid in Buenos Aires were to be made at the rate of exchange in London on the last business day of the month in which the vessel arrived; and the arrangement of more efficient regulations for discharging general vessels, in agreement with the stevedoring companies. The committee reported that its protest to the directors of the Royal Mail Steamship Company concerning the detention of parcels at Rio de Janeiro had elicited a reply from the agent in Rio promising that steps would be taken to prevent a recurrence of such delays.[36]

The merchants, of course, did not always agree upon political priorities. In 1845 four or five commercial houses strongly connected with the Buenos Aires government requested that the United Kingdom should not intervene in the differences among the states of the Río de la Plata and even asserted that they might censure any measures adopted by the British government. These merchants felt that since their interests were at stake, they had the right to judge the circumstances for intervention. However, many other merchants refused to sign the petition and sent letters to the British Consul supporting United Kingdom political decisions.[37]

British merchants seldom participated in local politics. Britons were not inclined to hold positions in either the national or provincial governments, although they were more than willing to perform services for the government.[38] Thus, British merchants avoided military service while subscribing to the public library, aiding education, contributing toward funds for the widows of men who died in battle, and donating funds for the repair of roads.

The British community, being self-sufficient and cohesive, devoted attention to the plight of Britons involved in South American adversities. In 1823 and later years subscriptions assisted British residents in Paraguay. By 1835 the British Friendly Society of Buenos Aires provided temporary relief to British subjects unable to support themselves because of sickness or accident. The committee helped widows and orphaned children and provided medical assistance. In 1843 a general meeting of British subjects established a hospital for Anglo-Argentines. Prominent merchants sat on the first board of trustees.[39]

When British merchants felt that the Buenos Aires government threatened their rights as British subjects, they protested to the British Consul. During threatened blockades committees of merchants demanded that the consul should obtain a time extension for vessels to leave before closure of the port. The consul ably arranged an extension with the French squadron during the French blockade but was less successful in protecting British interests during other blockades.[40] The British Consul in Buenos Aires was both receptive and vulnerable to merchant criticism. He received their appreciation for services rendered and their approbation for his inaction. He could expect their opinions about the designation of a temporary consul in his absence and their keen observations on the state of commerce in the Río de la Plata.[41]

The actions of British consuls in Buenos Aires did much to supplement the commercial treaty of 1825. For example, Woodbine Parish, first British Consul in Argentina, acted as an intermediary between British citizens and the local government by representing the interests of British subjects. Consuls also lodged protests against arbitrary actions taken by local authorities. For example, a protest was made on behalf of a merchant, Duncan Stewart, who had his visa to go to Santa Fe and Entre Ríos revoked and was informed he had to leave the Republic within nine days. Similarly, British representatives in Argentina supported Britons in such matters as their claim for exemption from service in the national guard.[42]

Consular representation of direct claims against the government gave British residents in Buenos Aires a considerable advantage over Argentines. Most of the claims made between 1828 and 1852 pertained to loss of property in the interior provinces because of civil disturbances.

British citizens successfully claimed compensation for cattle appropriated and houses ransacked by government troops because they possessed the services of a consul. Probably the surprising factor is not how large were the number of claims but how small in relation to the supposed political instability of the period.[43]

At times British merchants bypassed the consul to appeal directly to the United Kingdom government, usually with a conspicuous lack of success. During the Anglo-French blockade, the Foreign Office ignored a merchant petition for permission to pass through the British blockade. The United Kingdom authorities gave more sympathy to appeals for the protection of person and property during civil disturbances.[44] Even a neutral policy of the British government offered certain advantages to the commercial community. Britain's neutrality in the Wars of Independence and her refusal to permit other nations to intervene or to furnish military assistance against rebel forces almost guaranteed a successful revolution. Since the United Kingdom excelled in manufacturing and marketing, a policy demanding fair and equal treatment for Britons guaranteed British dominance in trade.

British merchants used their political and personal contacts in Great Britain to increase their trading advantages. During the Wars of Independence, British merchants urged the United Kingdom government to aid the belligerents rather than remain neutral. While unsuccessful in this endeavor, their pressure led to the enforcement of complete neutrality. The rapid growth of British trade with South America created influential pressure from merchants in South America and their partners in Manchester, Liverpool, and Glasgow for United Kingdom recognition of the new republics.

Once independence was assured, merchant organizations such as the Manchester Chamber of Commerce persuaded the government to appoint British consuls to all the chief commercial towns, including Buenos Aires. Not only did the combined pressure of the British community in Buenos Aires and United Kingdom merchants encourage independence, but the merchants made their influence felt on other subjects. Merchants in Buenos Aires, for example, never sympathized with the British blockade of Buenos Aires. Their protests probably influenced the naval commander of Buenos Aires to withdraw his warships on July 15, 1847, contrary to specific instructions from London.[45]

British merchants applied pressure not only on their own government to protect their interests but on the Buenos Aires authorities as well. As early as 1810 the British merchants, in a petition to the Buenos Aires government, called attention to their services to the Argentine Republic. After noticing their support of the government action against the contrabandists, they protested against the unequal rates of the tariff and complained about the requirement that cargoes should be imported and exported only by Spanish merchants.[46]

In 1852 a political crisis arose which terminated with Justo José de Urquiza's assumption of power under a banner of "federalism" and the adoption of a policy of freedom of navigation, with abolition of interprovincial duties and equalization of port and pilotage charges against foreign shipping. As a consequence of this crisis British merchants requested the Buenos Aires government to adopt a bonded system. The government provided warehouses and permitted goods to be stored at low rates until duties were paid on the goods or they were reexported. Since the government had already decided in favor of the system, it requested the advice of the merchants on how to implement it. The merchants specifically suggested that storage time of goods in the process of transshipment be extended from six to twelve months. The merchants also proposed the abolition of the law that exacted twenty-five percent more from goods coming from Montevideo than from other ports. In September the merchants' committee urged the Buenos Aires House of Representatives to reduce the storage rate on goods in the customshouse. In February 1853 the committee successfully petitioned the Buenos Aires government for an extension of time for the reshipment of goods, since the customshouse had been closed temporarily.[47]

British merchants' influence contributed to the acquisition of government concessions. During the Wars of Independence British merchants had responsibility for auctioning booty. They often obtained government contracts to import government supplies. The British import-export house of Hodgson and Robinson in 1841 and 1842 imported goods ordered by Simón Pereira, nephew of General Rosas, Commissary General, who was responsible for providing all the army and navy clothing and supplies. Thus Anglo-Argentine firms handled a large share of government-ordered merchandise.[48]

The effectiveness of merchant protest to the Argentine government may have reflected close personal relations rather than formal exchanges between merchants and officials. Thus, import-export merchants such as George Frederick Dickson, who served as Argentine Consul in England in 1855, sometimes represented the Argentine government in London.[49] Similarly, the Wars of Independence and the habit of Argentine politicians to spend some time in Great Britain aided Anglo-Argentine influence. Certainly such foreign residence led Bernardino Rivadavia and Bartolomé Mitre to conceive an enthusiasm for Anglo-Argentine commerce.[50] Nevertheless, British merchants occasionally voiced dissatisfaction about Argentine conditions, particularly about various decrees affecting commerce, the Consulado (Merchant Guild and Commercial Court), and antiforeign sentiment. Legislation before 1812 decidedly favored nationals. Although foreigners were permitted to import goods into the country, marketing was restricted to Argentines. After a period in 1811, when British merchants endured the threat of expulsion, the decree of September 1812 permitted foreigners to sell goods without consigning them to nationals.[51]

Most of the decrees British merchants protested fell equally upon national and foreign merchants. However, when the decrees directly pertained to the import-export trade, British merchants suffered greater difficulties. For example, various decrees prohibiting the export of bullion and coin worked to the detriment of British merchants because these measures hindered remittances to the United Kingdom. Decrees respecting the specific export of produce, although probably enforced with lethargy, primarily affected national merchants. In 1834 the government decreed that coypu should not be hunted, which restricted the trade in nutria skins. Two years later the decree expired. In May 1838 a decree prohibited the export of wheat and flour during the continuance of the blockade, but this had little direct effect upon the British merchants, who exported little wheat.[52]

All trade endured impositions from lack of legal protection. Not until 1856 was there a law that specifically sanctioned the formation of joint stock companies. And only in 1876 did the government approve a complete trademark law. Without a joint stock law, businessmen used a proprietorship or partnership form of organization. Before the passage of a trademark law, the government granted sole title in a trademark to the first person who registered the article. That person received the right ad infinitum. An individual would register the trademark and then write to a manufacturer and offer to market the article. The manufacturer could either appoint the person his agent or pay him a price for the right to sell the article under its original name.[53]

In the early period merchants complained that the Consulado was antiforeign. In fact, in the 1810 to 1820 period, the Consulado made efforts to obtain favorable trade preferences for Argentine-nationals. Specifically, it demanded lower duties on the imports and exports handled by nationals. Yet the treatment of the numerous British cases by the commercial court showed that the Consulado made every effort to rule fairly.[54] The British complaints of antiforeign feeling in Buenos Aires in the nineteenth century had only a degree of truth. Most of the xenophobic feelings in Argentina developed after 1880, when large foreign immigration and the international depression had greatly changed the social and political power structure of the country. Books written in the post-1880 period transferred an antiforeign bias onto the earlier period. Sociological-historical writers Julio Mafud and Leopold Lugones, for example, saw immigrants as always looking toward Europe, always desiring to remain foreigners, and always obsessed with the desire to return home.[55] Prior to 1880 some national resentment occasionally flared, particularly when British merchants profited in periods of depressed trade or enjoyed the rights of citizenship without the duty of military service; but on the whole Britons maintained good relations with Argentine nationals.

BRITISH merchants in Buenos Aires in the nineteenth century profited by the civil disturbances and blockades because they used the Anglo-Argentine community as a power base from which to press their commercial interests, which often coincided with government concerns. When government fiscal and political policy did not coincide with commercial interests, merchants effectively appealed to both the United Kingdom and Argentine government. The cohesiveness of the British community aided in the social adaptation to Buenos Aires while providing a channel for movement into the broader Argentine community. The Anglo-Argentine treaty of 1825, the institution of the mercantile house, the merchant's political and personal contacts in Great Britain, as well as the unity of the British community served as stabilizing forces for trade and investment in Argentina. Through individual proprietorships and partnerships British merchants expanded business operations to meet Argentine demands for industrial goods and international requirements for raw materials.

4.

The Organization and Operation
of the British Mercantile House

BUSINESS practices in the United Kingdom and the quality of communications determined the structure, finance, and functions of British mercantile houses in Buenos Aires between 1810 and 1880. British import-export firms adopted forms of organization and operation that had been developed to market United Kingdom cotton goods elsewhere in the world. However, mercantile houses were organized not merely to market Argentine and British goods but also to create local manufactures, introduce foreign skills, transmit information, and promote the flow of capital.

Innovation and business in Argentina depended upon effective oceanic communication for profit and even survival. During most of the nineteenth century British packets linked Europe and Argentina and provided the only regularly scheduled means of communicating the state of the international market. Changes in the technology of communications, such as the introduction of oceangoing steamships during the 1850s and the extension of the South American submarine telegraph cables to Buenos Aires in 1876, drew British merchants into ever closer contact with the supply and demand of the European market.

The variations of the international market only partly accounted for the fluctuations in the number of British import-export houses operating in Buenos Aires. The multifunctional nature of the houses, their reluctance or inability to preserve records, and the ease of bankruptcy or liquidation confused the identify and extent of merchant operations. British houses were sometimes indistinguishable from foreign or national houses, and few observers even ventured a precise enumeration of the British houses. This confusion came partly from the highly competitive character of the Buenos Aires market, where slow communications, variable prices, and local instabilities reduced profit margins and placed a

Table 4. Import-export houses in Buenos Aires for various years, 1818-1869.

Year	Total mercantile houses	Number of British houses	British houses as a percent of total houses	Sources
1818	—	55	—	UM/HR Green and Hodgson Letter Book, 6 Nov. 1818.
1820	—	38	—	Love, *A Five Years' Residence in Buenos Ayres during the Years 1820-1825.*
1825	85	28	33	Blondel, *Almanaque político y de comercio de la ciudad de Buenos Aires* (1826).
1827	—	37	—	Battolla, *Los primeros Ingleses en Buenos Aires, 1780-1830.*
1828	82	31	38	Blondel, *Almanaque* (1829).
1829	114	38	33	Blondel, *Almanaque* (1830).
1832	137	50	36	Blondel, *Almanaque* (1833).
1833	138	49	37	Blondel, *Almanaque* (1834).
1835	127	52	40	Blondel, *Almanaque* (1836).
1842	—	40	—	PRO/F.O. 6/153, 1842.
1850	—	52	—	PRO/F.O. 6/153, 1850.
1852	—	45	—	BA/HC, 16, B.A. 1857.
1854	162	37	23	*Almanaque comercial y guía de forasteros para el estado de Buenos Aires* (1855).
1857	—	40	—	BA/HC, 16, B.A. 1857.
1862	139	33	23	*Plano comercial y estadístico de la cuidad de Buenos Aires* (1862).
1863	—	26	—	Belgium, *Recueil consulaire,* vol. 9.
1863	111	27	24	Pillado, *Diccionario de Buenos Aires* (1864).
1866	150	27	18	*El Avisador: guía general del comercio y de forasteros* (1866-67).
1869	—	41	—	*Advisador general* (1870).

premium upon privacy. Although the variation in the number of functioning British houses appears to be great, as shown in table 4, an improvement in world business conditions and the Argentine political situation brought an increase in the number of houses. Between 1810 and 1818 merchants, who had arrived in large numbers in the Río de la Plata, realized that the trade would not support so many houses. Soon some were liquidated while others consolidated or went bankrupt. James Hodgson, a British merchant in Buenos Aires from 1817 to 1844, noted in 1818 that while fifty-five houses operated in Buenos Aires, "the trade appears to me to be greatly overdone at present so much so that if things do not mend, some of our establishments will find themselves under the necessity of giving up the trade."[1] Twenty-seven houses ceased business between 1818 and 1825, but trade soon recovered from the postwar recession and the uncertainties of Latin American political independence. Although a Brazilian blockade of the port of Buenos Aires partly accounts for house failures in 1828, a worldwide business recession certainly exerted more influence upon failures between 1835 and 1842 than did the French blockade from 1838 to 1840. The continued decline in the number of houses during an expansion of the world economy between 1852 and 1863 must surely be ascribed to the increasing insecurity and falling profit margins attributed to the Argentine civil war.[2] Given the political and economic risks in Argentina, the fluctuations of the world market, and the nature of trade from 1810 to 1880, the survival of the British mercantile house is more remarkable than a rash of individual bankruptcies.

Contemporary observers identified British houses in Buenos Aires only in a limited number of years and then without applying a uniform criteria. Because houses were defined as British if the principal volume of their trade lay with the United Kingdom or if they were managed by Britons, the number of British houses was overestimated. Martin F. Hood, the British Consul in Buenos Aires, provided the only systematically researched statement of British influence. He compiled his information in 1850 by personal questionnaires to each firm. Hood even distinguished those concerns mainly engaged in the import-export trade from those specializing in local business while occasionally indulging in foreign transactions on their own account.[3] British houses might be distinguished from other foreign houses by three criteria: the major countries with which business was done, the origin of the capital, and the nationality of the partners, which is the basic criterion for table 4.

British observers classified houses according to the origin of imported goods, since a large part of Argentina's imports came from the United Kingdom. This definition overlooked the entrepreneurship of other nationals and led to the conclusion that Argentines were unimportant in the import-export trade. Thus, A. Rivolta and Company, an Argentine concern trading with the United Kingdom, was certainly considered a British house.[4] Similarly, Daniel Gowland, an Englishman who traded with the United States, was married to a *porteña*, and served the Argentine government, was seen as the proprietor of a British house, although he might well have been classified as either an Argentine or an American.[5] Faced with such conflicting interpretations, the only valid basis for determining the nationality of a house remains the origin of capital. However, infor-

mation on origin and amount of capital cannot be calculated, since the
accounts rarely exist.

FINANCE governed the organization of British merchant houses in Argentina. In the absence of capital reserves, access to credit in the United
Kingdom not only provided merchants with the wherewithal for business
but also lubricated the whole structure of Argentine external trade.
Credit transactions, which involved the purchase or loan of goods, services, or money either in the present or for some future date with a
promise to pay at an even later date, were easily arranged. British manufacturers and other mercantile houses compensated for capital shortages
by extending credit through goods on consignment. Other devices serving a similar purpose for a shorter term included letters of credit and bills
of exchange. The arrangements were supplemented by an adequate commercial banking system during the 1870s. Before then, mercantile houses
in the United Kingdom bore the risk of exporting goods to Argentina,
while houses established in Buenos Aires sold imports on credit and took
the risk in the cash purchasing of Argentine produce for export, a process
that might take as long as a year in the 1840s.

British merchants in Argentina entered commerce to make their fortunes rather than to find a use for accumulated wealth. They remained
short of working capital. However, this state of affairs proved a decreas-
ing problem after the 1850s as communications improved and the banking structure became more elaborate. In regard to British houses, the initial capital of a new trading firm was generally British. There were exceptions to the rule, as in the house of Parlane Macalister, where both Duncan Wright and James Parlane acquired their initial capital in Argentina
while they were employed as clerks. But neither in the case of capital imported from Britain nor in the case of capital earned in the Río de la Plata
was the amount of initial direct investment large.

Consequently, an individual beginning in commerce used five devices
for obtaining sufficient capital. A person with good experience but without available funds might obtain opportunities by joining a secure, established firm, although this possibility gave little scope for individual initiative. If he had experience in the Río de la Plata trade or influential contacts at home, he might be fortunate enough to find the sponsorship of an
experienced merchant, banker, or manufacturer in the United Kingdom
who would be willing to supply the capital and might join the partnership. Alternatively, he might borrow the funds from relatives or friends.
Sometimes he might have minimal funds either saved from his time as a
clerk or made in speculations. However, the most practical solution lay
in operating primarily as a general commission merchant, making use of
credit.

The mercantile houses of Manchester, Liverpool, and London, the agents for manufacturers, provided the import-export houses of Buenos Aires with the greater part of the credit they required to maintain their operations. The *River Plate Journal* was not too far from the truth when it mentioned that before 1860 European merchants sold their goods on long credit and paid cash for the purchase of produce.[6] Mercantile houses in the United Kingdom favored the extension of credit, particularly when they held agencies for particular manufacturers. Thus, Robert Barbour and Company of Manchester, a firm of merchants and agents for cotton manufacturers, who specialized in stockings, men's shirts, and blankets, granted the Buenos Aires concern of Kerr, Heald, and Company credit up to 20,000 pounds for four months, renewable for another four months. Kerr, Heald paid its British correspondents a commission of two percent and interest on the credit at one percent over bank rates without involving Robert Barbour and Company in serious risk.[7]

Several other means existed for extending credit to merchants in Buenos Aires. A procedure advantageous to both merchants in Buenos Aires and the United Kingdom allowed for the sending of consignments to Argentina on the condition that payment would be made when the goods were sold.[8] Merchants in Buenos Aires, unlike their United Kingdom colleagues, benefited by receiving advances for the purchase and shipment of Argentine produce. Between 1810 and 1880 the forms of credit for the purchase and shipment of Argentine produce hardly changed.

Even more favorable to British merchants in Buenos Aires were the opportunities of acting as commission merchants and of dealing directly with manufacturers in the United Kingdom. When a house was operating on commission, the goods were not paid for until the house had received payment for the goods from its customers in Buenos Aires. Since no security was required, in effect merchants gained credit for as much as two years.[9] This arrangement caused friction because communications were so slow that debtors gained an excuse for dilatory payment. Mettam, Roberts, and Company of Sheffield wrote impatiently to Joseph Green of Liverpool in February 1831, stating: "We ought not to wait any longer for a settlement of our accounts with Mess. Green & Hodgson; besides the misfortune of goods laying so long at Buenos Aires unsold, we have now had the Account Sales in our possession nearly two years from which we learn that the last of the goods have now been sold about five years."[10] Manufacturers offered most generous credit facilities. Kerr, Heald, and Company, who obtained ponchos and poncho cloth from Sloan of Glasgow, received goods for a cash payment of only one-third up to the sum of £4,500.[11]

Letters of credit operating similarly to enclosed checks and drafts, otherwise known as bills of exchange, acted partly as the machinery of remittance but also as sources of credit in their own right. The commercial letter of credit issued by the merchant's bank authorized the seller of goods or produce to draw on the bank under certain stated terms. A letter of credit might be given to a young man just starting in business, or to a traveler, with the stipulation that a particular house in a given location supply him with funds and charge the amount to the house in some other location. The bill of exchange, an order from one person to another directing the payment of money at some future date, could be bought and sold on the open market, involving speculations in exchange rate and delayed payment up to ninety days. The bill of exchange functioned rather like a personal check with the addition of an acceptance, the acknowledgment of the bill by the drawee, the person to whom the draft was addressed. Drafts fell into two categories: the clean draft and the documentary draft. The clean draft needed no collateral documents. A documentary draft demanded accompanying records, usually the bill of lading, which was a document given by the master of a vessel acknowledging the receipt of certain goods on board. Bills of exchange could be drawn either at sight (sight draft) or at a specified number of days after sight (time draft). Most generally in the nineteenth century, time drafts were used which specified that a bill was to be paid thirty, sixty, or ninety days after sight. Four months were needed for a bill written in Buenos Aires at ninety days after sight to be paid—that is, one month for the bill to reach England and three months for the bill to come due. Paying by draft in Buenos Aires in August was equivalent to paying it in sterling on December 31 in Liverpool. The heavy use of bills of exchange in nineteenth-century international trade meant that most transactions were credit ones.

British merchants in Buenos Aires gained access to formal commercial credit only in 1862 with the founding of the Bank of London and the River Plate.[12] The Bank of London and the River Plate, representative of the large number of private joint stock banks which began operating in Buenos Aires during the 1860s and 1870s, offered various types of credit facilities to the merchants. By 1875 there were ten banks operating in Buenos Aires while fifteen years earlier only the Provincial Bank and the Mauá Bank serviced the market.[13]

The Bank of London and the River Plate attempted to assess the credit standing of its customers, although a good deal of business was carried on through personal contacts and oral agreements. The board of directors of the London and River Plate bank sought to establish credit guidelines. It stipulated that no credit exceeding £20,000 should be given to any single person or firm. The bank evaluated the respectability and soundness of mercantile houses and curtailed credit when necessary.

From 1875 the board of directors of the Bank of London and the River

Plate strengthened its controls against the easy credit prevailing in Buenos Aires. Thereafter, bills of exchange were negotiated only with known clients who exhibited letters of credit or produced shipping documents.[14] A house could obtain credit from the Bank of London and the River Plate under a third signature, on the standing and respectability of the firm, by providing the security of bonds, property deeds, shipping documents, or bills of lading, by arranging to overdraw its account, by taking a short-term loan, or by receiving small advances. Sometimes a firm simply overdrew its account and made arrangements later. Each credit case was worked out individually with the house, and the amount of credit extended depended on the bank's knowledge of the customer's reliability.[15]

Merchant banks operating in the Río de la Plata region, such as Baring Brothers, also gave credit to import-export houses. Unlike commercial banks, merchant banks preferred credits connected with goods they handled and were generally more reluctant to provide credit facilities. Baring Brothers rarely authorized unsecured credit and avoided advances to any house that had more than one account on London. Their "double account" policy prevented a correspondent from drawing on one merchant banker to pay another without either merchant banker knowing the circumstances of the transaction being financed. Baring Brothers would not handle bank accounts for exchange operations unless the parties kept a balance sufficient to meet the possible amount of protested bills (bills dishonored for nonpayment). They did allow credit on dry goods accounts on the condition that the house kept no other account in London and used their Liverpool house as the forwarding agent. When giving credit, Barings preferred that their correspondents use the bill of exchange. The merchants drew the bills on themselves to the order of the supercargo and thereby the bank did not risk its capital. The stipulations placed on credit by Barings Brothers meant that few mercantile houses operating in Buenos Aires either desired or received their credit in this way.[16]

BEFORE Britons founded their houses in Buenos Aires, they obtained credit and determined their form of business organization. The interconnected factors of finance and British commercial precedent structured the organization of the import-export house in Buenos Aires. The merchant who preferred to run an individual proprietorship rarely speculated in the overseas sale of Argentine produce, choosing instead to engage in local business and operate on a commission basis. Although it seems that merchants never engaged in joint stock company organization before 1880, they compensated by forming partnerships. The careful selection of partners allowed merchants to increase their company's working capital and strengthen its credit. In spite of the financial disadvantages of partnerships—unlimited liability and disconcerting dissolution in the event of death or incapacity of one of the partners—they allowed merchants to more readily expand their operations and extend their contacts in both the business and political spheres. In Buenos Aires the typical import-export house of two or three partners engaged in international speculations with Argentine produce while handling British goods on consignment. British houses generally employed a number of clerks to maintain accounts and undertake routine activities. Although British merchants used an organization and a system of credit already proven elsewhere in the world, practical considerations of Argentine trade governed the selection of both partners and clerks. The slowness of communications between Europe and Argentina meant that the wise choice of colleagues and employees could do much to make an individual house effective in the competitive market of Buenos Aires.

The individual proprietorship, a one-man directed business enterprise in which the owner is completely responsible for the conduct of the business, participated in the whole range of merchant business found in Buenos Aires. However, more often the proprietor engaged in local commerce and the consignment business because that branch of trade depended less heavily upon capital reserves and credit facilities. Frequently a clerk, working from his employer's premises, began small operations on his own account and sole liability. Duncan Wright, who served as a clerk in 1827 in the house of McCrackan and Jamieson, borrowed from his employer to purchase goods. He sent his goods to the interior, where he sold at a profit. Wright also profited on the currency market by purchasing Spanish doubloons and Uruguayan pesos in Montevideo. When carried to Buenos Aires, these coins yielded a one hundred percent profit on the exchange for pesos.[17] Wright later established the house of Parlane and Macalister in Buenos Aires and Montevideo in partnership with some friends and was also instrumental in the founding of a Manchester business, Wright, Parlane, and Company. Presumably both the limited capital needed to establish the houses and his experience came from his clerkship in Buenos Aires.[18] A few individual proprietorships were very substantial businesses. Thomas Armstrong, regarded in 1863 as one of the principal capitalists in Buenos Aires, owned extensive lands and a slaughtering house. He exported the produce of both to an agent in London. As early as 1837 he received the cargoes of five British ships on consignment and dispatched four others. Although considered very speculative by other merchants, he commanded a sizable amount of capital from various sources and possessed a personal fortune exceeding £10,000 in terms of the gold sovereign.[19]

The partnership was the primary mode of business organization of the mercantile houses in Buenos Aires in the nineteenth century. The dominance of the partnership as the form of business organization is clear from the list of British mercantile houses in existence in Buenos Aires in 1850. Of the fifty-two, only fifteen were individual proprietorships, while seventeen were jointly owned, eighteen included three partners, and two had four partners. The individual proprietorship allowed for flexibility but had limited capital and a modest organization. It is thus not surprising that in 1850 none of the individual proprietorship houses had branch houses, while 40 percent of the partnerships had branch houses in Montevideo.[20] Partnerships, based on either written or oral contracts between participants who agreed to accept joint liability for the business, were formed under four principal incentives: to increase working capital; to obtain foreign contacts, whether in business or shipping, in order to minimize the risks of the Argentine trade; to obtain commercial advantage through association with prominent Argentines; and to provide opportunities for close relatives or family friends.

The desire to increase working capital proved the fundamental reason for the formation of a partnership. Robert Barbour in 1850 operated as an individual proprietor. Principally engaged in local business, he occasionally imported and exported on his own account. By 1863 Barbour had formed a partnership with Robert Barclay. In 1874 the two partners evidently had a disagreement and dissolved the partnership. Barbour retired with £45,000, leaving Barclay with £35,000, a sufficient amount to enable him to join a new partnership, Barclay, Campbell, and Company.[21] Barclay was fortunate. When the partnership of Kerr, Heald, and Company terminated, Walter Heald not only lost his initial capital of £5,000, a loan from his father-in-law, but even failed to recruit a new partner of capital and could continue in business only on a limited commission basis.[22] The company of Green and Hodgson (1817-1830) formed with one partner in Argentina, the other in the United Kingdom, operated to maximize the available credit. The frequent use of partnerships in the trade of Buenos Aires compensated for the fact that British businesses were undercapitalized.[23]

The range and flexibility of merchant houses increased substantially when partnerships existed between Argentine and United Kingdom concerns, particularly when similar arrangements gave a series of related South American branches. Not only was capital increased but the political risks of war, xenophobia, and blockade became more manageable because cargoes could be diverted to other ports. Similarly, the captains or supercargoes of merchant ships seemed useful partners, strengthening shipping interests, increasing international contacts, and introducing into the firm associates who knew another aspect of the import-export trade. By 1819 James Brittain, one of the strongest British merchants, had formed a partnership with Captain Thomas Winter, who first arrived in Buenos Aires in August 1815 as commander of a Royal Navy frigate. The

company soon gained the services of a young German supercargo named
Claudius Stegmann, who joined the firm after Brittain's death in 1833.
Within eleven years Stegmann amassed a large fortune in Argentine
lands and urban dwellings while also contributing to the extensive German connections of the British house dealing in imported English manufactured goods.[24]

The problems created by the Argentine political system could be decreased by forming partnerships with influential nationals. In the early
part of the century it was particularly useful to have a Spaniard of Argentine national sympathies as a member of the partnership. David Curtis De Forest, an American who gained his interests in the Río de la Plata
while smuggling, formed a partnership with Juan Larrea around 1810.
Three years later his partner became the Minister for Finance. When De
Forest then formed a company with a close friend of Juan Martín de
Pueyrredón, he obtained protection against Argentine merchants and
received government contracts. De Forest left Argentina in 1818, taking
with him accumulated capital of 101,952 pesos, then equivalent to
27,840.8.0 in gold sovereigns.[25] De Forest's practices were not unusual.
During the early 1850s, for example, the British house of Nicholson,
Green, and Company was fortunate enough to recruit Señor Norberto de
la Riestra as partner. Riestra became Finance Minister of Buenos Aires in
1860.[26]

Partnerships were also formed with relatives or friends who possessed
some initiative, experience, or money. It was not uncommon to have
nephews or younger brothers working as clerks in the house. They became partners later, not because they had large amounts of capital to
contribute to the business or strong political connections, but because
they had mastered one phase of the business, and particularly because
their blood relationship offered some guarantee of integrity. Thus, before
the collapse of the partnership of Kerr, Heald, and Company, a nephew
of Kerr had been offered a partnership because he had demonstrated his
managerial ability during the illness of one of the partners and had become an excellent salesman in the Buenos Aires market.[27] On the other
hand, the firm of Milligan, Williamson, and Company was a partnership
between men who had know each other since their boyhood days in the
British community of Buenos Aires.[28]

Although partnerships offered substantial advantages to business in
Buenos Aires, they involved considerable risks. Bankruptcy, insanity, or
death of one of the partners automatically dissolved the partnership, and
each partner became liable for all the business debts of his colleagues.
Moreover, the partnership agreements were often so sketchy that
complications arose which the agreements did not cover. For example,
Walter Heald experienced difficulties in his partnership with Kerr in

Liverpool and Milroy in Buenos Aires. In January 1875 the partners did not know what to do about payment of salaries if there was a loss in the business. The partnership document had only considered the payment of salaries of £700 to Kerr and £500 to Milroy and Heald, providing for the division of profit and losses on a basis of 40 percent to Kerr, 35 percent to Milroy, and 25 percent to Heald. Milroy's death in 1876 ended the partnership and left Kerr and Heald responsible for Milroy's liabilities of £2,500. Following the death of Milroy, the choices became to find a new partner, to change the organization of the business so that Heald could go to Buenos Aires to take Milroy's place while Kerr continued to handle the business in Liverpool, or to liquidate.[29]

Liquidation and failure raised similar problems even when all the partners still lived, because one partner might be forced to sell personal property to redeem the debts of his colleague. The failure of the Darbyshire and McKinnel house of Liverpool to meet liabilities totaling £250,000 brought the liquidation of Darbyshire, Jordan, and Company of Buenos Aires and threatened Darbyshire, Krabbé, and Company of Montevideo. Claims were made upon the entire personal estates of all the partners. Jordan and Krabbé, who had only recently joined the Montevideo house, were even obliged to offer to sell their private property to settle the debts.[30]

THE INTERNAL organization of the merchant houses depended on establishing premises in the city of Buenos Aires, in which the whole establishment of partners and clerks often lived. The counting house, warehouse, and dwelling house were usually located in the same building.[31] Once a merchant had found a location and issued circulars announcing his business, he generally looked for a clerk to keep the books. He might find one in the community, but more likely he would send for a younger brother, nephew, or a friend's son. The clerk's job might involve long hours—9 a.m. to 6 p.m. six days a week and an occasional half day on Sunday, particularly if the packet was leaving shortly. Yet the personal diary of Walter Heald clearly indicates that the clerk was not always overworked, partly because one of his duties was to become acquainted with every aspect of marketing in Buenos Aires.[32]

Clerks undertook the clerical duties of correspondence and the maintenance of account books. Correspondence had to be written by hand, often in duplicate, although a simple method existed by which another copy of a letter could be made from the original: a clerk wrote a letter with a special ink; the paper was then dampened and placed in a press. The clerk had to be very careful in reproducing the copy—making it too wet or leaving it too long in the press would ruin both the original and the copy.

Depending upon the administrative precision of the house, clerks might also be required to keep as many as eleven sets of accounting books. Hodgson, Robinson, and Company had a journal for the day-by-day transactions of the business; a ledger in which all debits and credits from the journal were supposedly entered; rough sales books which were concerned with the accounts of the Argentine merchants to whom the firm sold goods, giving the amount paid for the goods and the name of the payee; and rough account sales which gave the goods and their markings, all charges, and the commissions. The rough sales and accounts were both transferred into the "account sales" book. The "account current" book included all the current expenses of the firm, from wages to duties paid out on goods. There were also the rough cash books of debit and credit, which dealt with the accounts of the storekeepers and which were finally transferred into cash accounts; the cash books, which were the day-by-day journal of the cash accounts; and the petty cash books, which kept a record of small cash amounts paid out. The order book kept track of the various goods requested from England. In addition to these accounting books the house kept outgoing letter books, and James Hodgson kept a private letter book. Joseph Green in England also kept a book of consignments and sales in order to double check the account sales books of James Hodgson.[33]

Argentine wages seemed attractive in Europe even though the cost of living in Buenos Aires was high and diminished profits. In 1818 James Hodgson paid 32 pesos or £70.0 per month for a suite of rooms containing one small front store, one ample room which served for a store, counting house, breakfast parlor, and sitting room, two bedrooms, and a small kitchen. Hodgson expected his living costs would be from 1,600 to 1,800 pesos (£360 to £400) a year. During this period an experienced clerk with a knowledge of bookkeeping and ability to be cash keeper earned £150 a year plus board and lodging. An inexperienced clerk who contracted for five years in the 1840s to Bradshaw, Wanklyn Jordan, and Company received £50 each of the first two years and £150 in the sixth year with a return passage to the United Kingdom.

Phenomenal inflation decreased the value of wages. Taking 1826 as a base year, currency depreciated 594 percent by 1836 and 2,100 percent by 1840. Although local wages adjusted to the inflation, prices rose still more quickly. The result was that the standard of living of the salaried individual and the wage earner was repeatedly lowered.[34] Room and board for a British clerk cost 500 pesos (£5) a month in 1866. Between 1868 and 1871 rent for houses varied between 900 and 2,000 pesos a month (£7.10.0 to £16.0.0). A British Consul in 1871 criticized the high price of staples such as bread. A four pound loaf, for example, cost three times as much as in the United Kingdom, 8 to 9 paper pesos (16 to 18 pence), although wheat per bushel fetched about the same amount. The different costs of baking the bread came from the high price of fuel, wages, and the large profits expected by the baker.[35] Only a well-established house could afford to employ a sufficient number of clerks so that its employees included men who specialized in the diverse functions of expatriate trade in Argentina.

THE VARIETY of functions performed by merchant houses in Buenos Aires depended upon the financial resources of the partners. In addition to the importing of manufactured goods and the exporting of Argentine produce, British merchants provided numerous other services, including extending credit to travelers, conducting market research, finding employment for friends or relatives, selling ships, and reporting on the Argentine political and economic scene. A British merchant in Buenos Aires might also serve as an attorney, examine insurance claims, or serve as agent for insurance companies based in the United Kingdom. Table 5 notes some of the services offered and the various charges. Although the British import-export house represented a trading institution connecting two areas of the world, its functions led it to modify market structure, create new production alternatives for the local market, and transfer skills, information, and capital. However, British import-export houses increasingly concentrated upon the external trade as specialization increased, so that by 1880 the brokerage functions as well as wholesale and retail trade had largely passed into the hands of Argentines or new immigrants. Nevertheless, the apex of the nineteenth-century business community in Buenos Aires was the import-export house.

The import-export business linked the local members of the commercial community and brought them in contact with the international market. As import commission merchants, they ordered goods contracted by purchasers in Argentina. As export commission merchants, they acted as purchasing agents for mercantile houses in London and handled the packing and shipping. Since the foreign buyer often stipulated the price that he was willing to pay and the quality of produce desired, merchants became familiar with the Argentine market. Mercantile houses made their largest profits when operating on their own account, buying products to send to the United Kingdom and manufactured goods to sell in Argentina. The risks of individual trade were high because as wholesalers they had to maintain a stock of merchandise sufficient to fill anticipated demands. Competition, price changes, tariff revisions, and foreign exchange made operating on one's own account both speculative and potentially profitable.

As brokers, the import-export merchants brought parties together to assist in negotiating contracts between them. In nineteenth-century

Table 5. Functions and charges of import-export houses of Buenos Aires in 1863.

Service offered	Fee charged by percent on transactions
Sell ships and merchandise	5
Sell all other goods	2
Sell specie	1
Purchase produce of the country or purchase products for ships	2.5
Purchase produce or repay in specie or letters of exchange without guarantee	1
Deliver, endorse, and negotiate acceptance of bills of exchange on Montevideo or Buenos Aires, or transfer funds from Montevideo to Buenos Aires or vice versa (brokerage included)	0.5
Furnish, endorse, or negotiate letters of exchange	2.5
Receive or pay funds without other commission	1
Handle ships in ordinary cases	2.5
Advance funds to ships in need, or to condemned ships, or to damaged ships unable to enter the port	5
Embark and reembark the cargoes of ships in distress (on the basis of the invoice)	2.5
Settle claims	5
Obtain freight for ships (brokerage included)	5
Pack freight on board ships	2.5
Receive and dispatch merchandise (fee charged on evaluation of the duty)	1
Take care of dispatches (fee charged on value involved)	2.5
Recover duty of reexportation	2.5
Store manufactured goods for six months and bulk produce for three months (after this term the rates double). Storage of all merchandise disembarked and reembarked is calculated on the evaluation of the duty	1
Insure against fire according to risk	.5-1

aTranslated and edited from the French. Report of Consul General DeRote of Belgium at Buenos Aires. Belgium, Ministère des affaires étrangères, *Recueil consulaire contenant les rapports commerciaux des agents belges à l'étranger. Publié en exécution de l'arrêté royal du 13 novembre 1855,* 9 (Brussels: H. Tarlier, 1863), 252.

Buenos Aires there were several types of brokers: the stock broker who dealt in such securities as shares and bonds, the exchange broker who handled bills of exchange, the produce broker who conducted business in produce such as wool and hides, and the shipping broker who arranged for the chartering of vessels. Although specialized brokers existed in the early part of the century, the import-export merchant often fulfilled the broker's many functions. For example, the ten largest shipping brokers in the period 1854 to 1856 were all import-export houses.[36] The clear distinction between the functions of the broker and merchant came only after the organization of the stock exchange in 1854. British import-export houses also participated in the development of Argentina's distribution system. As wholesalers of imported goods sold in large quantities and brokers of produce, they filled a position that few Argentines could match. In addition, houses occasionally undertook retail functions and encouraged peddlers to sell in the interior, report on the state of the provincial markets, and collect produce for export.

Packing and shipping services formed an integral part of the functions performed by British merchant houses in Buenos Aires. Like their counterparts in the United Kingdom, merchants in Argentina faced the problems of securing ships for the sending of goods and produce, arranging charters, establishing freight rates, loading and unloading, and handling the consequence of shipwrecks. However, the difficulties seemed less acute in Great Britain than in Buenos Aires, because the home company merchant could use shipping agents to make the arrangements, while the Buenos Aires merchant had to handle most of the details himself.[37] This proved quite time consuming because of the forms that had to be completed in order to export from Argentina. The merchant or a person he authorized requested the customs authority to examine the cargo, giving the number, type, and nationality of the ship and the destination of the cargo. The cargo was categorized as produce of the country, foreign merchandise being transshipped, or foreign merchandise exported from the city or province.[38]

Merchants preferred fast ships of smaller tonnage (150-200 tons) to large, slow ones because of the nature of the produce. Long voyages and delays in port were certain to ruin hides improperly dried and jerked beef carelessly cured. Hodgson and Robinson reported that, as the result of a prolonged delay in Buenos Aires, they had hides which had become disfigured because moths had bred in them and eaten the hair of the hides to the roots. They were quick to assure the receiver in Manchester that this would not affect the quality of the hides. Thus, merchants often reported to the United Kingdom that a particular vessel such as the *Mary Wall* was "a regular trader to this place as she is a most prime one and a fast sailer and the captain a most careful and experienced man in this trade." It was highly recommended that she be used, as merchandise would arrive safely and quickly.[39] Processing techniques and tariffs also affected the quality of packing. Products had to be packed in a specified manner. For example, wool was exported unwashed, unclassified, and usually tied with jute string because it was cheaper to classify in Europe. If manufacturers preferred that the wool be bundled without twine, the wool was rolled in grease to hold its shape.[40]

The chartering of ships raised additional problems because the port and market requirements of the United Kingdom and Argentina were so different. Thus, the ship D'Arcy consigned to Hodgson and Robinson presented just about every conceivable problem. Although she was able to begin discharging her cargo the day after her arrival, because of an oversupplied market only one-half the salt could be sold on board and even that amount at a ruinous price that hardly covered one-half the freight. But even the price of 13 pesos per fanega (a dry measure varying between 210 and 225 pounds) was worth taking, since the alternative was to secure places for its deposit at expensive rent rates, with additional costs for peons and carts. Only seventy lay days (days allowed by the charter party for loading or unloading a vessel) remained, whereas a vessel of D'Arcy's tonnage generally required one hundred. This meant that six guineas had to be paid for each day beyond the allowed number. Nor had Hodgson and Robinson been able to find a complete cargo with which to reload her nor someone to recharter the ship. Many days after her arrival they were still soliciting their friends to see if they would send tallow, salted hides, and other produce by her. To top off the problems, the crew, including the mate, were practically in a state of mutiny. The ship finally left port eighty-nine days after its arrival with a full cargo, but more than half of it was consigned to other individuals.[41] To the Buenos Aires based merchant it was of crucial importance that the charter agreements contain a particularly large number of lay days because of the problems of handling the goods at the port of Buenos Aires. Rarely was a ship in port less than three months. To the British based merchant it was important that the ship stop at Cowes or preferably Falmouth, for order, and from there proceed expeditiously to another port either in the United Kingdom or on the Continent.

The choice of vessel and the provisions of the charter agreement were largely governed by the variation of freight rates, an important factor in the profit and loss margin of import-export houses. Merchants sought the lowest freight rates possible and watched that packages were not overweighed by the ship's captain for increased freight payment. In December 1840, soon after the French blockade had been lifted from Buenos Aires, the British merchants at a general meeting with the masters of British vessels agreed that the following rates would be paid: tallow, £6; dry hides, £10; dry salted hides, £5.10.0; wet salted hides, £5.10.0; heavy bales, £5; wool, £4; horns, £2 per ton. Yet the merchants who had been paying between 5 and 6 pounds per ton of goods in 1820 considered these rates high. The rates fell only as the number of ships in port increased. In 1874 freight rates were £1.10.0 a ton, but in 1875 rates jumped to £3.10.0 a ton and then began to decline until by 1896 they were half of what they had been in 1876.[42]

The large number of ships which delivered damaged goods or which were shipwrecked led merchants to insure their goods. Before 1859 and the establishment of the Compañía Nacional de Seguros Marítimos in Buenos Aires, marine insurance had to be purchased in Great Britain. Even in the 1860s and 1870s after many British and European insurance companies had arranged for branches in Buenos Aires, shippers of merchandise to foreign ports tended to secure insurance in Europe. The Buenos Aires based merchant would write to his counterpart in Europe, indicating the value of the cargo and the type of insurance recommended. Broad coverage allowed for damage in loading and unloading at given ports and exchanging of one cargo for another of equal value, as well as for damage done at sea and complete loss due to shipwreck. A more limited policy might be for sea risk only. The cost of insurance, dependent upon the type of coverage, varied from two to three percent of the declared value. At other times a merchant might prefer not to insure in order to increase his profits. He took the risk himself by parceling out his goods among various ships.[43]

Shipwrecks and cargoes thrown overboard in efforts to save a ship presented yet another type of problem. London would request information on the goods or produce on board that were salvaged, damaged, or thrown overboard; particulars of freight, insurance, and passengers; and the amounts of funds drawn by the captain. The merchant in Buenos Aires might be asked to verify the poor quality of goods received so that an insurance company need not pay damages.[44]

Just as a British merchant in Buenos Aires received instructions on how goods were to be sold, he in turn sent specific orders of how produce sent on his own account was to be sold. Hodgson and Robinson gave instructions that produce was to be disposed of at the most advantageous time but sold for cash down only and preferably not held for too long a time. And just as the Buenos Aires based merchant chose to make other recommendations on how goods were sold, the Liverpool or London based house also made recommendations. Thus Wilder, Pickersgill, and Company pointed out that while they realized that the Hodgson and Robinson produce was not to be delivered until paid for, they offered to assume the risk of immediate delivery of hides to the buyers and to take the risk of debt on a payment of one percent guarantee. This would reduce the irritation and prejudice against sales by buyers accustomed to having credit.[45]

A British based mercantile house could handle the selling of the produce in a number of ways. He could send the goods to another market, sell directly to buyers of tanneries, sell by public sale himself, or turn the goods over to a broker. It was not uncommon to send a shipment of goods on to the Continent. Transshipping was done if the European markets looked better than those in the United Kingdom. For this reason charter parties usually called at some port in Great Britain for orders. Selling directly to buyers was probably preferable, but it was more common to sell by public auction of the house and, later in the century, by public auction by broker houses specializing in the produce of the Río de la Plata.

Complaints that the market was overstocked or depressed and that numerous failures had put a stop to commercial transactions were as common in the British market as in the Buenos Aires one. This was partly because shipments had recently arrived from other ports—wheat from Chile or the United States; tallow from the United States, Russia, or the Cape; hides from Brazil, the Cape, or East Africa; wool and sheep skins from Australia. The prices current for tallow and hides fluctuated in relation to supply, demand, and political climate. If the British based merchant could not comment on the depressed state of the market, then he was almost always sure to remark on the poor condition of the produce sent. Jerked beef was improperly cured; hides were damaged by worms and had to be sorted or were the wrong weight for the market; sugar was wet; and nutria skins, wool, and hair were so damaged from sea water that they could not be sold at any price.

An increasingly important function of the British import-export houses in Buenos Aires was to act as agents for United Kingdom insurance companies. Before 1880 the insurance business in Argentina was too slow to justify the establishment of branch offices. Merchants tended to have partners in Europe effect insurance on their consignments, and fire insurance was taken only on a very limited scale in larger cities such as Buenos Aires and Rosario. Because of low profits and low demand, insurance companies employed British merchants already located in Buenos Aires as their agents. Even the merchant agents had difficulty securing business, and the London companies considered a net profit of £4,000 a year excellent.[46] Agents made remittances monthly to the London office or when the balance on hand reached a fixed sum of perhaps £100. Companies prevented agents from insuring property that was too risky. They preferred that merchants issue insurance against fire to property in shops or warehouses and against damages to goods shipped. There was no demand for life insurance in Argentina. For his services the merchant received either 10 percent on the premium and 10 percent on the profits plus 2.5 percent extra on premiums received through brokers or a payment of 15 percent on premiums and 5 percent on profits.[47] However, the London insurance companies had difficulties in obtaining merchants to act as agents. The Alliance Assurance Company, for example, found in 1865 that respectable houses either were acting as an agent for another British insurance company or had investments in a national insurance company.[48]

The British merchant in Buenos Aires also performed services only remotely related to import-export. He might be asked to check about such specialized products as 182 planks of zebra woodware consigned to another house or to send eight cardinals to another port in South America. Sending special produce demanded a diplomatic handling of a captain. The captain had to keep the cardinals in his cabin and then undergo a reprimand from an admiral of the Royal Navy for his efforts.[49]

The merchant in Buenos Aires might be asked to find employment for a young clerk, the son, brother, or nephew of a correspondent in England. And quite often he was asked to help some new merchant begin in Buenos Aires, or assist a merchant traveler on the way to another port in South America, or befriend travelers in need of contacts with the British community.[50] Particularly in the first half of the century, commercial houses received small deposits for their clients and lent money on security.

A British merchant might be asked to sell a ship, a process that demanded a thorough knowledge of how business was transacted in Buenos Aires. Merchants had to make payments to various individuals for their services. For example, in 1852 in order to sell to the government the steamer Correo, a merchant house paid a fee to the port admiral for recommending that the government purchase the ship, and to the captain of the port for reporting favorably as to her condition. Without the agreement of both of these functionaries, the merchant could not complete the sale. All sales to the government had to be arranged in much the same fashion. The payment of special fees was the legitimate and accepted means of doing business in Argentina, and it was necessary for British houses to adopt the practices if they wished government concessions.[51]

Nor was it uncommon to give to the Buenos Aires based merchant the power of attorney to recover money due on goods from another merchant, to protest an unaccepted draft, to receive the dividend and interest on stocks, to pay wages to the captain of a vessel recently sold, to sell a ship, or to rearrange her charter to receive consignments from another house which had not sold them. With the power of attorney would go all

the legal power to act in default of payment. In 1832 Thomas Mendenhall, a resident of Philadelphia, gave Zimmermann, Frazier, and Company, power of attorney to obtain interest from stock that had been deposited at the Banco de Buenos Aires. Mendenhall wanted Zimmermann
and Frazier to give him a letter of credit equal to the value of the yearly
dividends, 1,200 pesos, which they did. In 1843 Zimmermann and Frazier requested the amount due them from the Casa de Moneda de la Provincia de Buenos Aires. In 1845 they took their case to court to force payment of 18,000 pesos. They finally won their case and received payment
in June of 1846. Power might also be given to act as insurance agent or
estancia manager.[52]

THE FINANCE, organization, and functions of the British mercantile houses
in Buenos Aires depended upon communications and transportation.
From 1810 to 1860 sailing vessels connected Europe and Argentina, but
from the 1850s the use of steam vessels for transatlantic trade increased
the speed of conveyance and enabled merchants to reduce their stocks of
goods. However, facilities in Buenos Aires hampered the rapid and efficient discharge of passengers and cargoes, while the inadequate structure
of internal transport limited the commercial benefits of improved oceanic
navigation. Commodity shipments assumed an importance unprecedented in the days of colonial Spain because nineteenth-century business
functioned in a competitive market. Success in overseas trade depended
upon postal services to confirm the integrity of any particular transaction. In consequence merchants were acutely aware of the movements of
packet vessels and exerted constant pressure upon the British consulate in
Buenos Aires, their agents in the United Kingdom, and the General Post
Office to adapt any innovations that might improve communications. In
1850 the Postmaster General endorsed a contract for the steam carriage
of mail between Southampton and Rio de Janeiro with transshipment to
Buenos Aires, only ten years after the introduction of steam packets between the United Kingdom and India. During the 1870s the laying of a
submarine telegraph cable between the United Kingdom and South America and its extension to Buenos Aires revolutionized the communications
services that supported British merchant operations in Argentina. On
April 1, 1878, the post office of the Argentine Republic joined the Universal Postal Union. The use of steam mail service, the submarine cable,
and improved internal transportation not only diminished United Kingdom control over Argentine communications but also made possible the
operation of the large joint stock companies, which made the import-
export houses almost unprofitable during the 1880s.

Until 1860 sailing vessels were the main means of transferring communications, goods, produce, and people between Europe and Argen-

tina. Merchants estimated that a minimum of 60 to 70 days were necessary for the passage between Europe and Argentina and another month to unload the goods in Argentina. In 1831 ships sometimes anchored off Buenos Aires for as long as 150 days, while as late as 1881, a five-hundred ton vessel required 100 days to unload.[53] The inadequacy of overseas communications obliged merchants in Argentina and the United Kingdom to invest large amounts of capital in stocks on hand and carefully calculate future demands and market trends. As early as 1825 a steam vessel operated in the La Plata region, but oceanic steamships were used with regularity only during the 1850s, when they reduced passage time to 30 days. This improvement coincided with the introduction of steam launches and lighter tugs at the port of Buenos Aires, which reduced handling time to some 16 days. The use of steamers of increasing tonnage accompanied a decrease in the number of sailing vessels entering the port of Buenos Aires.[54] Although the total number of ships entering the port of Buenos Aires decreased, average draft and tonnage increased from 13 foot, 200 tons in 1850 to sixteen foot, 400 tons in 1870.[55]

The port of Buenos Aires presented both merchants and shipowners with severe problems. Since the Río de la Plata was shallow with sand bars, large vessels could not approach near to the city. A vessel might have to wait in the outer road several days before a health ship visited it and wait several more before it could find a position in the inner road. Until 1845 there were no docks, piers, or moles. At the mouth of the Riachuelo (Boca) and at the Barracas two miles higher up the same stream, vessels drawing eight feet of water, or from 150 to 200 tons, could load and unload goods into lighters. The difficulties of securing lighters and peons and the high cost charged when a large number of ships were in port reduced the effectiveness of shipping facilities. Because of the use of lighters for loading, the mate had to issue receipts to the master of each lighter for the goods received. Receipts were given to the merchants, a slow, unreliable, and complex procedure. All goods shipped from the customshouse and other locations had to go through a double process of being first conveyed by river carts—large wheeled carts that could go through shallow water—to the lighters and then from the lighters to the vessels. A traveler in 1842 complained that he paid 200 pesos (£2.17.5, more than the monthly wages of a clerk) for a boat to take his luggage from the packet to the shore and half that amount again to take it from the customshouse to his place of residence.[56] Bad weather or just a moderate breeze would put a stop to the loading process. Finally, the Rosas administration constructed two wharves that lasted until the end of the century.

In 1855 the government inaugurated a 250-meter passenger mole which was in use until 1890. In 1856 a mole belonging to the customshouse was constructed. But even in 1871 vessels had to remain in the estuary. Those drawing over ten feet of water could not come within a mile of the shore, while those of fifteen feet had to anchor in the outer road, four miles out. Ocean steamers had to anchor twelve to fourteen miles off the shore. It was thus very expensive to discharge cargoes. In fact, the cost of discharging cargoes by lighters was sometimes greater than the freight per ton from England. In addition to the added expenses of loading and unloading and loss of time, the ships anchored in the outer road might be damaged by storms. Nevertheless, between 1810 and 1875 the number of ships entering the port of Buenos Aires increased over one thousand percent. In October of 1875 the Chamber of the Province of Buenos Aires voted a sum of 500,000 pesos for dredging and widening the Riachuelo. But it was not until November of 1878 that a new port of Riachuelo was open for oceangoing vessels. And only in the 1880s and 1890s was the port of Buenos Aires improved and extended sufficiently to handle the large number of oceangoing vessels. For most of the nineteenth century, Buenos Aires port facilities were very inadequate.[57]

Internal communications also reduced the advantages that came from technological improvements in overseas communications. Only after 1853, when a treaty was signed between the United Kingdom and the Argentine Confederation for the free navigation of the rivers Paraná and Uruguay, could oceangoing vessels use the interior ports. Although the government provided facilities for interior navigation and maintained beacons and markers pointing the channels, the rivers remained treacherous. Shifting channels, winds, and storms on the River Paraná made navigation dangerous, while during the winter low water made running aground a distinct possibility. But in spite of their peril, the rivers Paraná and Uruguay were important means of communication with the interior. The increase of the foreign trade of Buenos Aires stimulated the interior trade. The departure of river traffic rose from 999 vessels in 1810 to 3,877 in 1860. At the beginning of the nineteenth century the Argentines and Uruguayans controlled trade on their domestic rivers. But with the coming of foreigners and steam navigation, Italians and Spanish became important in river shipping.[58]

The use of the rivers was often preferable to the use of roads. Even the roads around the city of Buenos Aires were extremely bad. After rains mud holes seriously impeded and sometimes entirely stopped the transit of goods. Yet produce had to come from the country by these roads. Wagons equipped with high wheels to permit passing through the mud and drawn by four to eight oxen brought the produce to Buenos Aires. In 1860, 7,416 country carts entered Buenos Aires, bringing 181,279 ox and cow hides, 7,034 calf skins, 9,294 skunk skins, 19,185 horse hides, 67,716 deer skins, 71,724 sheep skins, 109,371 nutrias, 14,946 arrobas of hair (1 arroba=25 pounds), 544,951 arrobas of wool, 9,550 arrobas of tallow,

5,613 arrobas of grease, 3,363 arrobas of hide cuttings, 3,113 arrobas of feathers, 43,579 horns, 359 fanegas of wheat, and 781 fanegas of maize. The cost of bringing produce to market by cart at least doubled the price of the produce in Buenos Aires. The price of corn doubled if brought 60 leagues (1 league equals approximately 3 miles), wheat 75 leagues, jerked beef 95 leagues, tallow 226 leagues, salted hides 240 leagues, and wool 400 leagues. The result was twofold: the provinces farther from Buenos Aires could not compete with the province of Buenos Aires, and only certain produce was sent. Thus, it was more practical to send wool, tallow, and salted hides than corn or wheat.[59]

By 1879 the railroads brought produce to Buenos Aires, and it was freight rates that were important to the merchant, not the cost of transportation by cart. The construction of railroads decreased interior freight rates and made possible both the development of pampas and the greater export of produce from Argentina. In the 1880s the cost of transporting a ton of wool by cart for twenty miles was equal to transporting it fifty miles by rail. Railroad rates exercised an increasing influence on the costs of produce exported and of goods imported.[60]

The inadequacy of Argentina's transport system at the beginning of the nineteenth century paralleled the rudimentary character of postal communications. Letters traveled on merchant vessels or with friends and acquaintances. The development of a satisfactory external postal service began in July 1808 when the first General Post Office mail was made up in London and dispatched from Falmouth by a Royal Navy ship to Rio de Janeiro, care of the British Consul of that city. Mail for Buenos Aires was forwarded by irregular naval ships or occasional merchant vessels. By 1810 a postal agent in Rio administered the collection and distribution of correspondence not merely for Brazil but also for Buenos Aires, Valparaiso, and Lima.[61]

During the period when branch packets operated between Rio and Buenos Aires, the merchants were not always satisfied with the service. Thus, import-export houses often took care of the mail for friends in Buenos Aires and saw that it was forwarded with the captain on the first merchant vessel or that the letters were sent with the Brazilian government mail. Sending by packet to Rio meant that the mail had to be forwarded. The British postal agents at Rio dispatched mail only by packets or vessels of war. The result was that correspondence was greatly delayed until a regular direct packet service was established to Buenos Aires. Although mail service continued during blockades, the service by merchant vessel was more irregular then. Mail was sent indirectly, going first to Montevideo and then by blockade runners to Buenos Aires. However, the English packets were often allowed to enter the port of Buenos Aires to deliver the mail.[62]

Although merchants occasionally complained about the packet system, they were heavily dependent upon it. Not only did the mails carry correspondence but documents such as bills of exchange and letters of credit. Without these, British merchants could not conduct their trade. The packets also carried specie. In addition, the packets were invaluable as newscarriers. The packet commanders noted in their logs and journals the news at home and abroad. This news was dispatched from Falmouth ahead of the mails and open to public inspection at the General Post Office in London. [63] The first official mail packet to Buenos Aires arrived on April 16, 1824. For the first year the British Consul General acted as postal agent until a competent clerk could be appointed and a postal agency established. The packet vessel that sailed each month from Falmouth remained ten days in Buenos Aires. A mail was also dropped at Montevideo without delaying the packet, and in a similar manner a bag was collected on the return trip to Europe. Later, after pressure from the merchants, it was decided that the packet would wait twenty-four hours in Montevideo on the return to Europe. The close communications between the merchants of the two localities appeared to demand an official mail stop in Montevideo. [64]

The British community in South America agitated for a steam mail service as early as 1842. After some delay the Postmaster General recommended to the United Kingdom government that his department finance it. In 1850 the General Post Office signed a contract with the Royal Mail Steam Ship Company to carry the mail between Southampton and Rio de Janeiro. According to the contract, the ship was to take no more than twenty-eight days and nineteen hours to Rio, where correspondence would be transshipped for arriving at Buenos Aires within thirty-eight days and three hours after leaving Southampton. The first ship took almost double that time, but the service soon improved.

The mail service to Buenos Aires was further improved in 1854 when the Postmaster General contracted with the South American and General Steam Navigation Company to convey the mail once a month between Liverpool and Brazil and the Río de la Plata. The ship called also at Lisbon, Madeira, Bahia, and Pernambuco. By the establishment of this line of contract packets, in addition to the existing line of the Brazil mail packets, communications between England, Brazil, and Argentina were maintained regularly twice a month. There were periods of time when the packet to Buenos Aires was a branch packet and subject to delay because of the late arrival of the packet at Rio or ship repair in that port. Epidemics of yellow fever in the Brazilian ports occasionally reduced the services, but they were immediately resumed when the quarantine was removed. On the whole one can say that the mail service to Buenos Aires was fairly regular, although dates of packets were often changed with due notice. The addition in 1860 of French mail packets from Bordeaux twice monthly with slightly higher rates further increased services.[65]

Postage rates by the British packets were progressively reduced throughout the nineteenth century. In 1824 the rate of postage to Buenos Aires was the same as the rate for Brazil in the previous sixteen years, 3/6d for a letter of a single sheet and fourteen shillings an ounce. By February 1825 the cost of a single letter from London to Buenos Aires had been reduced to 2/7d.[66] On March 1, 1852, postage rates between Buenos Aires and the United Kingdom were reduced to 1 shilling for letters not exceeding one-half ounce in weight, two shillings for letters weighing one-half to one ounce, and four shillings for letters not exceeding two ounces. Letters to Montevideo and Brazil maintained their same rate of more than double the Buenos Aires rates. Thus, the British merchants in Buenos Aires had a decided advantage.[67]

During the 1870s the Argentine government began to assume the responsibility for much of its own external mail service. The British and French abolished their postal agencies in Argentina and the local post office handled the mail coming by packets. Although the United Kingdom signed a postal convention with Argentina on January 13, 1876, the entry of the Argentine Republic into the Universal Postal Union was delayed until September 1877 for political reasons. The rates charged were those of twenty years earlier—six pence or sixty-four centimes per half ounce. They were forty percent cheaper than the previous year. Through 1880 the Postmaster General had renewed contracts with four steamship companies who delivered the mail weekly to Buenos Aires, while the Argentine Confederation also contracted with the companies to carry the mail.[68]

Although the packet service improved greatly in the period from 1810 to 1880, British merchants continued to send letters unofficially by merchant and naval vessels, at least through the 1850s. Merchants in Buenos Aires desired to hear from their correspondents in Europe by every merchant vessel coming in from their port. And they certainly expected to hear from them by every official packet. Often, however, they were disappointed, and thus felt disadvantaged in trying to gauge the European market. Occasionally the Buenos Aires merchants prepared letters to send to correspondents by merchant vessel, only to have the ship leave without its mails. It appears that at times letters were thrown overboard because ship captains did not wish to concern themselves with delivery of letters upon arrival in port. Apparently United States ships were notorious for that practice, and merchants advised their correspondents to send letters via English ships for safety.[69] Merchants made use of unofficial mail service for practical reasons. They dispatched duplicate letters by merchant vessels. This method saved postage, since merchants did not have to pay postage by weight. Advantages increased if the vessel was scheduled to arrive in England as soon as the packet. Merchants especially recommended that market advices, which were usually printed on heavier paper, be sent by merchant ship in order to save postage. Hodgson and Robinson in Buenos Aires wrote their correspondent Owen Owens and Sons of Manchester on October 22, 1841, that their plan of writing by every packet was a good one, but writing only by packets was bad. They recommended that both duplicates and extra original letters be sent by direct vessels from Liverpool to Montevideo and addressed to an affiliate commercial house. Merchants criticized London correspondents if they closed their advices too soon and did not enclose the latest information.[70] The irregular mail service often put pressure on merchants to hurriedly prepare letters to send by any unscheduled means possible. Since the regular mail service to Buenos Aires was established before that to Chile and Peru, correspondents sent letters to Buenos Aires to be forwarded by any vessel going in that direction. If an individual were going to Mendoza, letters were sent that way as communications from there to Chile were frequent. But either way, the mail service from the east coast of South America to the west coast was far from regular.[71]

While the overseas mail service was improving, Argentina reorganized the internal postal system. Even in 1824, after the official packet service was initiated between Argentina and England, the British Consul received and sorted the packet mail. He selected the official letters and transferred the remainder to the local authority for delivery. Between 1839 and 1853 communications improved greatly. In 1853 the government adopted measures to provide more frequent and regular postal communications between the capital and rural districts. Mail for rural districts of the province of Buenos Aires was made up for various locations once a month on a set date for each district. Rates were determined in relation to weight and distance outside the province and were uniform within it. Postage stamps were not in use in 1853, but newspapers were sent through the post free of charge. Prepayment was compulsory for letters sent from the capital to rural districts of the province of Buenos Aires but optional for those sent from Buenos Aires to the remaining provinces of the Confederation.[72]

By the 1870s British merchants in Argentina could communicate with Europe by rapid steamships, an improved postal system, and a British-financed cable. By July of 1874 when a cable connected Rio with Lisbon, Buenos Aires merchants could have European news in less than a week from Rio at the cost of £10 per twenty words. By July 1876 Argentina was also linked to Europe. The commercial houses, who composed individual codes to communicate with correspondents in Europe, could now keep an assortment of goods for less capital by making frequent use of the cable. Items when sold could be replaced in 45 days, against 160 days when requests were sent by sailing vessels and 76 days when sent by steamers. The rapid means of transportation and communications ultimately changed the structure and function of the import-export houses.[73]

BRITISH mercantile houses, organized upon the proven models of individual proprietorships and partnerships, exchanged United Kingdom manufactured goods, notably cotton textiles, for Argentine produce. Successful operation depended heavily upon the manipulation of credit obtained from British banks, merchant banks, manufacturers, and other mercantile houses through letters of credit, bills of exchange, and goods on consignment. As they diversified their activities, British mercantile houses utilized new means of communication, more elaborate Argentine infrastructure, improved financial services, and widening markets. The increased use of steamships after the 1850s, better port facilities in Buenos Aires, and a regular mail service permitted British mercantile houses to operate more efficiently until increasing economic centralization led to the rapid spread of the joint stock company. In the period 1810 to 1880 the variety of functions performed by import-export houses made the mercantile house a competitive and efficient institution in the marketing of Argentine produce and British goods. Marketing demanded a knowledge of both local needs and international supplies, the institution of practices that would bring substantial profits, and the willingness to speculate in commodities and exchange through international trade.

5.

Operating in Argentina

COMPETITION from other foreigners increased the necessity for British merchants to adjust their marketing techniques to Argentine requirements. The French and North Americans offered strong competition at the beginning of the century, while by 1860 Italian and German houses had obtained a substantial share of the market by serving their immigrants, who were arriving in increasing numbers. The cargoes of ships were related to the nationality of the ships and the goods that particular nation produced. For example, British ships in 1825-26 brought textiles, American ships came loaded with flour, timber, and reexported United Kingdom cotton and linen goods, and French ships carried woolens, linens, and silk. Brazilian ships delivered tobacco, sugar, and coffee while United Province shipping, plying the coastal trade, also transported Brazilian produce. Hamburg, Dutch, Danish, and Prussian ships conveyed woolens, linens, and hardware; Sardinian vessels came with wines and liquors.[1] By 1830, as foreign knowledge of the Buenos Aires market increased, merchants were sending an increasing number of ships to the Río de la Plata. French trade soon lagged behind the increased activity of British shippers, while United States vessels arrived in greater numbers. However, after 1840 both American and British interests faced enhanced rivalry from French, Italian, and German ships and goods.

British merchants competed not merely in foreign shipping and manufacturing but also in the marketing of goods. By 1850 the French had established at least twenty-one mercantile houses and the United States five.[2] It was far more difficult to measure the amount of business controlled by French and United States citizens than by the British. The mode of operation of the French and United States citizens differed from that of the British and a large number of houses, both national and foreign, sold North American and French merchandise.

Although Argentine admiration for French culture may have provided a climate of opinion favorable to their commercial interests, French merchants faced greater political problems than did Britons because they did not have the advantage of a trade treaty. The French blockades of the port of Buenos Aires produced resentments that destroyed most of the French houses established at the beginning of the century. In the 1850s the French firms were of recent standing, although a number had just moved from Montevideo. The Franco-Argentine conflict transferred French commerce to Spanish, Italian, German, and British houses. Those houses transacting a large amount of business with France often had French junior partners to facilitate the obtaining of information on the markets. At the same time, those houses had other foreign or national partners to aid in their commercial transactions in Argentina.[3]

The small number of United States houses operating in Buenos Aires fails to indicate the extent of the trade being carried on with the United States. United States citizens managed their business in Buenos Aires without establishing houses by operating in the name of some established concern to whom they paid a small commission, usually 2.5 percent. They thereby avoided house rent, clerks' salaries, patents, and all the other demands that went with the establishing of a mercantile house. Another interesting feature of the United States business activities in Buenos Aires was the continuation of the merchant adventure mode of business operation well past the middle of the century. Like the British merchant, the United States merchant started in the trade when it was illegal. Instead of establishing a mercantile house once the trade was legalized, the North American merchant continued his speculative type of operations in a more informal manner. For example, an individual in New York would decide to speculate on a shipment to Buenos Aires. He would freight a vessel, perhaps three-fourths in lumber and the rest in the ordinary articles best adapted to the Buenos Aires trade. If he did not appoint a supercargo for the voyage, he would embark with his wife and family. On his arrival in Buenos Aires, he would consign his vessel and cargo to one of the few established United States houses, most likely Zimmermann, Frazier, and Company, who would dispose of his goods and invest the proceeds in the produce of Argentina. The United States merchant would then reembark with his family for New York to learn the fate of his speculation. The entire transaction would be accomplished in a period of eight or nine months.[4]

The nature of North American merchant operations was due less to the political relationship between the United States and Argentina than to the nature of the United States goods in the early years of the trade. A major part of United States trade to South America in the early years was reexport of European commodities. This was possible under the system of auction prevalent in the United States. British merchants sold goods at low prices to American merchants, who obtained more favorable freight

and charter rates. An American skipper might then combine a consignment of goods to Rio de Janeiro and the Pacific ports with a voyage to the
northwest coast for skins and furs and thence to Canton, picking up on
his return a cargo of dried beef at Buenos Aires destined for Havana.
United States merchants gained their profits by speculating in the goods
and produce of other nations.[5] However, not all United States individuals operated as speculators or through other import-export houses.
There were five United States houses in Buenos Aires in 1850. The largest
house, Zimmermann, Frazier, and Company, could trace its connections
back to the turn of the century and the establishment of a commission
house by David Curtis De Forest.[6]

All the major European countries had mercantile firms established in
Buenos Aires. In 1863 there were three Belgian houses, sixteen German
firms, twelve French houses, eleven Italian companies, and four Swiss-
German houses. In that same year the number of British houses had de-
creased to twenty-six, the number of United States houses risen to six; six
Argentine houses were in operation.[7]

Because of the foreign competition for the import-export trade in Buenos Aires, British merchants relied upon accurate marketing decisions to
provide a margin of advantage. Buenos Aires merchants based their decisions upon knowledge of the European commercial world and the Argentine economic and political environment. They preferred that correspondents follow advice on the type of goods in demand. By allowing colleagues in Buenos Aires freedom to decide upon the type of remittances,
merchants in the United Kingdom engaged in those types of speculation
which were often beneficial to all concerned.

Merchant correspondence ranged widely over commercial matters.
Complete information was recognized as the determining factor in sound
decision making. Information contained in mercantile correspondence
included the following: market prices of goods and produce; exchange
rates in London; the arrival and departure of ships, their cargo, and des-
tinations; the condition of and prices received for goods of specific merchants; acknowledged receipt of bills of exchange and account sales;
warning of competitor's efforts to undercut the market in a particular line
of goods; credit information on mercantile houses; an analysis of the general economic environment; news of political events; and the inclusion of
predictions of what would sell well in the future, often made in the form
of specific instructions. All of these might be formalized by the sending of
trade circulars.

For houses in Buenos Aires, news of the European market was of vital
importance. Houses based in Buenos Aires were the equal of their European counterparts and often appear to have had more decision making
power. For example, in the case of a working arrangement between an

English and a Buenos Aires house, one of the partners would be in charge of operations at each location. Each was responsible for the necessary decision making at his end. Further, as protection against bankruptcies, the houses were created as legally separate entities, operating independently of each other, although this did not preclude individuals from being partners in both the British and Buenos Aires based houses. Complicated and changing economic and political circumstances in South America and slow communications made it easier to make profitable decisions affecting Argentine speculation in Buenos Aires. Since the European political and economic situation was more stable, the Buenos Aires merchant's prediction of the European market was likely to be more accurate than vice versa. That larger profits were made from Buenos Aires rather than from Europe meant that often two partners were in Buenos Aires with only one in the United Kingdom handling that end of the transactions.

The importance of Buenos Aires as a decision-making base can be seen in the substantial number of houses that used British mercantile firms as agents. For example, James Hodgson, after breaking business ties with Joseph Green, apparently had no partner based in England. The firm of Rooke, Parry, and Company, commission merchants, had a counting house in London with a clerk in charge to look after consignments and answer inquiries while both partners, Alfred Wallace Rooke and William Griffith Parry, resided in Buenos Aires. When a Buenos Aires house was but a branch of a major London or Liverpool House, a British partner usually resided in Buenos Aires. Even in the case of merchants acting as commission agents, the decisions rested primarily in Buenos Aires. The type of decisions made and the amount of authority given to commission agents did not differ substantially from that of merchants operating almost entirely on their own account.[8]

Within the firm the partners made most of the decisions. At times they were not adverse to giving some responsibilities to experienced clerks or placing the house under a manager when they went to Europe. Because of the importance placed on resident partners in Buenos Aires, firms might add a new man to take charge of the house while the resident partner was in Europe, or ask a head clerk to join the house primarily to handle the operations while one partner was on leave. At times the partners placed the house under the permanent management of a nonpartner. Given the great extent of his decision making and the narrowness of profits in speculation, this was rather risky. A manager who saw the firm losing money might be more inclined than a partner to increase speculation to regain losses and so put the house into deeper debt.

Clearly a manufacturer or merchant sending goods and ordering produce had extensive authority over the types of remittances and produce sent and price of goods sold and produce bought. But the inclination was to leave the decision making in the hands of merchants in Buenos Aires, with limited instructions manifested in invoice price and demands for quick sales and returns. In the case of speculations on his own or joint account, the merchant was free to engage in such schemes when they seemed profitable and funds were available.

In the last resort, it was the political and economic environment of Argentina that determined final decisions. What the Buenos Aires market needed in 1838 was clearly dictated by the political situation as indicated by James Hodgson in his letter to Thomas Broadbent of Manchester. "Red, pink and scarlet ground print are now all the rage here—these being the popular or *Federal Party* colours and what is more: to every appearance, as far as can be seen forwards, they are certain to remain so, and accordingly you must exclusively in a measure run upon such and carefully avoid both in ground and prominent objects thereon, the colours of *Sky Blue* and *Green* which are the anti-party colours."[9]

While Argentine culture and family relationships influenced decision making, the British community and the house organization occasionally showed an unwillingness to innovate. Complaints by importers in Argentina that the British merchants were slow to adapt their operation to the South American markets were particularly strong near the end of the century when mercantile houses were changing their multifunctional base. Even during the early part of the century merchants tended to publish price lists only in English, and foreigners found the British imperial system and prices confusing. National retailers noted that packing was unappealing to local tastes. Manufacturers failed to send the cheaper articles desired. Too often British merchants spoke poor Spanish and their knowledge of Buenos Aires was limited. But if British merchants were to survive in the competitive Buenos Aires market, they had to introduce new marketing techniques and adapt their operations to the political and economic conditions.[10]

British merchant houses in Argentina suffered repeated impractical demands from their United Kingdom agents for the rapid turnover of goods and prompt payment. United Kingdom merchants never seemed to realize that the competitive nature of the Argentine market made retailers demand high quality, low price, and extended credit terms as a necessity of business rather than as a desirable opportunity. Similar misunderstandings prevailed upon the problems of exchange and remittance. British merchants in Buenos Aires disdained the pettiness and impatience of their United Kingdom agents because the highest profits came from international speculations in Argentine produce rather than from the marketing of British manufactures.

James Hodgson, whose experience was typical of British merchants in

Argentina, successfully faced the problems of the Buenos Aires market. He began operating in Buenos Aires as a general commission merchant of limited capital in 1817. During the following year Hodgson formed a partnership with a family friend, Joseph Green of Liverpool. When this arrangement dissolved in 1829, Hodgson formed another partnership in Buenos Aires with John Robinson, his former accountant. He then operated through manufacturers' agents, like Owen Owens and Sons of Manchester, until the business was liquidated in March of 1844, when both partners returned to the United Kingdom. For seventeen years James Hodgson obtained goods on consignment, marketed British goods innovatively in a competitive market, and speculated profitably on his own account in Argentine produce.[11]

Hodgson, like the greater number of his contemporaries in Argentina, began business as a commission agent. Before crossing the Atlantic he made some minor contacts in the United Kingdom, but clearly the bulk of his trade depended upon Green's initiative. Hodgson certainly experienced less difficulty than those merchants who possessed little property and no worthwhile family connections. When Green terminated the partnership in 1829 because he felt dissatisfied with Hodgson's dilatory settlement of accounts and slovenly bookkeeping, Hodgson returned to the United Kingdom to settle the affairs and to secure his overseas agents. While in Europe Hodgson also tried to expand his contacts by competing with other Buenos Aires merchants in the rate of commission offered to his agents. Thus, James Hodgson obtained the Argentine business of C. G. Becker, a Leipzig merchant, by offering one percent of his commission on all business between the two houses for a private purse for Becker's daughter. Hodgson secretly contacted many other German houses, particularly those active in the linen trade, to undercut his competitors in Buenos Aires. He suggested that there would be mutual advantage if the consignors were to prepare a complete master pattern card and set of textile patterns by their usual manufacturers so that consignments of unsalable goods should not be dispatched to Buenos Aires. Hodgson promised to show the samples to retailers in order to find which items would sell well and asked for quotations of the lowest cost for which goods could be sold, indicating such additional charges as packaging, carriage to Hamburg or Bremen, transit due, and freight and insurance rates.[12] As part of his effort to obtain consignments and compete favorably in the Buenos Aires market, James Hodgson stressed his fourteen years' experience and low commission charges of five percent on sales, one percent on warehouse rent, and two and a half percent on returns made in produce.[13]

Hodgson's experience and reputation even before 1829 encouraged overseas agents to request that he sell their goods. This aspect of the consignment business proved particularly helpful to British merchants in

Buenos Aires, provided that the new business did not compete with products already handled and did not come into an oversupplied market. As general merchants, British houses in Buenos Aires were quite willing to handle a variety of goods ranging from wines and luxury goods to textiles and ready-made clothing. However, merchants recommended trial shipments of an unknown product.[14] The reputation of a merchant depended on his ability to gauge the market, to receive good prices for consignments, to sell promptly, and to answer the letters of his correspondents. Trade principally benefited when the consignor followed specific instructions.

Along with the exact specification of goods that he desired at a particular time, James Hodgson also advised his agent, Owen Owens, to follow certain instructions. First and foremost, goods were to be invoiced at their bonafide exact costs to give a clear idea of the profitable selling price. All goods were to be measured accurately with the short stick of 36 inches and the full length to be marked. Patterns were to be sent of the full width of the articles, with each pattern numbered and with separate reference to the number, giving the names, lengths, widths, and prices. The consignor was to keep a reserve duplicate of the pattern with the number for reference so that if he had similar goods of different prices, the consignee could request those that sold best. Hodgson insisted that manufacturers should not learn the destination of purchases and recommended that Owens employ packers and shipping agents at Liverpool who were not intimate with other houses. The shipping agents were to select the best vessel of the quickest dispatch and a captain familiar with the Buenos Aires trade, and to have the goods stored in a dry place in the ship easy to reach so that they would be among the first unloaded in Buenos Aires. The bills of lading were to be drawn out to "order," endorsed by the captain, and made out in as general and as vague terms as possible so as not to give the competition undue information. Hodgson also needed advice as to the insurance effected upon goods. To lessen risk, uninsured consignments were generally shipped in two or three vessels while letters and parcels of patterns were put in the ship's letter bags. Hodgson placed considerable importance upon early warning of future consignments and urged Owens to advise the exact assortments of colors, widths, lengths, sizes, quantities, and costs as well as the name of the vessel and its possible sailing date. And, finally, Owens gave explicit instructions on how the returns should be invested and how much freedom Hodgson and Robinson could take in deciding on types of remittances.[15] At times, specific instructions were given to different consignees. Hodgson and Robinson asked George Faulkner and Company of Manchester to keep the accounts of each consignment separately. They further suggested that Faulkner employ Owens' shipping agent, Buchanan and Son.[16]

Buenos Aires merchants preferred to sell the goods on board the ship so that they did not have to worry about putting the goods on shore or taking them through customs. Occasionally, the merchant in London gave specific instructions that the goods were to be sold on board. But this meant that Buenos Aires merchants had to have samples on hand, because the dealers would not buy the articles without seeing the patterns.[17]

The successful marketing of goods depended upon their type, the market demand, and the merchants' ability to compete in terms of credit, price, and good will. James Hodgson instructed his Buenos Aires House that

> when you sell a shipment off all at once, the price demanded should be a shade lower than for single packages to enable the purchasers to sell by the piece or even single packages with a small advance . . . be wooed and don't woo purchasers, nor run down the market . . . where you can barter for produce pray do so . . . When you clearly see an article cannot be sold to pay, then don't show it even but wait for it to come round . . . In order to get going some new style of prints by hook or crook, get some dashing or leading families to get dresses made up of them. To show them in the streets give them some romantic sounding titles and ask about double the price for them and they are sure to go like a house afire.[18]

Hodgson in fact underestimated the problems of the Buenos Aires market. Thus in 1841 he complained to Fielden Brothers of Manchester that their recent consignment of textiles had ignored all advice, as it comprised mainly green and blue colors unsuited to the market for political reasons so that shopkeepers would not touch them. He added that competitors had recently received preferred patterns in red and pink colors and felt that Fielden's shipment would be unsalable unless the prices were reduced. Items such as ale and port, not consumed nor salable in the summer, were to be shipped to arrive in Buenos Aires from February through October, while butter and coal for winter consumption sold only from March to August. These types of consignments were not particularly desired, but profit could be made if they arrived at the right time.[19] Manufacturers were also blamed for supplying goods inferior to those of their competitors. Occasionally, a refund had to be made because goods ordered by a particular shopkeeper were not of equal quality to the first shipment. If, however, the goods were of the type preferred by dealers on the market and were well known to them but still did not sell quickly, merchants were quick to point out that the market was oversupplied.

The financial conditions of the Buenos Aires market further unsettled the stability of merchant affairs and intensified competition. Hodgson reported that shopkeepers were almost forced to take the goods and thereby could make their own terms not only in regard to price but also in regard to the credit desired. In May of 1838 he wrote that the house of McCrackan and Jamieson had sold all their stock of goods at auction at 30, 45, 60, and 75 days credit and that they brought but moderate prices. On the whole, other English houses were generally selling what they could on open credit, apparently on more liberal terms than those of Hodgson and Robinson, who only in 1838 were thinking of extending their credit to one month.[20] An editorial in the *Buenos Aires Standard* of 1876 expressed with some nostalgia that twenty-five or thirty years ago importers sold on current account, the dealers commencing to pay something on the account the first Saturday after the delivery of the goods and the goods being paid for in three months. By 1848 a system of promissory notes had been adopted, which gave definite proof that the goods had been delivered and that the accounts were correct. Soon after that, this system collapsed and credit was extended to seven or eight months with no document being taken because of the intense competition in the import market. The writer of the editorial argued that importers should agree to restrict credit, selling only on a cash basis or at the most giving credit for thirty days with stamped promissory notes. The problems of credit extension to shopkeepers by importers and the sluggish inventory turnover in goods plagued the entire period between 1810 and 1880.[21]

The British merchant in Argentina not only had to have a knowledge of the demands of the Buenos Aires market, be innovative in the selling of consignments, and extend credit to retailers, but he also sought to expand market demand by the introduction of new or modified merchandise. Hodgson and Robinson profitably duplicated Indian fancy rugs and ponchos at a cheaper cost than internal production. In 1828 James Hodgson wrote Robinson from London during a sales trip requesting that he buy a nice poncho from the interior of a popular shape, size, color, and texture that could be used as a model by a British manufacturer. To avoid British restrictions upon the import of foreign woolen goods, the captain of the ship was to bring the poncho ashore with his mattress and blanket, as if it had served him as a cover. Hodgson and Robinson were successful enough with this venture that other British firms followed their example, when they saw the high prices obtained for the product. Eventually the supply of ponchos greatly exceeded demand and a reexport trade began to Chile. The first trial shipment of one thousand ponchos was invoiced at 100 percent above the price paid by Hodgson. His agent in Chile was told to sell the ponchos without delay for the best cash prices he could obtain and to send the account sales immediately, along with a full report as to how well each pattern sold according to assortment, sizes, and fringes. In order to encourage sales, the letters to the merchant in Chile gave hints as to the high profits obtainable for sales at the invoice prices.[22]

Much the same plan was carried out with fancy rugs, although with rather less success. In January 1834 Hodgson and Robinson wrote to George Faulkner and Company:

> We hereby send you to care of Mr. Dan Campbell a native made woolen fancy rug as a pattern for you to execute on joint account 600 *as soon as possible* and which will of course put in at the lowest prices you can possibly make them for, but the quality of *wool, weight, pattern, specious weaving, breadth, tassels, brilliancy and fastness of colours of the pattern must be imitated to perfection itself down to the most minute particular so that in short the copies may not be distinguishable from the original, on the most rigid comparison.* At the same time these you make (so as to come under the lower duty) must come woven in pieces of 22 yard lengths (37 inches to the yard) and free of the fag ends . . . The tassels for the rug couriers must be sent separately packed up inside the bales.[23]

It was not until December of 1834 that Hodgson and Robinson received a reply in regard to the cost and the feasibility of producing the rugs. Since the cost was twenty shillings each, slightly higher than expected, the manufacturer felt that they could not satisfactorily reproduce the original pattern. When the rugs finally arrived, James Hodgson was delighted with the imitation but hoped that the manufacturer could make them for fifteen shillings. Initially the fancy rugs sold for 50 pesos each, but the Argentine retailers made only a 5-peso profit. Hodgson did not order more than one thousand since the demand was limited; prices decreased and competition threatened because the junior partner of the house of McCrackan and Jamieson had taken a sample with him to England to be reproduced. Hodgson sold some in Uruguay and Chile, where the fancy rugs imported from Buenos Aires fetched a slightly better price, since the people thought they were made by the pampa Indians. The profit margins on rug sales in Buenos Aires were so small that Hodgson devised an intriguing scheme for saving a little expense by selling the worsted line and yarn contained in the bales of rugs separately. Failing to receive an invoice from the manufacturer for one of the bales, Hodgson, Robinson, and Company had to open the unadvised bale and count the rugs in the presence of a customhouse superior. They then were accused of smuggling in the yarn to avoid duty. Moreover, the retailer had not known before that the yarn and line were for the rugs and they had to be given to him in the sale. Hodgson, Robinson, and Company finally discontinued the order of these rugs in June of 1836 when the price of 45 pesos each was the best offer they could obtain, leaving them but a trifling profit.[24]

The production and marketing of rugs and ponchos illustrates the adaptation of European technology and marketing techniques to the local area. Through their contacts with manufacturers in the United Kingdom, Hodgson, Robinson, and Company developed at a lower cost a product similar to ones already on the Argentine market. The goods produced specifically for the local market were introduced to national retailers in the city of Buenos Aires and the interior. Efforts were made to create further demand through contacts with import-export houses in other parts of South America, who in turn sought to interest their local retailers.

The ability of a given house to operate profitably depended upon its ingenuity. Hodgson, who was quite innovative in his marketing techniques, was often just as clever in his efforts at coastal trade speculation. In November of 1825, Hodgson suggested to Green, Hartly, Tully, and Company in Rio that they might speculate in Brazilian produce, noting that if the emperor were to declare war on Buenos Aires, the value of Brazilian produce would rise. To make use of this fact, they suggested that the British house based in Brazil use its political influence to obtain letters from the minister of foreign affairs to all the authorities commanding the Brazilian naval and military forces to permit their vessel to pass. The arrangement could be made under the guise that the vessel was conveying dispatches to the British Plenipotentiary in Buenos Aires, Woodbine Parish. To carry out the arrangement Hodgson suggested that Green and Hartly join an influential Brazilian or European Portuguese house in Rio, with the Brazilian house taking one-third and Green and Hartly taking two-thirds in the cargo—one-third on their own account and one-third for Hodgson and Robinson. The whole cargo should be taken in the name of the British house to avoid risk of detention in case the vessel fell in with any Buenos Aires privateers, and should be insured against all risk.[25]

Although Hodgson's activities proved generally successful, he occasionally encountered disastrous failure from reasons quite beyond his control. In December 1838 Hodgson suggested to Fielden Brothers of Manchester that a ship be chartered to pick up a cargo of salt at Cape Verde and then be sent to Buenos Aires. He assumed that by the time the ship arrived the blockade of the port of Buenos Aires would be terminated, salt would fetch a good price, and the ship would be easily loaded with produce to return to Europe. In July 1840, on Hodgson's advice, Fielden Brothers, W. Whitaker and Company of Santos, Brazil, and Owen Owens and Sons agreed to charter the brig *D'Arcy*, with profits and losses for the venture to be divided among the three houses. *D'Arcy* arrived at Santos from Liverpool in fifty-nine days. On September 25, 1840, she commenced to discharge her cargo of manufactured goods, primarily materials and piece goods. Although the discharging of goods was completed by October 19, the French were still blockading the port of Buenos Aires. Therefore, Whitaker and Company furnished the captain with a small quantity of firewood and the sum of £125 in specie with which to purchase salt and sent the ship to Cape Verde. The ship returned to Santos on September 7, 1841, with the cargo of salt; but since there was no market for the cargo there, and the port of Buenos Aires was now open, Whitaker and Company dispatched the *D'Arcy* the next day to Hodgson, Robinson, and Company of Buenos Aires. Since Hodgson and Robinson had trouble finding a cargo for the *D'Arcy*, she was not finally dispatched for Liverpool until August 21, 1841. Although a substantial amount of the decision making was left to the mercantile house in each port to which the ship was sent, the venture still proved disastrous—so much so that Whitaker and Company tried to withdraw from the initial contract. Because of the unstable political situation and the inability to relate market demands to shipping time, the advantages gained by international connections did not prove profitable in this case.[26]

Occasionally merchants speculated in fields rather divorced from the import and export of goods and produce. In 1882 James Hodgson and Alexander Brown of Buenos Aires sent a painting to London which they believed was San Antonia Abad praying in the wilderness. But their small speculation on joint account in the arts proved unremunerative, since the painting, at least in the nineteenth-century market, had little value.[27]

DURING the early part of the century, British import-export merchants, in order to expand their markets, sometimes sent goods directly into the interior rather than sell them entirely in Buenos Aires. Shipping into the interior usually meant going up either the Paraná or Uruguay River, the easiest way of transporting goods and produce. But it might also mean travelling to Ensenada or across to Colonia (fig. 3). After the several early trials, British merchants such as James Hodgson only occasionally sent consignments directly into the interior, preferring to sell to national dealers who took the goods into the interior. In the latter part of the century branch houses were occasionally set up at a port like Rosario, although even within the city of Buenos Aires the importers sold primarily to nationals, for the closing of markets in the province of Corrientes and the Republic of Paraguay meant that the market in Buenos Aires might be more than usually glutted with goods, particularly of the type that was ordered for the interior trade.[28]

Trading in the interior often presented special problems. Not only were there Indian invasions, civil disturbances, conflicts between the government of Buenos Aires and Montevideo, and the need to procure special licenses, but also there were communicational and operational

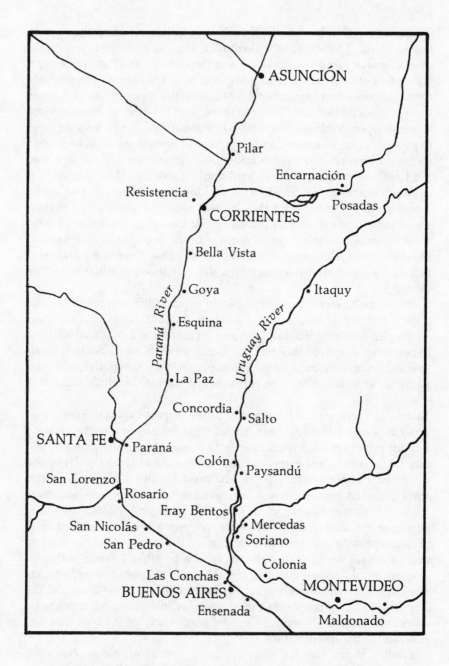

3. River ports on the Paraná and Uruguay rivers before 1860. (After Clifton B. Kroeber, *The Growth of the Shipping Industry in the Río de la Plata Region*, Madison, 1957, p. 36.)

difficulties. John Wilson, for example, wrote Dallas from Colonia that he waited in his schooner fourteen days for goods from José María Romero so that he could start up the river to procure hides.[29]

The interior trade depended upon both the marketing of imported goods and the collection of hides, skins, horns, hair, wool, and jerked beef because merchants often preferred to take payment in produce rather than currency. In the early years of the trade, operations in the interior were quite profitable. As early as 1811 John Parish Robertson, acting as an agent of British imported goods, went to Paraguay to sell merchandise. When expelled from Asunción in 1815 for political reasons, he established mercantile operations with his brother William in the interior of Argentina at Corrientes on the Paraná River, later expanding to Goya. In both of their major centers they owned offices, warehouses, and barns. The brothers succeeded because they adapted the previously used credit system, which involved the extension of credit in goods or currency for a designated time to the grower or collector of produce, and because they paid high prices for hides and charged low ones for goods. The Creoles found the new arrangement advantageous and the Robertsons' undercut their Argentine competitors. Between January and October of one year they shipped no fewer than fifty thousand ox hides, one hundred thousand horse hides, and numerous bales of wool and hair. Although the collection of this produce—purchased by barter, transported to the river in carts and shipped—demanded organization, the difficulties seemed small in comparison to their profit of over one hundred percent. For example, they contracted with an *estanciero* for twenty thousand wild horses to be taken from the estate for three pence each, slaughtered for three pence, staked and cleaned for three pence, carted to Goya for three pence—at a total cost of one shilling per hide. The market value in Buenos Aires yielded three shillings each and sale in the United Kingdom fetched seven to eight shillings. The hides thus sold from 2,800 to 3,000 percent of the cost of the horse. Deducting transportation costs between Goya and London (approximately three shillings per hide), profits would have averaged 166.66 percent of the cost of the horse.[30]

The transactions of the Robertson Brothers clearly varied from the typical mercantile operations in that the establishment in the interior was the original base and only later were connections established with Glasgow, Liverpool, and London. Nevertheless, quite early the Robertsons realized that they needed an organization in Buenos Aires to handle their import-export trade.

During the 1820s the interior trade became less profitable for British merchants. Argentine entrepreneurs, with their greater understanding of the interior political environment, operated more efficiently in the provinces than could British merchants. In times of civil disturbances, despite varying currencies, nationals were relatively unaffected by provincial prejudice against traders from the city of Buenos Aires. While the interior markets raised too many problems to attract much attention from British merchants, government policy and Argentine circumstance turned the activities of national entrepreneurs to the interior and by so doing enhanced the commercial importance of Buenos Aires.[31]

WHEN BRITISH merchants ceased to operate directly in the interior trade, they obtained products by financing expeditions to the interior, establishing contacts with persons in the provinces, or buying produce directly in Buenos Aires. Vast herds of cattle roamed the pampas and furnished the staple produce of the country. The cattle were either slaughtered on the *estancias*, the hides dried, tallow packed in the raw state, and the hair collected and forwarded to Buenos Aires in ox carts or sent by water if near the coast, or the cattle were driven to the outskirts of the city of Buenos Aires where men salted the hides, prepared the jerked beef and steamed the residue of the animal down for the extraction of tallow. British merchants in Buenos Aires procured products directly from other exporters, national dealers, *saladeros* (meat and hide salting houses), or the *barracas* (the hide drying sheds) during the produce season which began in late September.[32]

At the saladeros, hides, meat, tallow, horns and hair could all be procured. The basic function of the saladero was the salting, curing, and packing of beef, in effect the production of the jerked beef or *charqui*. After the animal was slaughtered and the beef removed from the bones in portions two to three inches thick, workers pickled the pieces in brine. Then the meat was piled in successive layers separated by dry salt and subsequently dried in the sun. When this process was finished, packers sorted the meat and according to quality packed it in canvas bags.

Produce might also be bought on credit or for cash in Buenos Aires. In 1828 James Hodgson advised the buying of ox hides to the full extent of funds in hand and the acceptance of payments at two and four months, allowing the seller one percent interest per month as part of the credit terms to be included in the bill.[33] Brokers sold hides by weight of thirty-five pounds per hide, charging a one-half percent fee for selection, examination, and procurement of the hides. Ostrich feathers were sold by arrobas or twenty-five-pound groups. By 1825 brokerage fees were not yet standardized in the selling of ostrich, chinchilla, or nutria skins. In the early years of the wool trade the import-export merchant was the intermediary between the interior and Europe. He bought the wool from a city broker, a local interior storekeeper, or the sheepbreeder. The merchant then baled and stored the wool in sheds and exported the wool to Europe either to order or for sale.[34] Whether in the interior or in

Buenos Aires, goods might be exchanged for local products. Produce was also paid for by cash or bills of exchange. Advances were generally required and credit might be arranged.

British merchants in Buenos Aires sometimes exported products by producer's request from the interior or from an individual in Buenos Aires, on joint account or on his own account, on the basis of orders sent from England or the continent, and as remittances to pay for goods he had imported. Most mercantile houses sent goods on their own account or on joint account; while this method increased the risks, it also meant increased profits if successful, particularly when the price of produce was low in Argentina and high in Great Britain.[35]

Merchants often had difficulty executing orders for produce, especially if it was requested in the off-season and if the request was too specific as to the quality required. Thomas and William March of London wrote Hugh Dallas in 1818, giving specific instructions on the hides they desired for the Antwerp market:

> The weight should be from 17-33 pounds each, if they are lighter than this they are difficult to sell, and if heavier the weight is generally too much in the head and nothing can be more objectionable than large clumsy hides with thick heads. The heads on the contrary should be thin and the hides generally compact without being stretched too thin in the body; they should also be strong in the back and should have been dried on the grass. The fleshy part should be clear, smooth, and of a yellowish or greenish colour and free from fat and all hides that have been pricked or improperly cut or which are either moldy or worm eaten to be avoided.[36]

The March Brothers also ordered that the ten to twelve thousand hides purchased by Dallas should not cost more than six pence per pound allowing for the costs of putting them on board the ship, exchange, freight, and insurance, calculated at 3 percent. This sanguine assessment was later raised to seven pence. A first class British ship of the proper size was to be procured, which would call at Falmouth or Cowes for orders and then proceed to London or to any port on the continent of Europe between the Elbe and the Garonne. For reimbursements, Dallas was to draw directly on March at sixty days sight at the most favorable exchange unless it was more advantageous to draw on Rio de Janeiro, where the necessary credit was arranged with Henry Miller and Company to the favor of Mess. March Brothers and Company.[37]

Not only did the British merchant in Buenos Aires receive orders for Argentine produce, but he also received orders for produce of other South American countries. Emanuel Bingham, a merchant of Le Havre, requested Hugh Dallas to send him 60,000 pounds of Spanish-weight unwrought Peruvian copper to be shipped for 10 to 11 Spanish doubloons—later raised to 15 doubloons. The copper was to be loaded aboard a French vessel bound for Le Havre. Dallas was to reimburse himself by drawing at seventy days sight on Mess. Campbell, Bowden, and Company of London, who would also effect the insurance.[38]

OPERATING in both the international market and the Argentine environment, British merchants faced complications in the payment for goods and produce whether they were bought on order, joint account, or the firm's own account. Payment took one of three forms: specie, produce, or bills of exchange. Remittances by their very nature involved a certain degree of risk and demanded a knowledge of both internal and international supplies and demands, since the value of bills of exchange and specie depended upon fluctuating exchange rates, while goods and produce were dependent on buying and selling prices in the open market.

Although payment in specie appeared the simplest method, it presented complications. First, the specie had to be obtained, then shipped and marketed, all involving speculation. Merchants thus recommended payment and speculation in specie to their correspondents only when the exchange rates were particularly favorable and when an order of the government prohibiting the export of specie could be evaded. When Henry Miller, a British merchant in Rio de Janeiro, shipped gold to his partner, Hugh Dallas of Buenos Aires, he violated the government order by sending the gold by Royal Navy packet with no bill of lading and sending the invoices, which debited the amount of the invoice in *reales*. The preferred but more expensive means of sending specie was either by Royal Navy warships or by British packets. However, gold could be sent in Royal Navy ships only when the South American governments permitted the export of specie. Rostron and Dutton of Rio de Janeiro pointed out to Hodgson and Robinson of Buenos Aires in March of 1833 that specie being shipped to London should not be landed in Rio, since it would be subject to one percent import duty on the current value plus expenses of guards and boat hire, and to two percent export duty on the current value plus one-half percent commission for handling. Freight rates on British ships of war or the packets were one percent from Buenos Aires to Rio and one percent from Rio to Falmouth unless the specie were sent directly to the United Kingdom. If bills of lading were made out to Falmouth, the transshipment at Rio was considered part of the total voyage, and freight rates would be one percent of the value of specie. When specie was transshipped from one Royal Navy vessel to another, the local authorities had no control over it and consequently could not impose duties. But the case was different for a merchant vessel.[39] In the early part of the century the Falmouth packets operated to Rio, with auxiliary packets to Montevideo and Buenos Aires. Transshipment increased the delay in arrival of the specie but not the duties because no business transaction involving the specie took place in Brazil.

Speculation in Spanish gold pesos was also considered an operation in specie. In April of 1818 Henry Miller wrote to Hugh Dallas:

> We wrote you under the date of 31 ultimate instant, having received a letter from London recommending an operation in Specie [Spanish Doubloons]; request you will be pleased to ship us in the Hyacinth to the extent of thirty thousand dollars [Argentine pesos] and draw for the amount one half on Mess. McIntosh Miller & Company and one half on Mess. Campbell Bowden & Company provided the exchange on London does not exceed 51° [pence] per dollar at utmost 52 and charging a commission of 1%. The order being given with a view to the advantage of the exchange operation, it will not allow a heavier rate of commission; but if the business be worthy your attention we pray the favor of your accomplishing it if possible, observing all possible secrecy; in respect to your view, you can pretend that you want them for Indies.[40]

According to the instructions, Dallas bought Spanish doubloons in Buenos Aires. These were shipped to Rio and sold for reis, while Dallas obtained payment for the pesos by drawing on London. Miller eventually used the reis to buy bills of exchange on London, calculating a profit of 20 reis on each doubloon. He thus would have made £170.3.4, a profit of 3.6 percent within two months of his speculation. When the rate of exchange jumped from 555 reis per doubloon to 865, Miller was able to make £271.5.0 returns and a profit of 7 percent within two months. However, it was important to watch the exchange rate for Spanish pesos; for if the rate fell between Argentine pesos and British pounds in England, profits would decrease since Dallas was drawing on England to pay for the Spanish doubloons shipped. As more persons speculated in doubloons, the price in Rio declined. Then it became more advantageous to ship pesos in any British vessel, not just a vessel of war, so that the coins arrived before prices declined. Although the cost for freight shipment was greater and security less on merchant vessels, insurance could be effected on the shipment of any registered British vessel. In addition, the sailings of ships of war were uncertain, so that the consignments of several merchants would arrive simultaneously, flooding the Rio market with Spanish pesos and raising the exchange between reis and Spanish doubloons. However, it should be clear that Dallas' shipments of pesos to Rio were not always a speculation but often a method of making remittances for produce.[41]

Produce might be substituted for payment in gold, silver, or coin. This too could be speculative, since its yield would be credited to the account of the merchant only after sale, while freight, handling charges, and duties had to be deducted from the amount. In some cases merchant creditors overseas would specifically request that remittances be made in produce and deliberately speculate. Thus, Buenos Aires merchants bought produce to the amount owed, while merchants in the United Kingdom paid freight and handling in the hope of selling the produce at a profit. Who assumed the risk in sending the produce as payments for funds owed depended primarily on the type of account held and on whether produce had been requested. Hugh Dallas, who had a standing account and credit with the house of Henry Miller, sent produce on his own account to be sold for his credit in Rio. But if other South American or European houses requested that remittances be sent in produce as payments for goods, those houses assumed the risk. In addition to the fact that remittances in produce might prove profitable, there were two other reasons for paying in produce: governments often prohibited the exportation of specie, and a significant incidence of mercantile house failures periodically shook confidence in bills of exchange.[42]

Bills of exchange were the most common means of making payments. When one merchant (the drawer) wrote a draft on another (the drawee), the payee (the person to whom payment was due) assumed that the drawee had the funds to pay the draft, or would have funds when the bill came due. It was important that the drawer inform the house on which he drew the amount of the bill and to whom it was drawn, so as to assure acceptance and prevent forgery. At the same time the drawer desired to know that the bill of exchange had been received and would be paid when due. If a house was in need of immediate cash, the draft might be sold on the open market at a discounted rate, the total sum of the bill to be paid to the buyer when it was finally due. Occasionally a merchant in poor standing would find his bills refused by the drawee. If this happened the bill was then sent to the payee or his correspondent in the city in which the bill was initially written and the payee sought to collect the amount due from the drawer. Should payment of a bill be refused, it was generally desired that the bill be protested and payment enforced, the proceeds to be invested in a bill drawn on a reputable London house.

A house might ask that the drafts be drawn to order so that the buyers would not know the names of the correspondents. If the drawee did not guarantee debts of the parties drawing, the bill might be required to be drawn in the drawer's own name. If a house charged two and one-half percent of the draft as a guarantee for debts, it was obliged to make good to the payee. A merchant might create further difficulties for himself by an irregular endorsement. Rostron, Dutton, and Company of Rio sent a bill to Buenos Aires, evidently with a British countersignature, on the assumption that it was needed to guarantee payment and that their own signature was insufficient.[43] The date on which a bill was initially drawn was equally important, since it depended on the exchange rate either at the time the bill was authorized, at sight, or when the bill was due. A merchant who drew prematurely might be both criticized and penalized for his action; for not only did he risk dishonor of his bill, but he might miss the opportunity for a more favorable exchange rate. If it made no difference to the payee, the drawee might ask that a bill made out to him be dated for a certain time or be paid at a particular exchange rate. A bill carelessly written could be drawn at any exchange rate. Generally a carelessly written bill led to complicated and long discussions about which exchange rate should be used.

To make payments with less speculative bills of exchange, a merchant might decide on a fixed exchange rate. In 1843 Owen Owens and Sons wrote Hodgson, Robinson, and Company that their stipulation of fixed exchange had worked to their own detriment. Hodgson and Robinson replied quickly that neither they nor anyone else could predict any movements in exchange rates. Preferring the security of pounds sterling to risks on varying and unguaranteed currencies when selling on several months credit, Hodgson and Robinson adopted the method of fixing exchange for the safety of Owen Owens, despite the reluctance of their buyers to fix the exchange so far in advance and stipulate the price of gold. Charles Holland, a British merchant in Buenos Aires, solicited business by writing to Baring Brothers in 1829 and emphasizing that all his transactions centered upon a sterling base.[44]

Since mercantile houses operated on an international scale, speculation in exchange was often both a profitable adventure and a necessary hazard. International connections became crucial in the speculation in exchange on drafts. A particular house might be instructed to draw on either London or Rio, depending upon which offered the more favorable exchange rate. Because London was the center of the financial world, the arrival of the packet bringing news of the exchange rates in London often meant a shift in the local exchange rates. But it was not always the relationships between the national economy and the international economy that determined exchange rates. In 1838 James Hodgson attributed the rise in the exchange rate in Buenos Aires to the scarcity of currency due to the suspension of sales and the cheapness at which produce could be bought, which had induced some individuals to draw for the purpose of investing their funds. While it was possible to use bills of exchange for speculative purposes rather than as a form of payment, this was generally discouraged because the risk involved was disproportionate to the limited profits that could be expected from such ventures. In 1818

James Hodgson wrote to his brother Thomas Hodgson in the United Kingdom that a profit of 15 percent might be realized in the exchange of remittances through Rio de Janeiro by merely purchasing bills of exchange on Rio and reinvesting the proceeds there in bills on London.[45]

Before any international transfers occurred, parties might decide that funds be held until a favorable rate of exchange existed. Joseph Green signed an agreement with Yates and Company of Liverpool that the proceeds of iron sold in Buenos Aires for 2,005 Argentine pesos and 5.5 reales be held for one year. Unless directions were given at the end of the year to hold the funds longer, they were to be remitted at the current rate with the interest accruing from the time when it was in cash at the rate of 6 percent per year. If a favorable rate of exchange occurred during the year so that Argentine pesos increased in value in relation to pounds sterling, the funds were to be remitted at that time. If the exchange rate was particularly poor, a request might be made that remittances be placed in bonds, such as the Buenos Aires government 6.5 percent issue. The correspondent would eventually order the bonds sold and bills of exchange bought on London.[46]

Bills bought and sold on the market were subject to speculation, since exchange rates were taken into account and discounting was affected by supply and demand. A brokerage fee was also added. A given firm might request that its bills be bought if they appeared on the market. Too many bills of a given house on the market suggested poor credit standing. Further, it was the custom that indirect bills (those bought and sold on the market) cost one farthing to one half-penny more than the current rate of exchange no matter how good the paper was. If a house had a poor credit standing, the exchange rate on its bills declined. In 1879 Darbyshire, Jordon, and Company and Barclay and Campbell's bills, near the time they were going bankrupt, could be obtained at 50 pence exchange on the peso while other house bills might be bought for 49.25d. Although these differences in exchange rate appear minor, the amount on a bill of substantial size could increase or decrease profits substantially. Furthermore, this was profit or loss in one day's transactions when bills were negotiated daily.

Although some houses might choose to make their returns primarily in one medium, generally payments involved the use of all three forms— specie, bills of exchange, and produce. Charles Taylor and Company, a wealthy firm with a branch at Montevideo and houses at Liverpool and Buenos Aires, imported on its own account and preferred to make its returns in bills of exchange. On the other hand, Parlane, Macalister, and Company with houses in Buenos Aires and Montevideo, importers of British manufactured goods on consignment and on their own account and exporters of produce to Europe on their own account, preferred to make remittances in produce to their Manchester house of Wright, Parlane, and Company. The Manchester house then paid their correspondents in specie. A particular correspondent might ask that remittances be made in good bills, Spanish pesos, or produce. A house decided on its form of payment by considering the market and choosing the method of payment which would prove most profitable to all concerned. Correspondents might express a preference for one form of remittance over another, but the preference was almost always qualified to allow the final decision to the house making the remittances. In April of 1820 Thomas Coates of London wrote Hugh Dallas that he would like his remittances in hides, although the price seemed to be falling and it might be preferable to ship gold if it could be transmitted safely. Since the exchange rates on both gold and good bills were miserable, the final decision was left to Dallas.[47]

ALTHOUGH marketing posed numerous risks for British merchants, speculations in produce—buying or selling with the expectation of profiting by fluctuating prices—presented both the greatest hazards and the most remunerative profits. In addition to their European trade, merchants in Buenos Aires exchanged produce and goods with houses in South America as distant as Lima and Havana, or as close as Rio de Janeiro and Montevideo. Profits depended upon market demand at the port of final destination of the cargo. The greater the distance of the ports and the larger the number of transfers in different commodities, the more hazardous proved the speculation. Risk could be lessened only by operation on joint account and by accurate knowledge of market demands for the produce in which merchants speculated.

Hugh Dallas, a Scots businessman in Buenos Aires between 1816 and 1822, operated in partnership with Henry Miller, an import-export trader of Rio de Janeiro and London. Dallas, with limited capital and credit, gambled unwisely in both the produce of other South American countries and Argentine produce. As long as Dallas limited his risks to the coastal trade of Montevideo and Rio de Janeiro, where he had adequate contacts and valid information, he was able to make small profits. When he speculated in Chilean wheat and Argentine jerked beef, which demanded sound market knowledge of several countries and a willingness to leave the details of the operation in the hands of others, Dallas found himself bearing heavy losses which neither his reputation nor limited capital could withstand.

Hugh Dallas, like many other British merchants, frequently speculated in the coastal trade of South America. In November 1819 he engaged a ship to carry tallow and hides to Miller, Nicholson, and Company of Bahia and requested that the ship be sent back as promptly as possible

with a full cargo of white sugar. Dallas also shipped produce or goods to
Montevideo and Rio. In June of 1821 Henry Miller sent a cargo of coffee
down to Buenos Aires and asked that the ship be loaded speedily with
2,500 to 3,000 hides to be sent back to Rio.[48] From 1817 to 1820 Dallas
shipped hides, tallow, hair, and jerked beef to Miller, who sold the products on board the ship to another exporter whenever possible to avoid
payment of duty and unloading charges; otherwise the produce was unloaded and stored until sold and reshipped.[49] Although many of the large
commercial houses had branches in Montevideo to supply the Uruguayan
market, branch houses offered other advantages. Freight and local expenses were often cheaper in Montevideo than in Buenos Aires. Rather
than send produce to Montevideo to sell, the merchant sent partially
freighted ships, which were to be loaded with more jerked beef or hides.
The ships were then dispatched to Rio or Europe where the produce was
sold. If a Buenos Aires house did not have a branch in Montevideo or Rio
de Janeiro, it at least had strong working connections with a house at
those ports so as to be able to engage in the coastal trade, to exchange
goods from Europe, and to obtain additional news on the various markets in South America and Europe. The fact that Hugh Dallas did not
have a branch in Montevideo did not prevent him from having textiles
sold there, if he could receive a better price.[50]

When Dallas moved from coastal trade to speculation in Chilean
wheat, he experienced a severe financial reverse. In February 1819 Dallas
shipped four casks of hardware, including tools, screws, nails, and so on,
and one hundred and five mining bars (wrought-iron rods from six to
nine feet long used for pulling down loose pieces of ore or stone from the
roof and sides of a mine) to Winter, Brittain, and Company of Santiago.
The proceeds from the sale were to be used to purchase wheat for his account and shipment to Rio. Although the speculation initially appeared
profitable, Dallas immediately ran into problems. Winter and Brittain
sold the mining bars below invoiced price. They purchased 10,000 fanegas of wheat at a good price, under 10 reales a fanega. However, Winter and Brittain's difficulty in securing a ship for the wheat and the decline in the price of wheat in Rio de Janeiro forced Dallas to instruct them
to sell the wheat in Chile. By that time Winter and Brittain had succeeded
in finding freight to Rio for 1,000 fanegas at the rate of 2 pesos per fanega
and 5 percent primage (allowance paid by the shipper to the master and
crew of the vessel for the loading and care of wheat which is now included in freight rates). Dallas had hoped that the remaining wheat could
be sold at Santiago to yield a small profit after purchasing, handling, and
storage costs. However, no vessels were loading, the new harvest was
advancing, part of the wheat was from 1818 and packed in hides to protect it through the rainy season, the worm was setting in the wheat, and

warehouse costs were rising. Brittain and Company consequently sold 4,000 fanegas of wheat at 9 reales per fanega to cover their costs. That price cost Dallas a loss of one reale per fanega before he even deducted the expenses of storage and commission charges. Winter and Brittain then advised the shipping of the remaining wheat to Rio. The wheat caused a heavy loss on arrival in Rio because of its poor condition, which was rather worsened by leaks in the ship.[51]

The speculation failed because of difficulties in assessing market demand through the length of time involved in communicating the order, the effort of Dallas to make all the decisions on the buying and selling of his wheat from Buenos Aires in relationship to two markets of which he had limited knowledge, and the political instability in South America. Dallas bought his wheat before the rainy season started. He then had to have it stored for lack of a ship, because a Spanish frigate was blockading Santiago and merchant vessels could easily find freights elsewhere. When he requested it be sold, Dallas placed his price too high. He failed to follow the initial suggestions of the Chile-based house to have the wheat shipped to Rio. Finally, Dallas was forced to ship it in poor condition to the depressed market of Brazil.

Dallas' experience was not exceptional because the communications system was such that all houses received their information on profitable markets at the same time. They would then at once seek to purchase produce for the market, pushing prices up; seek to find ships, incurring inflated freight rates; send the produce to another market, flooding it and bringing prices down. Like Dallas, merchants often suffered heavy losses at every level of speculation in the local trades of South America. However, Dallas possessed too few reserves to be able to weather such large miscalculations.

Dallas' most speculative investments lay in jerked beef. On joint account with Henry Miller, Dallas sent a cargo of 5,376 quintales (approximately 537,600 pounds) of beef, 390 quintales of tallow, and 8,000 horns on board the vessel *Spring* bound first for Rio de Janeiro for orders. From there the vessel continued to Havana. The *Spring* proved a poor sailer and reached Cuba well behind many other ships that had departed from Buenos Aires at the same time. As a result, when the ship reached Cuba the market was depressed. In February of 1820, the cargo fetched 17 reales per quintal for good beef, 9 reales for damaged beef, and 24 reales per quintal for tallow; later the buyer reduced the price of tallow to 15 reales per quintal because of its inferiority. One-third of the cargo was to be paid for in fifty days, one-third in eighty days, and one-third in one hundred and ten days. Fifty working days were allowed for unloading. The length of time needed for loading and reloading brought the vessel on demurrage; but there was no alternative without accepting a worse offer of 16 reales for the good beef with thirty days for unloading. The *Spring* was then reloaded with sugar and coffee and dispatched to Falmouth for orders.

Sending the ship first to Rio proved disadvantageous, for such a route had increased both the time and expenses involved. Because Henry Miller disagreed with the customhouse as to whether duty was to be paid on re-exported beef, additional lay days were required. On her voyage from St. Thomas to Havana, the *Spring* ran ashore and had to throw overboard twenty-five to thirty tons to lighten the vessel. Since the exact amount thrown overboard could not be fixed, the Havana house furnished Dallas with a certificate showing that losses on cargoes of jerked beef coming from Buenos Aires ran from 8 to 15 percent. With this certificate, Dallas hoped to recover the amount from the insurance underwriters. The brig *Spring* was further delayed in loading in Havana because of holidays and the reparation of the customhouse. After the first thirty lay days were over, the captain insisted on the demurrage being advanced at 26 shillings per day in remuneration for the heavy charges to which his vessel was liable in Havana. On May 20, 1820, the ship left with a full cargo of 637 boxes of sugar; but the proceeds from the beef did not half load the *Spring*.[52] All of Dallas' beef speculations in 1820 and 1821 appear to have concluded much as the one for the *Spring*. The amounts received for the beef in glutted markets with increased competition did not more than half load the ships with sugar or coffee.

Dallas' speculations were only a part of his unsound business practice. He failed to safeguard his interests by efficiently disposing of the few consignments forwarded by Henry Miller. Dallas not only failed to pay his creditors judiciously but even handled his correspondence in a dilatory fashion. In May 1821 the partnership of Miller and Dallas dissolved in acrimony. Dallas lost his last respect and his most reasonable opportunity of profitable business. For three years he lived in Buenos Aires watching the diminution of his slender capital and credit until in December 1824 he found that his only refuge from bankruptcy and poverty lay in suicide.

THE FAILURE of the Hugh Dallas house was more dramatic than the general patterns of bankruptcy or liquidation. Although merchant houses failed regularly, the successful operation of many concerns was more significant than the failure of particular individuals. Of forty British houses in existence in 1842, ten were no longer in existence in 1850. This would put the bankruptcy and liquidation rate in an eight year period at 25 percent or about 3 percent per year, a not unusual failure rate for small businesses even in the twentieth century. In 1852 there were forty-five British houses in Buenos Aires, of which forty remained in 1857, one firm having liquidated and four having failed—a 1.8 percent failure per year. Because the practice of deferring payments was so common, it often took a great deal to make a house fail in Buenos Aires. The failure among British houses appears smaller than among other houses. In 1857 only 5 percent of the bankruptcy cases before the commercial court, which also included cases begun in previous years, concerned British houses, although they made up at least 25 percent of the total mercantile houses in existence. The most dangerous aspect of failures, whether British or non-British, was that it often jeopardized numbers of other houses, since their creditors were usually other merchant houses.[53] Seven factors, all indirectly linked to faulty decision making, accounted for failure: corruption or mismanagement by employees or partners, risky speculations and overextensions, minor losses in a large number of apparently safe speculations, inability to obtain payment from creditors, heavy involvements in other houses that failed, fluctuating currencies and unstable exchange rates, and failure to innovate.

Corruption or mismanagement by employees or partners of non-British houses frequently made news during the century. One of the more celebrated cases was the failure of Sebastian Lezica Brothers in September 1835. The manager of the house, a German named Frederick Hornung, apparently forged bills of exchange without the knowledge of his employers, three Argentine brothers. After the failure of a British house, Thwaites and Company, and after the retention of money in the Chilean branch, the Lezica Brothers had to raise money. Originally Hornung procured the signatures of a number of people, including Thwaites; but when persons declined, he began to forge names on bills of exchange—both the drawer's and drawee's names—in order to prevent bankruptcy. He thought this would need to be done for only a short time, but he became more involved until the total sum owed the market was over one and a half million pesos. Included in the sum were forgeries of bills from a number of British houses.[54]

Risky speculation and overextension also explained major failures. Samuel B. Hale and Company, which fell in the late 1880s, clearly overextended itself in the 1870s, particularly regarding government loans. Connections with the Mercantile Bank, which suspended payments, further taxed their resources.[55] Minor losses in a large number of apparently safe speculations might eventually bring down a house. For example, in 1836 the American house of Davison, Milner, and Company went bankrupt. The house owed its creditors 508,229 pesos and 4 reales, but had assets worth only 279,017 pesos and 6 reales after suffering losses on thirty-five speculations between January 1832 and April 1836. These losses varied from 542 pesos and one reale on remittances to a ship going to Boston, to 99,559 pesos and 2 reales on remittances on flour sent to

Punto del Pacífico. The failure to Duguid, Holland, and Company can also be attributed to losses on a large number of speculations, although Baring Brothers felt they took unnecessary risks in borrowing money at the exorbitant interest rate of some 25 percent per annum.[56]

Unpaid bills from other firms might occasionally bring about the failure of a house. The difficulty houses encountered in collecting bills can be noted in the large number of cases before the Commercial Court concerning payment of bills. Generally the respondent argued that he did not owe the money because a contract had been broken or the goods were of poor quality. But no matter what the reason for the respondent's failure to pay his bill, unless the plaintiff could collect, he was in a poor position. Thomas Armstrong argued in 1834 that his failure was due to "absolute, unavoidable and inculpable accidents and misfortunes," and that the principal cause was the failure of other commercial houses, who owed him large sums of money.[57] Bills might not be paid because a house was liquidating its affairs or going bankrupt. The liquidation of the Green and Hodgson firm took some twenty years. During that time creditors carried on lawsuits to try and force the speed of payment. Liquidation of affairs always involved a minimum of two years due to the nature of the import-export business, since investments were tied up in produce in the process of shipment and in lands and property.[58]

If a rash of failures occurred, confidence was greatly shaken and other failures soon followed because houses with heavy investments in bankrupt firms could not sustain business. The failure of Simón Pereira, a porteño merchant who owed seven British import-export firms the sum of 1,735,000 pesos (£21,687.10.0), precipitated such a crisis. Similarly, the Darbyshire and McKinnell failure, which took place at the end of the produce season, caught at least five British mercantile houses with their bills. The John and William Black failure in 1835, with liabilities of £46,162.12.10 covered by assets of £37,254.3.5 3/4, affected a further ten British houses in Buenos Aires.[59] Repayment from the failed companies rarely approached one hundred percent. Duguid, Holland, and Company paid 45 percent in 1831; William and John Black by 1837 paid 42.5 percent; McKinnell and Company repaid debts amounting to 42 percent, while Darbyshire, Jordan, and Company refunded only 31.5 percent.[60]

Creditors discouraged bankruptcies because they offered less chance for the recovery of investments than either liquidation or the continuation of business under supervision. When a firm had not behaved in a fraudulent manner, creditors usually granted permission to continue operating in the hope that that house might recoup some of its losses. Thus, the creditors accepted Simón Pereira's proposal that he should gradually liquidate his affairs, confining himself in the meantime to his consignment business with the government. They granted him ten months to pay the first 30 percent of his debts, fourteen months to pay another 30 percent and eighteen months to pay the remaining 40 percent. This concession was made because an auction at that time would not have realized even half the value of his assets. Pereira was allowed to hold sufficient funds to pay an interest of 10 percent on the whole of his debt, providing that he balanced his books each month and submitted them for the inspection of his creditors.[61]

Failure and bankruptcy were also related to broader economic and political situations. Fluctuating currencies and unstable political or economic situations further contributed to failures. William and John Black blamed their failure in 1837 on their speculations in Britain and the variation that existed between Argentine pesos and pounds sterling. They further argued that bankruptcy became necessary not because of lack of responsibility but because of uncontrollable events, particularly the ruin of other foreign houses and the commercial crisis in the United Kingdom.[62]

BY ADAPTING to Buenos Aires, British merchants influenced trading patterns in the Río de la Plata, because the overseas marketing of hides, tallow, and wool developed Argentina into a major exporting country. By forwarding correspondence, securing jobs, and acting as attorneys, British merchants extended their influence in Argentina and their opportunities to develop profitable innovations. Merchants brought produce from the interior to Buenos Aires and financed exports to the European market. From the demands of the Argentine export economy grew a need for better port facilities at Buenos Aires and faster means of communication with the interior. From the mercantile houses came demands for locally processed raw materials, the basis of twentieth-century Argentine industry.

The ability of merchants to survive depended upon their appraisal of the European and Argentine political and economic environments. The willingness of British merchants to take these risks and to make the right decisions created capital that was often reinvested in Argentine economic development and balanced the interests of trade and politics in the Republic. The profits made in the import-export trade in the early part of the nineteenth century and the political and social contacts developed by British merchants through commerce encouraged diversified investments in Argentina in the latter half of the nineteenth century.

6.

Merchants, British Investment, and the Economic Development of Argentina

BETWEEN 1810 and 1880 mercantile houses opened up new resources and financed the expansion of Argentina's economic growth. The investment occurred primarily in finance, transportation, and extractive industries. These developments usually were tied to efforts to promote additional trade. Although British merchants possessed slender reserves for investment, before 1880 Argentina was a preindustrial society that required only limited funds to provide capital formation.

During the nineteenth century the economic development of Latin America depended primarily upon private investment. Efforts at government finance were sporadic and of little consequence. From 1824 to 1825 Britons purchased Latin American government bonds with a face value of £17,000,000 and subscribed to an authorized capital of £35,000,000 for some forty-six ineffective joint stock companies.[1] British investors, in Argentina as in most South American countries, rapidly became disillusioned when the bonds depreciated and the governments defaulted on the loans. The failure of Argentina to attract sufficient foreign capital to finance the Republic's development gave the mercantile houses their opportunity to assume the responsibility for expanding the infrastructure.

Mercantile houses acted as an essential catalyst in Argentine economic development, not only because foreigners refused to risk their capital but also because national institutions possessed very little investment money before 1880. Spain was no longer willing to finance development in the remote frontiers of South America, and internal bodies such as the Consulado found their duties restricted to the protection of national merchants and the operation of a commercial court. Between 1810 and 1880

Argentina's new economic and political institutions were too impecunious to make advances to individuals or for the economic development of
the Republic. The Banco de Descuentos y Banco de Buenos Aires (1822-
1826) offered only limited short-term credit to the merchants. The Casa
de Moneda de la Provincia de Buenos Aires (1836-1854) issued currency
and made loans to the government and to private individuals which were
short-term but renewable. Only after 1856 and the establishment of the
Banco y Casa de Moneda del Estado de Buenos Aires (1856-1863) was
there an institution with more adequate credit facilities for entrepreneurs.
The Banco de la Provincia de Buenos Aires, established in 1863, continued to provide some credit facilities for private individuals. In 1871 the
government organized the Banco Hipotecario de Provincia de Buenos
Aires and allowed it to lend money, although only on the security of land
valued at double the amount of the loan. Only in the 1870s did the Argentine government borrow funds for specific development projects—
railroads, public utilities, and port facilities.

British investments in Argentina fell into two categories. The first consisted of portfolio investments, public investments, publicly floated
government bonds, and stocks of private corporations. The second cate-
gory was made up of direct investments—the financing of Argentine
manufacturing or commerce by individuals or companies of the United
States or Europe. In 1875 M. G. Mulhall, the proprietor of the *Buenos
Aires Standard*, estimated that United Kingdom interests controlled a
capital of more than £27,000,000 in Argentina.[2] By 1890 the total
nominal British investment had risen to £157,000,000.[3] Mulhall, who enjoyed access to informed government sources, quoted the nominal
investments in British mercantile houses at £1,500,000. This initial
capital excluded the subsidiary interests and diversification of the Buenos
Aires import-export houses.

From the perspective of development and international balance of payments a distinction must be made between foreign factors, which remit
their earnings abroad, and domestic factors, which spend their income
within the country, even though it may be to purchase imports. Thus,
British nationals investing money in Argentina may be considered foreign or domestic depending upon the use and function of investment and
payment of income. For instance, British merchants' investment of the
profits of commerce earned through Argentine produce represented
domestic capital. Similarly, British entrepreneurial skills applied to the
economic, social, and political development of the Republic can be considered Argentine. The British merchants of Buenos Aires even contributed both Argentine capital and leadership in the London registered
joint stock companies that were traditionally considered to be British
foreign capital investment. Anglo-Argentine participation proved vital

to the vast majority of companies that Britons owned and directed as well as those in which British investors held a minority interest.

THE IMMIGRATION of Britons with talent and experience proved as important for capital accumulation as the influx of United Kingdom capital. Although in 1865 British depositors—4.1 percent of the total immigrant depositors in the Banco de la Provincia de Buenos Aires—owned no less than 14 percent of the total paper dollars on deposit, the greater part of this wealth represented the reserves of merchant houses.[4] British merchants, who made their money through mercantile operations in the 1830-1850 period, financed many successful investments during the 1860s and 1870s. Among the more influential British merchants in Buenos Aires who adapted to their environment, generated capital in the import-export trade, and reinvested profits and ability in the Argentine economic development were the Robertson brothers, Thomas Armstrong, and Thomas Gowland. All of the same generation, they used their ideas and enthusiasm to cultivate the political and social contacts in Buenos Aires that led them to set precedents for the investment of funds by their contemporaries.

The brothers, William and John Parish Robertson, made perhaps the most notable contribution to Argentine economic development by stimulating the initial organization of the internal hide trade, helping to establish the first bank in Buenos Aires, encouraging immigration, and arranging the 1824 loan for the Argentine government. John Parish Robertson took up residence in South America at the end of 1807, when he was fourteen years old. For four years he acted as a commercial clerk, first in Rio de Janeiro and later in Buenos Aires. In 1811 he went to Paraguay to dispose of a cargo of merchandise. By 1816, when his brother William joined the partnership, John Robertson's house had developed a substantial hide business in the interior. In 1820 the Robertsons extended their business to Chile and later to Lima, Peru, and then began to invest in Buenos Aires Public Funds and in the stock of the Banco de Descuentos y Banco de Buenos Aires.

John Robertson, appointed as commercial agent of the government of Peru in London, profitably supervised the Peruvian loan of 1822. In January 1824 William Robertson, on behalf of John Parish Robertson and Company and in association with the Argentine merchant Felix Castro and three other merchant houses, arranged a loan from Baring Brothers on the instructions of the government of the Buenos Aires province. The government also commissioned the Robertsons to arrange for the settlement of two hundred families in the southern part of the province. In 1825 John Robertson optimistically promoted the Famatina Mining Company, and received a commission of 5 percent. Peru suspended interest payments on its loan in 1825 and Buenos Aires in 1827. The Famatina Mining Company laid claims to the same mines as the Río de la Plata Mining Association, formed six months earlier. The outbreak of the Brazilian-Argentine war completely destroyed plans to develop the mines and led to the dissolution of the colony. The result of overextension of business activities and overoptimism was the liquidation of the house. After twenty-two years in South American investments, John Parish Robertson returned to the United Kingdom in 1829.

The Robertson brothers lost the capital they accumulated from trade in South America. However, their role in the founding of the Banco de Descuentos y Banco de Buenos Aires laid the basis for later government efforts. Although their efforts in mining proved ruinous from the beginning, these exertions buttressed the government's continued efforts to develop Argentina's natural resources. The colonization scheme showed the disadvantages of encouraging immigration by contract, but it became the forerunner of more successful efforts. The Buenos Aires loan helped to keep the defaulting Argentine government functioning in a period when the government's expenses in war exceeded its meager revenues.[5]

Thomas Armstrong, an Ulsterman who arrived in Buenos Aires during 1817, made substantial profits from speculations in the import-export trade. Although Armstrong operated an individual proprietorship, he quickly diversified his interests. His ownership of extensive estancias, slaughterhouses, and an import-export house set precedents by creating an integrated structure which supplied exports for his merchant house. In addition, he was prominent in banking, insurance, finance, and railways.

Thomas Armstrong married into an old colonial landed and merchant family in 1829, remained a Protestant because he received the dispensation to marry a Catholic, and raised his children in the Catholic faith. He was also active in the British community, contributing to such causes as the hospital and participating in the committee of merchants. Armstrong became director of the Banco de Descuentos, a member of the Municipal Commission, and a friend and adviser to presidents Rodríguez and Avelleneda. He belonged to the Foreign Club, the Sociedad Rural Argentina, and was one of the founders of the stock exchange.

Although Thomas Armstrong failed in business in 1831, he recouped his losses because his wife inherited large amounts of property at the death of her mother. This property remained in his wife's name so his creditors could not secure it. From his new financial base Armstrong, along with other British and Argentine merchants, was instrumental in the founding of two insurance companies, the Compañía Argentina de Seguros Marítimos and La Estrella. He was connected with the construc-

tion of the Western Railroad, the Central Argentine Railway, the Great
Southern Railway, and the Ensenada Port Railway. He also gained interests in an Argentine flour mill and extensive speculations often placed
him in the position of a banker.

At their deaths Thomas Armstrong and Justa Villanueva de Armstrong
left substantial wealth, consisting almost entirely of houses and lands in
the city of Buenos Aires and ranches in the provinces, valued at 29,428,-
000 pesos, the equivalent of £235,424 in 1876. Unlike John Robertson,
Thomas Armstrong, who took the leadership in a large number of enterprises that benefited Argentine economic development, died a wealthy
man. Although his contacts and influence in both the Argentine and British communities were a contributory factor in his personal success, he
also used the same contacts to help develop the Argentine economy. His
role in founding the Argentine insurance companies prevented the complete dependence on British firms. His investments in flour milling promoted an Argentine industry and his interests in railroad construction
helped to lay the basis of a transportation system that finally opened the
interior of Argentina to profitable wheat growing.[6]

Thomas Gowland, born in London May 23, 1803, arrived in Buenos
Aires with his parents and brother, Daniel, in 1812. Both of the young
Gowlands married Argentine women and brought up their children as
Catholics. Thomas Gowland founded an auction house in 1825 and an
import-export house in 1830. In 1853 he served in the military and received Argentine citizenship for his meritorious service. In 1854 he became the first naturalized citizen to occupy a place in the Chamber of
Deputies (Sala de Representantes) of Buenos Aires. He was a founder of
the Compañía Primitiva de Gas and a member of the directorate of the
stock exchange. Daniel Gowland was also active in the Argentine commercial and political scene. His import-export house rivaled the house of
Zimmermann, Frazier, and Company for the United States business. He
served for a time as a director of the Banco Nacional de la Provincia Unidas del Río de la Plata and a member of the immigration commission. At
his death he left his seven children property worth 84,000 pesos (£13,062)
in lands and railroad shares.[7]

THE LEADERSHIP of the Robertson brothers, Thomas Armstrong, and
Thomas Gowland, who made their fortunes in import-export, set precedents for mercantile investments in Argentina. For example, merchant
initiative stimulated the growth of banking and insurance. Gaining experience in negotiating loans, issuing currencies, and marketing Argentine
loans abroad, merchants soon realized that the institution of commercial
banks would further their own operations and incidentally promote economic expansion in Argentina. Banking was in fact a natural outlet for

merchant capital because houses routinely made individual loans by letters of credit, obtained goods on consignment so that they could further extend credit to Argentine merchants, paid interest on customer deposits, and transferred money by means of bills of exchange.

In 1822 merchants assisted in organizing the first bank in Argentina, the Banco de Descuentos y Banco de Buenos Aires, and actively supported later banks, particularly the government controlled Banco Nacional de las Provincias Unidas del Río de la Plata and two private banks, the Bank of London and the River Plate and the Commercial Bank of the River Plate. Banking services and the growing political and economic stability of Argentina led to the foundation of national insurance companies under merchant sponsorship. Banking and insurance provided crucial services for the development of the Republic because locally based concerns showed a lesser propensity to remit their capital overseas than did expatriate concerns.

During the early years of the nineteenth century, the newly independent Republics relied upon mercantile houses to market their bonds in London. Mercantile houses or merchant banks, which most efficiently marketed government bonds, also engaged heavily in foreign trade, owned mobile assets, possessed influential contacts, and actively traded acceptances and exchanges. South American governments and London investors followed quite a uniform procedure in the 1820s when they floated loans. Their representatives traveled to London where they negotiated contracts with issuing firms, who bought space in newspapers to praise the countries whose securities they were to market. The merchants drew up a list of subscribers from clients and friends and gave bonds to them in bulk. Then banker and syndicate friends entered the market and bought heavily, forcing up the price of the bonds. The syndicate would buy up bonds that came on the market to prevent the price from falling below par until the purchasers had paid off their installments. When the bonds were dumped, they declined in value. A banker, in effect, needed only enough capital to insure the publicity of the loan and to cover margins upon the quantity of bonds he would have to buy and sell to himself on the stock exchange during the first few days. Thereafter, he might continue his operations out of the proceeds of the loan itself.[8]

The loan contractors for South American issues were primarily small mercantile firms engaged in foreign trade, with the exception of the Barings and Rothschilds. The small firms, active in the foreign remittance market, possessed connections abroad that enabled them to profit by handling South American loans. Their commission was calculated upon the nominal amount of the loan, not the proceeds. Since the mercantile houses and merchant banks controlled the entire issue of a particular loan, they could benefit from a rising market. They might also be called upon to handle undistributed interest and principal balance. The merchants received fees for making dividend payments and operating sinking funds. In addition, performing these services kept them in touch with investors and increased their supply of foreign exchange. Although most of Argentina's bonds were sold by the reputable London based Baring Brothers, firms such as Stern Brothers, Morton, Rose, and Company, and C. Murrieta Company also marketed Argentine securities. However, British merchants in Buenos Aires generally acted as government agents in the negotiation of the loans or represented the claims of bondholders against the national government.

In 1824 the government of the province of Buenos Aires negotiated its first bond issue of £1,000,000 on the London market. Although this transaction proved less corrupt than the general pattern of South American loans in the 1820s, it nevertheless gave some individuals useful opportunities for speculation. The government deputed six individuals to arrange the terms of the loan. Five—Felix Castro, William and John Robertson, Braulio Costa, and Miguel Riglos—were import-export merchants; the sixth, Juan P. Saenz Valiente, was a wholesaler. Felix Castro and John Robertson, both with excellent London contacts, traveled to the United Kingdom where they contracted with Baring Brothers to issue the loan of £1,000,000 at 85 percent of par (a discount of 15 percent) in 6 percent bonds. For a year or two the bonds were subsequently traded on the market at 90 percent, the highest rate of all foreign loans at the time. Of the £1,000,000, the government of Buenos Aires received £700,000 but had to pay interest on the face value. Baring Brothers paid the expenses of issuing the loan from their fee of £30,000 supported by a one percent commission charge. Barings also exercised their option to purchase bonds valued at £200,000 for 70 percent of their par value. Felix Castro and John Robertson, who were held personally liable for the integrity of the Buenos Aires government, took the greatest risk and made the largest profit. They received £120,000 for their services, with the understanding that if the government of Buenos Aires defaulted they would refund £120,000 to Barings.

In 1828 the government of Buenos Aires defaulted because inadequate resources, inflation, internal disorders, and war with other states was not conducive to paying high interest rates. By then John Parish Robertson, who had gone bankrupt, and Felix Castro, who was active in politics, could not be held responsible for the government default, and the bondholders carried the loss. Barings, who held £200,000 of the bonds, assumed the representation of the stockholders. In the 1840s, when the province of Buenos Aires appeared to be regaining stability under Rosas, Barings unsuccessfully sought repayment of the loan. Barings' representatives relied heavily upon their introductions to leading British merchant firms, who gave them advice and provided them with further introductions to government officials. In 1844 the representatives arranged with Rosas for a monthly repayment of 5,000 pesos fuertes (£62.10.0 on exchange rate of one peso equal to three pence) payable to the house of Zimmermann, Frazier, and Company, which remitted the funds to Barings by buying bills of exchange on London. The government again suspended payments in 1845 but resumed small payments again in 1849. Only in 1857 did the government of Argentina agree to a loan settlement, whereby it sent remittances directly to Barings by purchasing bills of exchange on London. The government agreed to redeem gradually the original bonds and to issue new bonds for the payment of interest. They planned to raise the repayment funds by rent charges on certain public lands. The Buenos Aires legislature passed a bill on October 28, 1857, implementing this settlement. In the loan of 1824, as in subsequent bond issues, British merchants and British import-export houses were active in every phase from the initial issue to the final settlement.[9]

British merchants provided financial services for both the public and the government. This interest in providing customer credit, just as their involvement in the raising of state loans and their concern for the economic stability of the Republic, encouraged the mercantile community to participate in banking. Britons engaging in the import-export trade were instrumental in the formation of two government banks and two commercial banks. Banks offered both substantial profits and needed services. Not only did banks increase credit facilities for individual merchants and aid in the stability of government finances, but they also made it possible for merchants to continue actively as government loan agents and gave their own currency manipulations a sounder basis.

Anglo-Argentine merchants provided over one-third of the capital of the Banco de Descuentos y Banco de Buenos Aires. Merchants helped design the bank's prospectus and later as directors dominated policy in general meetings of the company. The Banco de Descuentos proved a profitable enterprise which paid substantial dividends and provided needed services. Merchant participation in the founding of this bank early in the 1820s was a gesture of confidence placed by the British mercantile community in the new Republic, an optimistic belief that the availability of credit and other banking facilities would stimulate the Argentine economy and thereby the volume of the import-export trade.

On January 15, 1822, Manuel José García, under the direction of the governor of the province of Buenos Aires, General Martín Rodríguez, called a meeting to discuss the formation of a bank. A committee of nine persons, three of them British merchants, prepared the statutes and solicited subscribers for 1,000 shares of 1,000 pesos each. Shareholders paid 200 pesos on subscription, 200 upon the opening of the bank for business, and the remaining 600 pesos on the demand of the directors. The shares could be sold or transferred only in Buenos Aires and then only with the previous approval of the directors.[10] On March 18 a general meeting to consider the statutes of the bank attracted the attendance of twenty-four shareholders, nine of whom were Britons. Three British import-export merchants, James Brittain, William Cartwright, and Robert Montgomery, were appointed to the board of directors.[11] In June 1822 the government approved the foundation of the Banco de Descuentos y Banco de la Provincia de Buenos Aires. By decree, the government empowered the bank to discount bills for up to ninety days and to issue small bills. James Brittain attended to the equipment of the bank, ordering a safe, account books, and seventy-three thousand bills of different value printed in the United Kingdom in addition to five thousand printed in Buenos Aires for immediate use. The total value of currency issued by the bank amounted to 250,000 pesos.[12]

British merchant leadership dominated the Banco de Descuentos by soliciting proxy votes for the general meetings. On September 10, 1823, when the British merchants represented 92 shares out of 238, they elected four directors to the board of thirteen. At the meeting of September 3, 1824, when the British merchants held 183 shares out of 352, they elected six directors. The board also comprised six Argentines and one Spaniard. The British merchants built up their representation until in January 1826 they controlled 631 out of 838 votes, or 75 percent. Thomas Armstrong alone represented 454 shares, William Robertson voted 51, and James Brittain 39. The power of these men was out of all proportion to their capital investment.[13]

The interest of British merchants in the bank came from their dependence upon a depository for surplus money. Out of 204,883 pesos deposited by individuals from March 1 to August 31, 1824, the British merchants accounted for 77,437 pesos or 32 percent and they also obtained large allocations of credit.[14] However, the limited capital did not allow for extensive long-term credit which might have encouraged the formation of new industries. The war with Brazil diminished the bank's gold reserves, increased the government's debts, and encouraged the state to form a new bank.[15] During its four years of operation the Banco de Descuentos paid dividends of 12, 19, 19.5, and 19.5 percent.[16] On January 28, 1826, an act of Congress reorganized the Banco de Descuentos into the Banco Nacional de las Provincias Unidas del Río de la Plata with a capital of 10,000,000 pesos. Because the government contributed 3,000,-000 pesos (£387,500 at the exchange rate of one peso equals two shillings and seven pence) from the Barings' loan of 1824, it could control policy, and accordingly British merchants exercised much less influence. The Banco Nacional de las Provincias Unidas del Río de la Plata proved un-

fortunate in its attempts to raise a further 6,000,000 pesos by public subscription and began operation with a paper capital of only 4,840,000
pesos. It sold subscriptions valued at 440,600 pesos and received the capital of the Banco de Descuentos, 1,000,000 pesos, for which it paid a
bonus of 40 percent by issuing seven shares for each 1,000 pesos invested
in its progenitor.[17] Despite these initial difficulties, the new bank gained
widespread authority. It attempted to sell shares in other provinces and
possessed a larger capital. However, the influence of the Banco Nacional
de las Provincias Unidas was restricted to the Argentine Republic, because it had no European correspondent.[18] For overseas transactions, the
bank relied upon merchant help, even in arrangement with other South
American countries such as Peru and Chile.[19]

The principal activities of the Banco Nacional de las Provincias Unidas
were the issuance of currency and the provision of government credit
totaling 2,000,000 pesos. Consequently, the bank operated under constant government supervision and interference. The state had to approve
the sixteen directors elected to the board, and the power of the shareholders was limited to thirty votes, with the provision that the number of
votes per share diminished as the individual ownership of shares increased.[20] The shareholders elected only two British merchants, James
Brittain and Joseph Twaites, to the first board.[21] Anglo-Argentines controlled only 20 percent of the votes at the February 9, 1827 meeting, 12
percent at the meeting of December 10, 1827, 16 percent at the meeting of
February 13, 1829.[22] In contrast to their power in the Banco de Descuentos, British merchants who held shares in the Banco Nacional de las
Provincias Unidas turned over voting power to nationals.[23] By August
31, 1831, no Briton sat on the board of directors.[24] Between 1826 and
1836 the British merchants never held more than 1,412 shares worth
282,000 pesos, 5 percent of the 27,865 shares held by individuals in 1836.
Nevertheless, British interest in the bank was highly concentrated; in
1832 James Brittain held the largest number of shares with 520 and in
1836 the house of Brownell and Stegmann owned 306 shares which paid
annual dividends of 12 percent.[25] British merchants took little interest in
the Banco Nacional de las Provincias Unidas because the shareholders
possessed very limited power. The fact that a given individual could not
control more than thirty votes made a far more concerted effort necessary to exercise control. And while the government was also limited to
thirty votes, its influence and interference far exceeded its number of
votes because it could veto directors and made itself the principal debtor.
The amount the government owed the bank rose from 9,678,906 pesos in
1827 to 24,628,873 pesos in April 1836.[26]

From 1826 the bank, plagued by a shortage of capital intensified by
government indebtedness, offered fewer services to merchants than had

the Banco de Descuentos. Rather than the merchants' borrowing from the bank, the bank borrowed from the merchants. In 1827 the bank, acting for the government, borrowed over 140,000 pesos from British merchants to pay dividends due on the London loan of Barings.[27] Finally the Banco Nacional de las Provincias Unidas, with constant government interference, offered less hope than the previous bank had in stabilizing the economy. Since the bank brought neither the economic stability desired nor threatened the banking function of the import-export houses, the merchants lost further interest in the bank and turned to other investments. The dissolution of the Banco Nacional de las Provincias Unidas by General Rosas in May 1836 ended the experimental cooperation between the government and the commercial community in the operation of a national banking system. In later banks formed to replace the Banco Nacional de las Provincias Unidas, the government exerted strict control. These included Casa de Moneda de la Provincia de Buenos Aires, the Banco de la Provincia de Buenos Aires, and the Banco Nacional of 1872. The British merchants had no further opportunity to participate directly in the ownership and operation of a bank in Argentina until 1862 when overseas capital founded the Bank of London, Buenos Aires, and the River Plate. They did, however, occasionally serve on the boards of directors in the government banks. Thus, Edward Lumb sat on the board of the Casa de Moneda in 1854, while Thomas Armstrong and George Drabble served the Banco de la Provincia de Buenos Aires in 1860.[28]

The origin of British joint stock banks in Latin America depended upon trade and the use of the sterling bills drawn on London. It was but one step further from British import-export houses to British owned banks. With the protection offered by the United Kingdom Act of 1862 regulating joint stock companies, British banks opened throughout South America. The stockholder's liability was then limited to the amount of his investment.

The Bank of London, Buenos Aires and the River Plate, founded in London during 1862 and reorganized as the Bank of London and the River Plate in 1865, was dominated from the beginning by investors located in England. The nominal capital of £1,000,000 in 1864, doubled in 1870, made the Bank of London and the River Plate competitive with the Latin American domestic banks, the merchant bankers, and the mercantile houses. Its reserves enabled the bank to undertake two distinct functions: the issuance of loans and overdrafts and the discount of promissory notes and bills. Further, the bank's international connections facilitated the transfer of funds from one area to another, the collection of bills drawn in one country payable elsewhere, the purchase of securities, and the issuance of letters of credit. It also advised London companies of the credit standing enjoyed by Argentine companies. In fact, mercantile business was the main staple of the bank's operation.[29]

The Bank of London and the River Plate provided its most useful services for United Kingdom businessmen trading to South America, rather than for merchants based in Buenos Aires. An editorial in *The Brazil and River Plate Mail* declared that few Buenos Aires merchants believed in or patronized the Bank of London and the River Plate.[30] The original shareholders, with the exception of the import-export merchant John Rivolta, were all London men. The bank's first ledger of current accounts listed but thirty Anglo-Argentine merchants and import-export houses out of a total clientele of 260. Major import-export houses such as Milligan, Williamson, and Company, Nicholson, Green, and Company, Jordon Krabbé and Company, William Bigson and Company, and Darbyshire and Company held current drawing accounts at the bank.[31] Few British merchants in Buenos Aires used the bank because many of them executed their own banking functions. However, the bank needed the services of import-export house bills of exchange to remit funds to London.

The Bank of London and the River Plate lessened business risks for the merchants and provided some help to the Buenos Aires government by purchasing shares in government loans, as in the payment of £100,000 to the Argentine loan of 1871 issued by C. Murrieta and Company. This was a means of asserting its interest in the welfare of Argentina and building a good image in Argentina.[32] Previous to 1871 the bank was willing to lend the government up to £100,000. As the bank increased its resources and the government showed its stability, the government's credit limit was raised to £200,000 in February 1871.[33] The bank also aided the import-export trade by granting credit to British houses in Argentina, who could then open current accounts if they had proper introductions and could receive 3 percent annual interest on the credit balances. Customers could use checks, have approved bills discounted, obtain loans upon negotiable securities, and deposit valuable property for safe keeping. In increasing the amount of capital available in Argentina, the bank reduced interest rates.[34]

Argentine banking laws imposed few restrictions on the kind of business that a bank could do. Thus it was important that capable management was chosen who could invest wisely and make sound judgments. From this perspective, British import-export merchants served an essential leadership role. The fact that merchants familiar with Buenos Aires and British trade filled administrative positions of the bank was a factor in both its contributions to Argentina and its success. The first manager of the bank, J. H. Green, had been involved in merchant trading for the firm of Darbyshire and Green in Buenos Aires. Although he had no experience in commercial banking, his trading experience served him well. He received the cooperation of both David Robertson and John Fair who were in the import-export trade in Buenos Aires. Norberto de la Riestra, formerly minister of finance of Buenos Aires, served as a local director.[35]

While London merchants turned traders established the Bank of London and the River Plate, import-export merchants Frederic Wanklyn and Edward Lumb of Wanklyn and Company created the Mercantile Bank of the River Plate, later retitled the Commercial Bank of the River Plate. Wanklyn and Company dealt in Argentine public securities from 1869, when it received power to negotiate the sale of 6,000,000 pesos of bonds in conjunction with Lumb, Wanklyn, and Company of London. They were to dispose of the loan for the account of the government upon the best terms possible, the surplus over 70 percent of par being divided between the government and the banking agents who advanced to the government the sum of 1,000,000 hard pesos in exchange for exchequer bills until the final placing of the loan.[36] In 1869 Ambrosio Placido Lezica, Edward Lumb, Frederic Wanklyn and Alfred Lumb, all of whom engaged in the import-export trade, established the firm of Wanklyn and Company to deal primarily in foreign exchange, discounts, and commissions under the administrative control of Wanklyn and Edward Lumb. Edward Lumb contributed 200,000 pesos, Frederic Wanklyn and Alfred Lumb each gave 100,000 pesos, and Ambrosio Lezica promised 200,000 pesos.[37]

The failure of Wanklyn and Company to obtain the business of handling a further Argentine loan in 1871, granted to C. Murrieta and Company, probably led to the formation of the Commercial Bank in 1872.[38] In April 1872 Frederic Wanklyn sold his business to the Mercantile Bank of the River Plate, receiving 5,000 shares worth £6 each and the managing directorship. Lezica received from Wanklyn as his part of the former partnership 1,166 2/3 shares.[39] The first object of the company, according to its charter, was to carry on the monetary business previously carried on in Buenos Aires and Montevideo by the firm of Wanklyn and Company. The nominal capital of the company was £1,500,000 divided into 74,950 ordinary shares of £20 each and 1,000 founder shares of £1 each. Nine of the original fourteen signers of the charter, who subscribed 500 shares each, were merchants; the remainder were financiers. In November 1872 British merchants in Argentina held a little over one quarter of the 50,950 shares subscribed.[40] The Commercial Bank of the River Plate performed services similar to the Bank of London and River Plate. It received deposits, discounted letters, handled foreign bills, and offered credit in London. The bank had but temporary success and soon ran into financial trouble by overextending its credit.

British merchant interest in banking, promoted by a need for more efficient means of remitting money and for a secure deposit for surplus funds, paralleled merchant involvement in the development of national insurance companies. Although only two national insurance companies were established before 1880, they depended upon British initiative, management, and capital and set precedents for the establishment of national insurance companies in the 1880s and 1890s. In 1860 the government authorized an Argentine to establish the Argentine Marine Insurance Company (Compañía Argentine de Seguros Marítimos). The company, with a capital of 1,000,000 pesos fuertes, insured vessels in both the river and oceanic trade. In 1869 forty individuals, all residents in Argentina, held the shares of the company.[41] La Estrella, a marine and fire insurance company, established in 1865 with a capital of 2,000 hard pesos, also obtained merchant leadership and capital. Its board of directors included the British merchants Thomas Armstrong, Edward Lumb, and George Drabble and the United States merchant Samuel Hale.[42]

ANGLO-ARGENTINE merchants invested more talent and capital in transportation than they did in public utilities. Shipping and railroad interests promised not only lucrative profits but also the necessary means of linking internal Argentine markets with the international economy. While the tramway system of Buenos Aires offered no tangible advantages to the import-export trade, it increased the rapidity of movement within the city and demanded little capital which merchants could readily provide. On the other hand, public utilities demanded wide investment of technology and capital, which generally were beyond merchant means and interests.

Throughout the nineteenth century the primary interests of merchant houses focused upon the movement of produce from the interior to the coast. During the 1820s and 1830s merchant houses financed steam navigation on Argentine rivers. British capital and Argentine industry in Buenos Aires built the first screw-driven steamboat in South America. Esteban Rams y Rubert, one of the most prominent promoters of steam navigation in the 1850s, was an influential merchant in the Paraná River trade. British interests in Buenos Aires owned the first steamers running regularly on the Paraná. Prominent British merchants, including James Brittain, Thomas Nelson, John Robertson, and Robert Taylor, owned small river steamers as well as oceangoing ships. Many of the Britons who became great Argentine landowners after 1850 made their money in the maritime industries.[43]

Although trading and shipping had historically been long connected, during the course of the nineteenth century a clearcut separation developed between the two interests. Fewer and fewer firms still used their own ships for transportation of the goods they marketed. Even when a merchant was owner or a part owner of a ship and a partner in a mercantile house, trading and shipowning were separate businesses. The partner's own firm provided little of the ship's cargo.[44] In Argentina most import-export merchants had but limited interests in the ships that carried their consignments. By the middle of the century rarely did a house completely fill a ship with its own goods, even though it received the ships on consignment. However, merchants continued to invest in shipping companies. Although all the ocean steamship companies of the nineteenth century were European based, some of these companies had merchant capital invested in them. The Royal Mail Steam Ship Company and the Pacific Steam Navigation Company, noted for their mail, passenger, and freight services, had on their boards of directors individuals who had previously been engaged in the Río de la Plata trade. Shipping, even when driven by steam, still failed to tap the wider productive areas of Argentina. By 1850 efficient and economical land transport was needed if merchants were to maintain their profits from the export of produce.

According to Herbert Gibson, merchant and *estancia* owner, "The greatest title British industry and capital has to the recognition of the Argentines, is the development of the country by railway construction."[45] In 1867 English companies owned three railroads—Northern Railway, Great Southern Railway, and the Central Argentine Railway. Between 1858 and 1878 Britons invested more than £10,500,000 in Argentine railroads, some of which was surely Argentine domestic capital under the control of United Kingdom citizens. Railroad companies and the British import-export houses of Buenos Aires enjoyed a close relationship. The interest of merchants in carrying the goods from the interior created their initial interest in the railroads. Thus Edward Lumb, the first chairman of the Great Southern Railway, operated a mercantile house for twenty years in Buenos Aires and in 1862 obtained a concession from the provincial government.[46] Both import-export houses and merchant banks provided capital for the construction of railroads. While it was not only Britons who were interested in building railroads in Argentina, much of the initial investment, at times through loans, was British. A notable exception was the Argentine-financed Western Railroad.

London companies depended on contacts in Argentina to obtain railroad concessions. When a company was formed to build a railroad, the founding members confidentially approached the Public Works Department to ascertain whether a concession had already been granted for the route. Then the minister of public works received a list of arguments canvassing the advantages of the proposed line and the company selected a patron to present the plan to Congress. Once the Public Works Department approved the plan, the support and assistance of the Engineering Department was required. More diplomacy and payments were needed to obtain the signature of the government assessor for the concession. The company then applied for the grant of a right-of-way and demanded a government guarantee.[47] British merchants in Argentina had the contacts with the government officials and could make the proper introductions. They knew the political and economic situation in Argentina and those individuals who could more readily be convinced.

Railroad companies relied on merchants and their contacts not merely to obtain the concessions but also to secure effective management. The Western Railroad, Argentina's first line, set a precedent in the use of domestic leadership and capital that subsequent concerns emulated. On September 17, 1853, Jaime Llavallol, Daniel Gowland, Mirano Moro, Adolfo Van Praet, Norberto de la Riestra, Manuel F. Guerrico, and Bernardo Larrouda requested the government to approve a railroad concession for the route between the Plaza del Parque in the center of Buenos Aires to the western suburbs of Flores, with extensions toward the interior. By decree on December 19, 1853, and by law on January 9, 1854, the government approved execution of the work by a joint stock company empowered to sell shares, preferably only to individuals in the province of Buenos Aires or to those who had import-export houses or local businesses. The authorized capital consisted of four thousand 2,500-peso shares, of which the government was to buy one-third. An import-export merchant, Felipe Llavallol, became the first president of the company, and a British merchant, Daniel Gowland, the first vice-president. The Western Railroad was inaugurated August 30, 1857, with a ten-kilometer section finished and plans to continue the road on to Chivilcoy.[48]

The directors experienced difficulty in selling the shares. Of the final cost of 6,900,000 pesos, the government paid 1,300,000 pesos and the shareholders 2,000,000 pesos; the rest was made up of loans covered with the personal guarantee of the directors.[49] Merchants in Buenos Aires provided most of the capital. Although British merchant capital consisted of 136,500 pesos out of 3,269,809 pesos in 1863, or 4.1 percent, English leadership was important in both construction and organization.[50] English engineers built the railroad and Daniel Gowland imported the first railroad engine to Argentina.

When the Western Railroad proved unprofitable, the shareholders sold the 39 kilometers of track to the government of Buenos Aires. In 1862 the Banco de la Provincia de Buenos Aires paid the shareholders 4,222,816 pesos. This included the initial cost of the shares plus 6 percent annual interest on the original capital. This arrangement was most satisfactory because the company paid dividends of only 2.36 percent in 1857, 4.85

percent in 1858, and nothing in 1859 and 1860 when the line ran a deficit. The government began administration of the railroad on January 1, 1863.[51] Although the Western Railroad did not remain long in the hands of shareholders, its construction marked the beginning of the railroad era in Argentina. The Western Railroad attracted more British capital and interest in longer and more profitable railroads in Argentina. Constructed by the efforts of the Argentine citizens with the aid of a few British merchants, it was encouraged and financed by private domestic capital and the Argentine government. Later railroads also received the cooperation of the Argentine government, the interest and leadership of Anglo-Argentine merchants, and substantial amounts of capital from the United Kingdom. The government encouraged British investment in railroads by land grants and by guaranteeing profits. Of the fourteen railroads built between 1857 and 1880, seven had central offices in London.

Contact with influential people in Argentina remained a major factor in insuring the success of a railroad. In the case of the Great Southern Railway, influential Río de la Plata interests served on a board of directors in Buenos Aires which advised the London board of directors. The company built a line some seventy-five miles from Buenos Aires to Chascones, issuing a capital of £750,000 divided into 37,500 shares of £20 each. Edward Lumb, one of the wealthiest and most politically influential British merchants in the Río de la Plata region, obtained the concession for the railroad from the national government in 1862. He attracted the interest of other British-Argentine merchants such as David Robertson, John Fair, and Frank Parish, who were all members of families long involved in British trade in Buenos Aires. Thomas Armstrong, George Drabble, Enrique Harratt, H. A. Green—all import-export merchants— held substantial blocks of shares in the Great Southern Railway, and even the London board of directors consisted substantially of men with commercial experience in Buenos Aires. The Anglo-Argentine firm of Wanklyn and Company served as the railroad auditors. With the aid of political contacts, the company received a government guarantee of 7 percent annual profit, a concession for forty years, permission to construct branches, free duty for forty years on the import of all railroad equipment, and a promise of tax exemption for the same period.[52]

Other railroads such as the Central Argentine and the Northern railways had Anglo-Argentine merchants on their boards and made use of Argentine contacts to sell shares. In 1864 the Central Argentine Railway sold 1,000 shares to General Urquiza of Entre Ríos and 2,000 shares to the government. By 1870 the Argentine government possessed 17,500 Central Argentine Railway shares.[53] Few individuals in Buenos Aires owned shares of the Northern Railway. Less than 2 percent of the shares were held in Buenos Aires in 1873 and none of these by influential British merchants. No Anglo-Argentine merchants were on the Board of Directors of the Northern Railway.[54] In fact, none of the railroads with London directorates had as many individuals familiar with Argentina on their boards, nor sold as many shares to individuals in Argentina, nor were quite so profitable as the Great Southern Railway.

Tramways—street railways—attracted much British merchant capital and leadership. Mariaño Billinghurst, along with Méndez Hermanos and La Croze Hermanos, received the concession for the first tramway in Buenos Aires during 1869 and commenced operations in 1870. Billinghurst, a second-generation Anglo-Argentine merchant, possessed primarily Argentine contacts and associates. His activity in government aided his commercial endeavors.[55] Of the nine tramway companies operating in 1870, only two had their headquarters in London. This in itself is an indication of a greater amount of local capital investment. By 1875 merger had reduced the number of companies to six, with the directorates of three being based in London and three in Buenos Aires.[56]

Tramways required relatively small capital investment while their convenience value made patronage and profits likely. However, other public utility companies such as electric and telephone companies developed in Argentina only in the 1880s and 1890s. The two exceptions were gas companies and telegraph and cable companies. As early as 1852 the merchant firm of Federico Jaunet y Hermanos suggested the formation of a joint stock gas company. In 1853 the province of Buenos Aires authorized the formation of the Primitiva de Gas de Buenos Aires with a nominal capital of 6,200,000 pesos. In 1862 the board of directors of the gas company consisted primarily of merchants, with a British member. By 1885 there were two British-owned gas companies in Argentina. Although both the Argentine government and Argentines provided a large amount of the initial capital for public utilities, gradually the companies moved toward London directorates and British capital.[57]

ANGLO-ARGENTINE merchants applied their talents and capital to shipping, railroads, and tramways. They also sought profits from the extractive industries of mining, meat preservations, and agriculture. At the beginning of the nineteenth century the dream of El Dorado attracted speculation by merchants and others in mining. In time, merchants realized that it was far more profitable to invest in those enterprises that directly benefited the import-export trade. Although investments in most industries offered no advantage to Anglo-Argentine merchants since they could import manufactured goods more cheaply, they saw decided advantages in the processing and preservation of meat. However, for Anglo-Argentine merchants the soundest and most profitable investments were in land and agriculture. Although development of colonies seemed speculative in the 1860s, the ownership of cattle or sheep ranches provided a safe investment for surplus capital. By operation of *estancias*, merchants needed to invest only small amounts of capital while assuring themselves of produce to export.

As part of the investment boom of the 1820s two companies proposed to mine silver in Argentina. In 1824 the Río de la Plata Mining Association, with a nominal capital of £1,000,000, and the Famatina Mining Company, with a nominal capital of £250,000, received concessions from the government covering apparently the same area in northern Argentina. Both companies had a large amount of merchant involvement and obtained London capital. Hullett and Company, the Buenos Aires government agent in London, launched the Río de la Plata Mining Association with a British board of directors but depended upon mercantile houses in Buenos Aires for contacts, supplies, and credit. It formed an association with two mercantile houses in Buenos Aires, one national and the other one foreign. The national house was to provide means of conveyance to the mining area, to send cash and credits to the principal towns on the road, to find trustworthy laborers in the neighborhood of the mines, and to provide letters of introduction to respectable persons in those towns in which it was necessary to have resources and contacts with the local government. The foreign house, presumably British, landed the stores and personnel for the mines, transacted business with the government, and, along with the national house, gave the agents of the company all the information that was to be needed to execute the enterprise successfully.[58]

Unlike the Río de la Plata Association, the Famatina Mining Company was Argentine. The parties who originally received the concession were all merchants residing in Buenos Aires. Among the shareholders were the merchants William Robertson, James Brittain, and Thomas Fair. John Parish Robertson, who represented the Buenos Aires company in the United Kingdom, transferred the concession to a London company of the same name for speculative gain. While the new directorate contained individuals familiar with the Argentine situation, most of the shareholders were British. The Famatina Mining Company failed in spite of the large leadership involvement of Anglo-Argentines and national merchants.[59]

Both the Famatina Mining Company and the Río de la Plata Mining Association faced basically the same problems. They needed very large investments to develop an area of difficult access with low-grade silver in a politically unstable territory. Neither company was willing to put that type of capital into a locale in which the possibility of success was slim. Although the mining investments were certainly not successful examples of merchant investments, direct merchant leadership and capital were clearly evident.

Failures in the speculative mining business in the 1820s later discouraged British merchants from investing heavily in the development of Argentine industry. For example, Frenchmen, Germans, and Argentines financed flour mills in the period 1846 to 1858, although the machinery came from Britain or France.[60] Adolfo Dorfman in his *Historia de la Industria Argentina* contends that it was the French who developed Argentine industry, while the English concerned themselves primarily with selling manufactured articles and guarding the secrets of production. J. Fred Rippy also agrees that there was relatively little British capital engaged in manufacturing except in the meat processing industry. Only small capital sums were invested in the sugar refining industry, the brewery business, and the manufacture of chemical, pharmaceutical and other products. Although the firms of Tornquist and Bunge y Borne invested in Argentine industries, these mercantile houses had largely continental associations. Few British names appear in the industrial listings of the annual *Almanaques*, in contrast to the enumeration of French, German, and national investments.[61]

Before 1880 relatively little foreign or national capital was invested in industry. The Argentine government discouraged industry in the nineteenth century by unfavorable tariffs and failed to promote protective legislation. Industrial entrepreneurs had difficulty obtaining credit and found investments in land or cattle to be safer and more profitable. When British capital began to invest in industry, funds were used to buy out national firms. London capital bought out the Catalinas Warehouses and Molina Company of Buenos Aires in 1890, which was originally founded as an Argentine company in 1875. In the 1890s London capitalists purchased Bleckert's Brewery, established with Argentine capital in 1860. The industry that did develop before 1880 was often tied to the agricultural economy of the country—flour mills, candle factories, and meat processing plants.[62]

Meat packing and preservation proved the one exception to the reluctance of British merchants to invest in Argentine industry. In 1810 Staples, McNeile, and Company opened in Ensenada the first meat curing plant. As early as 1832 Hodgson and Robinson issued a circular announcing arrangements made with Duncan Macnab and Duncan Stewart, British import-export merchants, and Francisco Agell, Argentine merchant, to form a partnership to conduct a meat storage and meat drying business. According to a British consular report in 1850, two British import-export houses in Buenos Aires—Thomas Armstrong and Anderson, Maerae, and Company—among fifty-two mercantile houses were managing large slaughtering and meat salting establishments. A large number of other houses most certainly must have had at least some shares in the meat packing and preserving houses.[63] Interests in slaughtering and salting plants gave import-export merchants decided advantage. The supply of hides, tallow, and jerked beef from these establishments eliminated middlemen. Even if a merchant bought his hides directly from the cattle ranchers, he often had to arrange for at least further drying of the hides. Moreover, the amount of capital needed to open such a plant was minimal. Staples, McNeile, and Company paid less than 16,300 pesos to install their plant, while Armstrong's purchase of a saladero in 1845 cost but 8,500 pesos fuertes.[64]

Investments in salting and slaughtering led merchants to experiment with more effective means of preserving animal products. In 1862 a group of exporters of jerked beef, frustrated by the fall in price, sought to extend their market to the United Kingdom. However, even in the industrial towns there was no demand for the tough, indigestible, moldy, and sour meat that had been fed to slaves in South America. British demand for Argentine meat increased only after the development of refrigeration. In the 1880s British capitalists invested in two of the three largest abattoirs and refrigerating plants. George Drabble founded the River Plate Fresh Meat Company in 1882, while Hugh Nelson, connected with a merchant meat firm in Liverpool, Dublin, Manchester, and London, set up the Las Palmas Company in 1886. Nelson not only administered an import-export house but operated his own retail shop. Generally in Argentina the meat packing houses operated an integrated system of processing and distribution. The stock was bought, processed, then shipped on vessels either owned or chartered by the company. The meat packing firms sold the meat through their own outlets abroad. By 1910 approximately half of the directorates of nine important meat packing companies were Anglo-Argentines who had been involved in import-export trade.[65]

ANGLO-ARGENTINE merchants found their most profitable investments in land. Even the smallest commission merchant generally owned some property. Merchants invested in three different types of land development: small properties with houses in the city of Buenos Aires; colonization projects; and large tracts of land for sheep and cattle estancias. Most British merchants in the city of Buenos Aires sought to own at least their place of business and their residence. In 1875 Thomas Armstrong, for example, owned thirty-six residential houses in the center of Buenos Aires.[66] Generally, however, merchants preferred to invest in the provinces where land could produce commodities for export.

The ownership of land in the interior might be tied up with colonization schemes. British merchants' involvement in colonization projects began in 1825 when John and William Parish Robertson founded the colony of Monte Grande. Under an agreement with the government of the

United Provinces of La Plata, the Robertson brothers brought 250 agricultural colonists from Scotland. The colony failed due to the civil wars in Argentina, conflicts with the government over the land, and the financial difficulties the Robertson brothers encountered in other investments. But the establishment of the Monte Grande colony was to foreshadow an era.[67]

In the 1830s Hodgson and Robinson received permission from the President and the Chamber of Deputies to colonize their land in the province of Córdoba with European immigrants. The colonists were to enjoy the same privileges as the nationals in the province plus certain special privileges. The government exempted the colonists from taxes and military service for ten years, exempted stores from sales taxes for five years, and exempted the colonists from extra taxes for the defense of the frontier for five years. Green and Hodgson were to assume all the risks and expenses involved in the establishment of the colony.[68] Sixty years later the house of Gibson Brothers considered colonizing its lands. It noted that the government made colonization very easy, even though laws defined the size of the farm lots, roads, and towns. In a labor-short area, colonization schemes at times proved profitable enterprises.[69]

In the period 1856 to 1876, thirty-nine colonies were established. Between 1877 and 1884 another thirty-nine agricultural settlements were promoted. The wealth of these colonists more than tripled in value from 1873 to 1881, amounting in 1881 to 27 million Argentine pesos, of which 63 percent was represented by lands and cattle, 37 percent by houses and agricultural machinery. Fifty-seven percent of the colonists were Italians, 14 percent Swiss, 8 percent French, 6 percent German, 2 percent Spanish, 2 percent English, and 11 percent other groups.[70] As could be expected from the small percentage of British colonists, British merchants in Argentina did not care to risk a failure in founding colonies as had the Robertson brothers. Of the seventy-eight colonies founded between 1856 and 1884, only one was clearly established by a London company. A few other foreign merchants, some Swiss and German, were willing to invest in the companies. Otherwise, individuals, the governments of the various provinces, or various other nationalities established the colonies. The large risk involved and the small profits discouraged import-export houses from establishing colonies, although settlers' needs further encouraged the import trade and their produce increased the export trade.

Anglo-Argentine merchant failure to invest in colonies did not preclude large *estancia* interests in the province of Buenos Aires, the interior, or Uruguay. In 1902 Herbert Gibson, the heir of a British family long active in Argentine commerce, ranching, and politics, wrote his father that:

there are many "town agencies" which manage estancias. They usually charge a fixed sum; the others charge a percentum, varying from 2½ % to 5 % on the gross proceeds of all sales, stock and produce. They procure a manager for whom, of course, the owners pay. This is the person who really manages the estate. If they buy sheep, rams, or other live stock for the owners, they charge a commission. Indeed, everything comes to pay a commission. They assume no responsibility with regard to the technicalities of stock breeding and general estancia management. They are in fact "agents" pure and simple.[71]

A relatively small amount of capital developed a successful sheep ranch, thus tieing the relationship between the mercantile houses and the sheep breeding industries. Individuals such as Richard Newton, David A. Shennan, John Fair, Edward Casey, and John Gibson, who made money through the import-export trade, quietly reinvested the money in sheep farming.[72] Merchant investment in sheep farming offered definite advantages. In the first place, a merchant did not need a large amount of capital because land and labor were cheap and employees could be paid by a percent interest in the flock. Investors also received quick returns on their capital, since a flock doubled itself in three years and the import-export house had the contacts in a growing world market to sell the produce.

Import-export houses supervised *estancias* through a manager whose books would be inspected by the house accountant. The house also imported all the necessities for the *estancias,* from new breeds of animals to barbed-wire fencing. All the major British mercantile houses appear to have been willing to import livestock. Very early in the nineteenth century British merchants began investing in *estancias.* Yates, Cox, and Company in the United Kingdom wrote Green, Hodgson, and Robinson in 1829 that they had heard that land 200 and 300 miles from the capital cost only 6,000 pesos per square league. They asked that the funds which the mercantile house held for them be invested in an estate without cattle. The property was to be held for a few years until the value of the land increased.[73] It was but one step more to move from purchase and management of lands for a client to the ownership of lands by the mercantile house. An *estancia* might be bought with a firm in Buenos Aires or London on a partnership basis. The merchant appointed a manager just as he did for his clients. The *estancias* served as an investment from which to pay debts incurred in the import-export trade during a bad year. By exporting products from their own *estancias,* the import-export merchant decreased the need to buy produce from others to fill orders. Thus, merchants invested in *estancias* as soon as possible after beginning in the import-export trade.

Gibson Brothers, a mercantile house established in Buenos Aires in 1819 and a family business until 1969, exemplified the typical dependence of the import-export business on landed property. In 1819 John Gibson was sent by his father, a merchant of Glasgow, to establish a branch of the family business in Buenos Aires to import British textiles and export Argentine produce. John Gibson soon found that to engage successfully in the trade it was necessary to purchase pastoral estates, and he convinced his father of the value of investing in land. Between 1821 and 1825 John Gibson purchased five large cattle farms in the vicinity of Buenos Aires and later formed a partnership with some brothers. The financial crisis that hit Argentina during the war with Brazil proved disastrous for the house. Gibson Brothers had made commitments in sterling but could collect from customers only in Argentine currency, which had depreciated to 4 percent of face value. Since the parent house in Glasgow could not pay the heavy burden, the Buenos Aires house liquidated its land and cattle holdings in Argentina at ruinous prices. However, it retained one sheep *estancia* of 60,000 acres in the province of Buenos Aires. It was from this *estancia* that the family recouped its losses, adjusted to the local environment, and again entered the import-export trade in the 1880s.[74] Investments in *estancias* served not only as a means to increase the profits of the import-export house but as a profitable enterprise to compensate for losses in the import-export trade.

Duncan Wright, a partner in both a Buenos Aires house and a Manchester house, was not satisfied with simply combining import-export trade with *estancia* ownership and management. Along with Robert Macalister and James Parlane, former partners in the import-export house of Parlane and Macalister in Buenos Aires, and several British friends, he established a joint stock firm, the Yerúa Estancia Company Limited, in 1878 when his mercantile house was liquidated. The Yerúa Estancia had been purchased by the house of Parlane and Macalister in 1835 in the name of the several partners. The government of Argentina recognized the rights of the owners to seventeen square leagues of land in 1863. The formation of the joint stock company took place in order to obtain the needed capital to buy out partners who no longer had an interest in it and to settle claims against it. Basically, it was easier to set up a joint stock company with an office in London with its name on the door and a secretary as required by British law than to raise loans on signatures. Also, the different owners could then easily be given their part of the *estancia* in shares. Although operating as a joint stock company, import-export houses had the management of the *estancia*. Thus the house of McLeane and Parland handled the financing and managing of the *estancia* in Buenos Aires and exported produce and remitted proceeds to the partner firm at Liverpool, Parlane, Graham and Company. The shareholders received a dividend in 1880 of 8 percent on their investment.

The object of Yerúa Estancia Company, as defined by its statutes, was the working of an *estancia* in Entre Ríos, the import and export of livestock and produce to and from Great Britain and other areas, the maintenance of buildings on the *estancia*, and the purchase, hiring, and chartering of vessels. In effect the mercantile house carried out all of these activities for the company. The company provided only the £50,000 capital divided into one thousand shares of £50 each. The Yerúa Estancia Company, although listed on the British Stock Exchange and of British capital by that listing, was in fact created and developed by Argentine capital. Nine hundred of the one thousand shares were held by those individuals who initially had interests in the original purchase or by inheritors. The investors had earned the initial capital, which bought the *estancia*, in the British-Argentine import-export trade.[75]

ANGLO-ARGENTINE merchants determined their types of investments in relationship to profit, the time needed for adequate returns, the amount of capital possessed, their own cultural values, and the opportunities available. The goal of Anglo-Argentine merchant investments was profit, not the economic advancement of Argentina. The gains derived by the recipient country were a product of personal interests. Assuming a completely self-interested motivation, private capital in the period 1810 to 1880 brought more benefit than injury to the recipient country because it made available funds for investment in public works, finance, commerce, and land development in a period of time when national capital was unable to finance these needs. Indeed, before 1880 profits proved minimal. The Anglo-Argentine tramways were yielding 4 percent on a nominal capital investment of £200,000, Buenos Aires gas was yielding 5 percent on a nominal capital investment of £270,000, and the Great Southern Railway 10 percent on a nominal capital outlay of £1,600,000.[76] The Yerúa Estancia Company yielded 8 percent on a capital investment of £50,000.[77]

When a merchant made his investments, he made his decision on the basis of anticipated profits calculated not merely by dividends but in relation to the profits of the import-export house. Thus, British merchants invested most heavily in land, especially *estancias*, which provided produce. Similarly railroads and shipping carried produce while insurance and banking protected investments. Merchants invested least in industry, which would have competed with imports, and in public utilities, which did not directly affect trade. Merchants anticipated that investments in certain areas would increase the amount of trade, which in turn would increase their profits.

Anglo-Argentine merchants further considered the element of time; that is, how long it would be before an investment realized dividends. Investment in shipping, for example, would bring almost immediate returns by making overseas trade more profitable and convenient. Investments in railroads were slower in paying dividends either directly or indirectly. Companies had to obtain concessions from the government and then build the line. Thus, British merchants in Argentina were less inclined to invest in railroads than their counterparts in London and were more likely to invest in sheep ranching where 100 percent returns could be expected within three years.[78]

Merchants also attempted to use investments to gain financial and political influence. The greater interest in the Banco de Descuentos y Banco de Buenos Aires than in the Banco Nacional de las Provincias Unidas del Río de la Plata can be explained in part by the greater influence and control exercised with smaller amounts of capital.

The British culture of the merchant further explained heavy investments in land. In nineteenth-century Britain and Argentina, social position was determined by land ownership. By investing in land, merchants improved their economic position and social esteem. British merchants, unlike their Argentine counterparts, hoped eventually to obtain the wealth to return to the United Kingdom, where their social and political positions would perhaps be enhanced by being landowners in Argentina. Probably not more than thirty percent of the British merchants in Buenos Aires returned themselves and their capital to the United Kingdom. Merchant remittance of substantial amounts of capital, of course, would have hindered Argentine economic development, since the export of capital aggravated the Argentine balance of payments. Moreover, it appears that many who did return to England left their capital largely invested in Argentina.[79] The Argentine merchant, in contrast with the British merchant, hoped to use his land holdings to increase his position and power in Argentina and to expand from trade to politics. Those Anglo-Argentine merchants who used their land ownership to move into politics in Argentina rather than into British politics had come to accept Argentine social values. British merchants, desiring to return to Great Britain, invested in Argentine development rather than dissipating money in high living. In fact, the credit ratings of mercantile houses criticized those partners who seemed to live too high.[80]

Merchant investments responded to changes in trading patterns. Investments in land throughout the seventy-year period were usual, but the purpose for which land would be used changed. Although British merchants in Argentina invested in colonization in the 1820s, the failure of these colonies and the realization that small farming was difficult without better transportation to send produce to the market delayed further experiments. Thus, in the pre-1850 period merchants found their safest land investments in cattle *estancias* which increased their profits in the export of hides. By the 1860s land was devoted to sheep ranches, reflecting the increase in wool exports. Only in the 1870s when railroads were beginning to make wheat farming and wheat export profitable did merchants again find investments in colonization a useful supplement to the export trade.

The collapse of the foreign-owned joint stock companies in the 1820s gave British merchants an opportunity to invest in the economic infrastructure and the processing industry. British merchants invested in banking during the 1820s, but when the first two banks failed to bring the hoped-for results and the national government took increased responsibility for establishing a banking system, merchants turned to other investments. Anglo-Argentines helped to finance national insurance companies in the 1860s and 1870s, when London capital was still not optimistic for the long-term political stability of Argentina. Similarly, British merchants in Argentina took a large part of the leadership in establishing the first railroad, but from the 1870s encouraged London companies with larger reserves of capital to finance the greater part of construction costs.

Surely, British import-export merchants promoted Argentine development through their cultivation of trade that provided the Argentine government with needed revenues, through their tapping of idle resources for essential enterprises, through their provision of employment opportunities for an expanding population, and through their leadership and capital in the development of the economic infrastructure and extractive industries. The ability of import-export merchants to take advantage of the risks and opportunities of Argentine trade promoted both merchant profits and Argentine economic growth and development.

7.

British Merchants
as Entrepreneurs

BETWEEN 1810 and 1880 British merchants provided the link between European demand and Latin American supplies. Differences in products and variations in the political, economic, and geographic circumstances altered marketing and investment practices within Latin American nations. Making use of the various risks and opportunities and within the limits imposed by nineteenth-century commercial practices, British merchants proved their entrepreneurial abilities. Although British merchants throughout Latin America had access to capital, credit, and technology and could draw on the political prestige of Great Britain, they had to learn to adapt to new environments in order to profit. At the beginning of the nineteenth century, British merchants in Argentina were able to sell inexpensive but high quality goods on long credit at low interest rates and to develop the social and political contacts that enabled British industry to supply local markets without penalty and to undersell indigenous handicraft manufacturers. But even in the early days of the Río de la Plata trade, British businessmen faced competition from national merchants who attempted to restrict the import of foreign goods; from French merchants who controlled the trade in fine clothes, silks, and luxury items; from Germans who brought wines and products from the Mediterranean; and from United States citizens who undersold British houses by their reexports of United Kingdom industrial goods. As a result, British merchants quickly learned to diversify their operations.

At first British mercantile houses in Argentina concentrated upon the interior river trade in which they sold goods, collected produce, or bartered. As the competition of Argentine nationals, aided by government policy and political instability, reduced this trade, British merchants concentrated their interests upon the city of Buenos Aires, where direct investments beyond external trade could be made in safety. The fluctuations in the prices of produce and manufactured goods encouraged investment, particularly in land which could be used to produce exports and in infrastructure that supported trade.

In the 1860s accelerated trade and increasing specialization changed Argentina's principal exports from hides to wool and then to wheat and began to transform the function and organization of the mercantile houses. Nevertheless, the mercantile houses, organized in partnerships, continued to import and export on a commission basis or on their own account. During the late 1870s, with increased technology and a more rapid communications and transportation system, changes in the organization and operation of the mercantile houses intensified. Greater specialization became possible, and by the 1890s the function of import was separated from export. Not only did technology make possible more rapid means of communications, but it led to greater industrial complexes. By the beginning of the twentieth century industrial managers no longer desired to work through middlemen. They sent their own agents to sell their goods and to buy raw materials. Business thus passed from the hands of the import-export house.

Throughout the nineteenth century, Argentina's foreign trade was financed by sterling bills drawn on London and credit extended by British companies. Even in the 1870s the great bulk of business was still financed by credit in Europe or the United States, whether in the nature of direct arrangements with shippers or by bankers' credit. But there continued to be a certain amount of business done by direct draft on the importer in Argentina. The usual terms of credit in the dry goods trade was five-months promissory notes signed three months after the end of the month in which the sale was made. In the hardware trade it was six-months promissory notes signed at the end of the month following that in which the sale was made. Prices on imported goods were quoted in gold, and buyers could choose to sign promissory notes in gold or convert to currency at once, leaving the risk of gold variation to the seller. The frequent auctions or efforts by some sellers to sell for cash or accept discount of 8.5 percent were as much a result of the long credit and risk of gold variation as of keen competition. Local factors usually sold in currency at six-months promissory notes dating from the end of the month following that in which the sale was made or less 5 percent for cash in thirty days.

With the rise of more sophisticated means of production, distribution, communications, and transportation, partnerships found themselves unable to compete with foreign or Argentine joint stock companies, which bought produce directly and appointed their own agents to market manufactured goods. By the turn of the twentieth century, import-export houses, once an important part of British commercial enterprise, had either failed or moved into other forms of business. Some firms, discouraged by new protective tariffs for local industries, moved completely into *estancia* management and land ownership. Others remained in distribution but moved out of importing and exporting to handle the products of local industries. Those houses remaining in import-export under local ownership and management became subsidiaries or agents of particular British companies.

The changes that came in the handling of wool illustrate the eroding of the function of the import-export house. In the early years of the industry, import-export merchants purchased large quantities of wool and baled and exported their parcels on order or on their own account for British or continental markets. Argentine wool producers sold to storekeepers or to traveling wool buyers who, in turn, sold to the export house. But before the beginning of the twentieth century, this pattern had changed because railroads put *estancia* owners in direct contact with the market in Buenos Aires. French, German, and Belgian manufacturers sent their own buyers, with instructions as to class and price limits, to purchase directly on the Buenos Aires market. In 1893 a central market built in Buenos Aires further concentrated the business, while other collection points were established at railroad terminals. At these markets wool was exposed in piles with a ticket attached denoting place of origin, weight of parcel, and name of the consignment broker. Manufacturing agents could inspect the produce and make their offers. Although wool was at times auctioned, most transactions depended on private contract. The import-export merchant steadily lost his business to the manufacturing agents and to the consignment brokers. By 1903 75 percent of the Argentine wool parcels were shipped directly to European manufacturers.[1]

British import-export houses rapidly lost ground to United Kingdom joint stock companies and continental competitors at the end of the nineteenth century. Italian and German houses, supported by large immigrant minority markets, profitably supplied goods of inferior quality at lower prices than the British houses. British houses, satisfied with earlier opportunities, depended on the British industry of the earlier nineteenth century. Later industrial development based on heavy industry, shipbuilding, and transport had no relevance for mercantile houses used to handling the trade in cotton goods. The collapse of mercantile houses contributed to the relative decline in British trade at the close of the nineteenth century despite a massive inflow of capital. British manufacturers failed to comply with requests for change in quality of goods and for different styles. Goods were not packed in the best method possible and other foreign merchandise—for example, Italian exports—obtained cheaper freight rates. The competition made more effective use of trade circulars and advertising matter. False markings and piracy of trade marks further hurt British trade. And the failure to use the metric system discouraged business with the British. Competition from other Europeans and national industries demanded revisions in ways of doing business. A report to the House of Commons in 1899 suggested that longer credit be extended, more care be paid to market demand, and more effort be made to select agents with a zeal for British trade.[2]

Import-export firms which survived changed their business functions and operations. The Gibson house, which entered the Buenos Aires import-export trade in 1819, moved into investments in land and *estancia* management and even abandoned external trade during the late 1820s. By the 1870s the house was back in the import-export trade, concentrating upon wool and *estancia* management. By the 1960s Gibson Brothers operated as *estancia* managers and cattle brokers. They no longer imported goods other than whiskey because of the high tariffs, nor did they export wool. They did, however, handle vaccines for cattle and products needed for *estancias*. But these items were for the most part produced locally. By the 1960s only a small amount of business was in the hands of import-export merchants, but the mercantile house was again beginning to become important. In Europe small firms which produced very specialized products such as navigation instruments for airplanes or rare wines could not afford their own agents for a limited business in Argentina. Thus, new opportunities arose for mercantile houses which would handle a large number of specialized products.

A NUMBER of examples of trade flexibility existed in South America, and a few of these—Cuba, the British West Indies, Chile, and Columbia—present instructive comparisons. They demonstrate the adaptation of marketing techniques, financing, reinvestment of profits, and the demands and fluctuations of the international market to the geopolitical demands of the local society.

British merchants in Cuba, operating under the same general organization as their counterparts elsewhere in the world, adapted their marketing techniques to the requirements of the local market as fully as did British import-export houses in Buenos Aires. Working from premises that served as offices and residences, merchants in Cuba provided a similar range of marketing services except that their credit facilities were much more developed. Cuban society and economy, particularly the sugar planters, relied upon loans and advances on hypothecated crops. After merchants had made the initial investment of credit to sugar planters, they had to continue to finance harvests or lose previous investments. Until 1856 plantation owners, protected by law from forfeiting slaves, animals, or furniture in payment of debts, also prospered under the legal privilege that creditors could only appropriate a certain portion of the harvest. Thus, the government of Cuba insured the continued operation of sugar plantations under established proprietors, while merchants often waited many years to recover their loans. Consequently, high interest rates were charged. In the 1840s and 1850s a planter might have difficulty obtaining a loan at 20 percent annual interest in a time when loans in Europe were from 4 to 5 percent.[3] Merchant houses in Cuba focused their business on exports rather than imports. Although the capital reserves of Cuban planters were limited, their property enabled them to purchase stores on credit from United Kingdom manufacturers, so that the import-export firms simply handled ordering and shipping in return for a commission. Exports—which involved the competitive complexities of the international sugar market, presented greater risk, and demanded greater capital reserves—were delegated to merchant houses.[4] Merchants in Cuba further extended their investments into related industry. Many operated sugar plantations while others such as Drake and Company (which later became the London Merchant Bank of Kleinwert Benson) also engaged in sugar refining, shipping, and civil engineering.

Throughout the nineteenth century the British West Indies faced a chronic shortage of capital and extreme competition in price and quality from other producers of sugar. British merchants operated successfully by exploiting the needs of planters through the provision of financial and investment services rather than through the arrangement of external trade. John Pinney, one of the most prosperous British merchants in the West Indies during the earlier nineteenth century, began in the import-export trade but soon derived his profits from the interest on loans to planters. Nevertheless, the greater part of his £200,000 capital during the 1860s came from his initial investment of £7,700 in Pinney, Tobin, and Company.[5] Like most West Indies houses, Pinney at first loaned money to attract consignments of sugar for sale on commission. Pinney soon realized that finance was more profitable than an uncertain export market, and during the 1840s his commissions were between £2,000 and £2,500 a year, but interest on loans came to £12,000 a year. The house of Pinney succeeded through conservatism—extreme hesitation about accepting other people's bills of exchange, care in preventing its own bills from going into the hands of strangers who might dishonor them, and good judgment in evaluating the sugar market.

The movement from trade to finance was a response to the indebted planter class that desired imported goods and had to obtain good prices for sugar in order to pay mortgages. Merchants demanded collateral on crops or property and varied payment between bills of exchange or sugar according to individual circumstances or market fluctuations. Successful operation in the face of world overproduction of sugar, inefficient plantations, wide variations in market prices, and financial speculations demanded intimate knowledge of West Indian society. The Pinneys married into the West Indian planter class and into the merchant families of Bristol, traditionally the suppliers of West Indies slaves. Like some British merchants in Argentina, their social contacts and political acumen helped to create their business success.[6]

Just as in Argentina, Cuba, and the West Indies, British mercantile houses in Chile made their profits by adapting to the national society while tailoring international requirements to the demands of internal production. Stephen Williamson and David Duncan, two young Scots, opened a consignment business in Valparaiso, Chile, in 1852 with a capital of £5,000, while the third partner, Alexander Balfour, remained in Liverpool. Although the two houses remained interdependent in terms of produce and goods, separate books were maintained to protect investments against bankruptcies. Beginning on a strictly consignment basis, they operated on their own account, moved into merchant banking, and established branch houses. Good profits earned in Valparaiso depended on knowledge of overseas markets. Sales reports were sent to Liverpool by the fortnightly packet and correspondents were appointed in Panama, Guayaquil, Lima, Santiago, Bolivia, and Mendoza.[7] Williamson, Duncan, and Company made their profits in South America rather than in the United Kingdom. When the Liverpool house nearly failed in 1857, the monthly sales of Williamson and Duncan sometimes exceeded £20,000. Only when the Valparaiso partners credited the Liverpool house did Balfour, Williamson, and Company have sufficient operating capital. Retaining surplus capital, the Valparaiso house in the 1860s sought to rid itself of the consignment business and rely on its own resources to finance trade. It also invested in the copper, cobalt, and nitrate mining, the wool industry, a Chilean railroad, insurance, and shipping.[8] The sound basis of the house allowed active financial participation in the British community. The partners supported the British School in Valparaiso, the Union Church, the Valparaiso Bible Society, the YMCA, the hospital charities, as well as facilities for sailors and for persons orphaned in the War of the Pacific. In Chile the convertible currency reflected political stability. Only in 1880 did the house of Balfour and Williamson of Valparaiso comment on the declining value of the currency, when the partners decided to invest all their credits in sterling. At that time the realities of Chilean business were recognized when the Liverpool house was reorganized as a mere agency for the house in Valparaiso.[9]

In contrast to Chile, where political stability encouraged trade, the import-export business in Colombia faced wars and civil disturbance. But in spite of the political limitation of Colombian trade and the geographic hazards of tropical climate and rugged terrain, British merchants adapted to the environment. Although the British community was small, merchants created a market in Europe for tobacco and cinchona bark and diversified their assets in investments related to trade. As elsewhere, British merchants in Colombia dominated the import-export trade.

BRITISH entrepreneurs in South America possessed advantages that were not available to local citizens. They enjoyed access to capital and credit, often under arrangements made before departure from the United Kingdom, where London was the banking center of the world. The national merchant could not so easily tap the capital resources of Europe without spending extensive time making arrangements. Nor could South American capital compete with foreign capital. In Buenos Aires, capital was worth 12 to 18 percent a year during a period when capital in Europe received 4 to 5 percent a year. Interest rates for upper class Colombians with good credit reputations ranged from 9 to 18 percent annually in times of peace and 24 percent in times of depression; no credit could be secured at any price during civil war.[10]

British merchants also had access to greater technological knowledge and business experience. Great Britain had long been involved in international trade, and many British merchants in South America had gained experience in the counting houses of London or in the shipping ports of Liverpool. British merchants and craftsmen had learned skills in a nation moving rapidly into the technological age. Even if a national entrepreneur could obtain the necessary capital to begin an industrial enterprise or involve himself in trade, he was often dependent on foreigners to provide needed skills. Thus, in almost any type of activity requiring new types of machinery, foreign technicians played an important role.

British merchants and their investments were protected in South America by the threat of "gun-boat diplomacy." In many South American countries foreigners enjoyed special privileges that could not be obtained by nationals. Treaties made with the United Kingdom exempted aliens from military service, forced loans, and many ordinary taxes. If property were seized or destroyed during civil disorder, British consuls filed claims against national governments, which sooner or later made a settlement. Along with these treaties went a certain amount of imitation of British values by the South American upper classes.

Coming from a respected society with needed skills and capital, British merchants sought acceptance or at least sufficient toleration to permit trade and investment. By instituting British customs and procedures or by modifying their values to meet new environmental demands, British merchants imposed new fashions, modes of behavior, and attitudes—from business practices to afternoon tea. Migrant groups were among the more innovative of their nation. Britons came from a land without a peasantry, a land of civil order, prosperity, popular politics, and influential monarchy; the nation instituted factory production, steam power, and railroads, and exercised hegemony over the ocean. These circumstances opened more alternatives to British merchants—alternatives suggested either by their values and ways of doing things or by their new cultural setting. The nature of the British community abroad provided the social acceptance that both reinforced old values while encouraging adaptations.

The decided advantages enjoyed by British merchants in South America have led national historians to conclude that their citizens were rarely entrepreneurs and that aliens dominated business. To the contrary, every South American country had its national entrepreneurs. Colombia had Judas Tadeo Ladínez, who initiated a rather complicated banking system in Bogotá, and the Francisco Montoya family, which developed Colombian tobacco. Brazil had Viscount Maúa, who was involved in a wide variety of enterprises from railroads to banking. Norberto de la Riestra, Jaime Llavallol, and Braulio Costa were Argentines involved in trade, railroads, and banking.[11] All these countries had small industries established by nationals with the help of European technical aid. Citizens, in fact, overcame the disadvantages they faced, by generating their own capital or borrowing at higher interest rates and using foreign skills to advance their own interests. When citizens obtained the necessary capital and skills, they found themselves in a political position to remake the laws to their own advantage.

Because of the handicaps that national entrepreneurs faced in the import-export trade, they directed their entrepreneurial ability toward other areas. Therefore, nationals dealt in interior trade or in agricultural enterprises where they had decided advantages. In these areas they could use political contacts and familiar ties to economic benefit. Furthermore, the social system might be such that a career in politics was preferred above business. For example, an Argentine merchant might find it more advantageous to obtain a high position in government than to devote his time to trade. Through politics he could receive contacts that improved his economic position with less effort. Politics opened more positions for friends and relatives and improved the merchant's social standing. On the whole, Argentine merchants who moved into politics allowed their trade interests to lag.[12]

Foreigners succeeded when they learned how to operate in the political and social spheres. The foreign merchant in Argentina learned how to avoid taxes and how to gain concessions for railroads from Argentine merchants and landowners. Foreigners did not share the same basic assumptions as the nationals. When British merchants interpreted their new social environment in terms of the home country, their explanation proved inadequate. They lacked the extended familial ties possessed by national merchants.

THE MERCANTILE house, a major capitalistic institution for several centuries, operated throughout the Western-influenced world. Britons utilized the mercantile house to expand their commercial influence into developing areas. After 1810 and the collapse of Spanish power, British mercantile houses operated in Latin America and played a central role in states such as Argentina. In the late nineteenth century they declined in importance when marked innovations in transportation and communication and the growth of the Argentine market resulted in specialization in industry, finance, and trade which was more suited to the joint stock company. During most of the century the mercantile houses linked the developing Argentine economy through Buenos Aires to worldwide markets.

Over the decades the British merchants adapted to changing circumstances. Originally, they traveled abroad to make their fortune in the hope of returning to England with wealth and social position. First and foremost they sought profits. These merchants were speculators, often bold and daring in risk-taking. Political disturbances and economic instability made projections of the future hazardous. Although market information was sketchy, communications feeble, transportation unreliable, and currencies and specie fluctuating, the successful merchant overcame the difficulties to profitable advantage. Those merchants who succeeded ably balanced the risks of the unpredictable future and the large potential rewards. Some merchants, such as the Gibson family, won and lost a fortune, and survived to found new business enterprises. Others, such as Dallas, fell into financial failure which for him ended in suicide. Over the years greater political stability arose and improvements in transportation, communication, and finance decreased the risks in commercial transactions. It took time to learn how to form the necessary social and political contacts to which the national upper classes had easy access and to adapt to the Spanish Roman Catholic culture. The inability of some Britons to adapt to the new society, to learn how it operated, and to form the needed contacts explains why not all immigrants were entrepreneurs and why some went into bankruptcy.

British mercantile houses had decided effects on Argentina. Although merchants acted in nearly every case from self-interest, the overall effect on Argentina was positive. Merchants repatriated little capital to England, and the drain on Argentinian capital does not appear to have been significant. On the contrary, mercantile houses provided essential credit and invested earnings in Argentina in efforts to create and organize greater trade. They purchased land, developed *estancias*, and processed wool, hides, and meat. Capital promoted transportation improvements such as roads, tramways, railways, and port facilities. Finally, mercantile houses developed and improved banking services, provided insurance, and contributed to the founding of financial institutions. On the other hand, British mercantile houses were adverse to establishing industry which would compete with imports from England. But in this area the French, Germans, and others provided capital and technical knowledge.

Finally, British mercantile houses had a social and cultural impact on Argentina. British immigrants brought their cultural heritage with them and sought to perpetuate English business practices, education, and religion. But many, such as Thomas Armstrong, took Argentine wives and became prominent in national political and economic circles. Second and third generation Englishmen blended evermore deeply into the greater Argentinian society, just as nationals adopted English commercial practices.

British mercantile houses in Argentina played a significant role in capitalistic institutional development and South American economic growth. They brought Argentine produce into world markets and opened markets for European manufactures. Mercantile houses also provided the basis of development of modern business institutions and trained a generation for participation in the complex institutions of the twentieth century.

Notes
Bibliography
Index

Abbreviations

AGN/BN	Archivo General de la Nación, Buenos Aires, manuscripts from the the Biblioteca Nacional
AGN/DA	Archivo General de la Nación, Buenos Aires, documents, acquired donation
AGN/DC	Archivo General de la Nación, Colonial Division
AGN/GN	Archivo General de la Nación, National Government
AGN/MH	Archivo General de la Nación, Buenos Aires, documents of the Museo Histórico Nacional
AGN/TC	Archivo General de la Nación, Commercial Tribunal section
AGN/TS	Archivo General de la Nación, Tribunal Succession section
AHP	Archivo Histórico de la Provincia de Buenos Aires, La Plata
AMB	Archivo y Museo Histórico del Banco de la Provincia de Buenos Aires
AMB/HD	Archivo y Museo Histórico del Banco de la Provincia, Hugh Dallas manuscripts
BA/HC	Baring Brothers archives, London, House correspondence
B.A.	Buenos Aires
BL	British Library, London
BN	Biblioteca Nacional, Buenos Aires
CPA/BP	Canadian Public Archives, Ottawa, Baring Brothers papers
GH	Guild Hall Library, London
GP	Gibson papers, held by Clement Gibson, Buenos Aires
GPO	General Post Office archives, London
JRL	John Rylands Library, Heald Family manuscripts, Manchester, England
KB	Kleinwort, Benson Ltd. archives, Newbury Berks, England
KW	Krabbé and Williamson papers, held by John Lough, Buenos Aires
LRO	Liverpool Record Office, England
PRO/B.T.	Public Record Office, London, Board of Trade
PRO/F.O.	Public Record Office, London, Foreign Office section
Rio	Rio de Janeiro
SAI	Sun Alliance and London Insurance Group archives, London
UL/FH	University of London, Frederick Huth and Company Ltd. papers
UL/LB	University College London, London and River Plate Bank Ltd.
UM/HR	John Rylands University Library of Manchester, Hodgson papers
UM/OO	John Rylands University Library of Manchester, Owen Owens papers
WP	Wright papers, held by Hugh MacIntyre, United Kingdom

Notes

1. A Perspective

1. For a discussion of commerce and trade in colonial Latin America see Bailey W. Diffie, *Latin American Civilization: Colonial Period* (Harrisburg, Pa.: Stackpole Sons, 1945), pp. 146-164, 386-441; John Lynch, *Spain under the Hapsburgs*, vol. 1: *Empire and Absolutism, 1516-1598* (Oxford: Basil Blackwell, 1964), pp. 152-156; John Lynch, *Spain under the Hapsburgs*, vol. 2: *Spain and America, 1598-1700* (New York: Oxford University Press, 1969), pp. 140-141, 148-149, 153-172; and Tulio Halperín-Donghi, *Politics, Economics and Society in Argentina in the Revolutionary Period* (New York: Cambridge University Press, 1975), pp. 29-40.

2. The material on the Popham invasion is quite extensive. For example see Henry S. Ferns, *Britain and Argentina in the Nineteenth Century* (Oxford: Clarendon Press, 1960), pp. 17-51.

3. B.A., 26 July 1809, William Dun to Alex Cunningham, *Mayo documental: documentos para la historia Argentina* (Buenos Aires: Universidad de Buenos Aires, Facultad de Filosofia y Letras, 1964), vol. 9, p. 159. Rio, M. de Courcy to J. W. Crocker, 5 March 1810, ibid., vol. 9, pp. 116-118. PRO/F.O. 72/90, no. 1180, B.A., 29 September 1809, Mackinnon to Canning.

4. R. W. Eastwick, *The Master Mariner, Being the Life and Adventures of Captain Robert William Eastwick* (London: Fisher, Uneven, 1891), pp. 20-21, 219-241, 321-323.

5. An analysis of trading company charters is given by Edward Potts Cheyney, *European Background of American History, 1300-1600* (New York: Harper and Brothers, 1904), pp. 143-146.

6. Based on a discussion with the archivist of Baring Brothers and an examination of the materials of Barings' international operations in the Baring Brothers archives in London. Also see Philip A. S. Taylor, ed., "Merchant Bank," in *A New Dictionary of Economics* (London: Routledge and Kegan Paul, 1966), and J. L. Hanson, ed., "Merchant Banks," in *A Dictionary of Economics and Commerce* (London: MacDonald and Evans, 1965), pp. 275-276.

7. E. J. Hobsbawn, *Industry and Empire: The Making of Modern English Society*, vol. 2: *1750 to Present Day* (New York: Pantheon Books, 1968), p. 103.

8. Several indicators illustrate growth within Argentine society between 1810 and 1880. Increased revenues of the province of Buenos Aires, 1810-1850, and of the Argentine Republic, 1864-1880, are noted in Miron Burgin, *The Economic Aspects of Argentine Federalism, 1820-1852* (Cambridge: Harvard University Press, 1946), pp. 49, 167, 195-196; Ernesto Tornquist and Co., *The Economic Development of the Argentine Republic in the Last Fifty Years* (Buenos

Aires: Tornquist, 1919), p. 287; table 26 ("Revenues and Expenditures of the Province of Buenos Aires 1810-1860") and table 27 ("Total Revenues and Expenditures of the Argentine Republic 1864 to 1880)" in Vera Blinn Reber, "British Mercantile Houses in Buenos Aires, 1810 to 1880" Ph.D. Diss., University of Wisconsin at Madison, 1972, pp. 217-218. Or examine the statistics on Argentine exports between 1810 and 1880 as indicated in Burgin, *Economic Aspects*, p. 277, and Francisco Latzina, *Sinopsis estadística Argentina* (Buenos Aires: Compañía Sud-Americana de Billetes de Banco, 1914), p. 44, and Reber, tables 12 and 13, pp. 304-305. Railroad mileage grew from 6 miles in 1857 to 1,570 miles in 1880 as indicated in James R. Scobie, *Revolution on the Pampas: A Social History of Argentine Wheat, 1860-1910* (Austin: University of Texas Press, 1964), p. 171.

9. Rodolfo Irazusta and Julio Irazusta, *La Argentina y el imperialismo Británico: los eslabones de una cadena, 1806-1833* (Buenos Aires: Editorial Tor, 1934), pp. 51-55, 171-178. Julio Irazusta, *Balance de siglo y medio, 1810-1860* (Buenos Aires: Ediciones Theoría, 1966), pp. 8, 39-47. D. C. M. Platt, *Finance, Trade and Politics in British Foreign Policy, 1815-1914* (London: Oxford University Press, 1968), pp. 81-147.

10. José M. Mariluz Urquijo, "El capital y la técnica en la industria porteña, 1810-1835," *Boletín de la Academia Nacional de la Historia*, 36 (1965), 69-93; "La industria molinera porteña a mediado de siglo XIX," in *Boletín de la Academia Nacional de la Historia*, 39 (1966), 143-151; and "Las Sociedades Anónimas en Buenos Aires antes del Código de Comercio," *Revista del Instituto de Historia del Derecho*, no. 16 (1965), 31-74.

11. Susan Migden Socolow, "Economic Activities of the Porteño Merchants: The Viceregal Period," *Hispanic American Historical Review*, 55, no. 1 (February 1975), 1-24, provides supporting detail for the shift of commercial influence from the porteño merchants to British merchants.

2. Risk and Opportunity in Argentine Trade

1. Halperín-Donghi, *Politics, Economics*, pp. 65-107, discusses in detail how the revolution led to the breakdown of the hinterland commercial system. He also recognizes that the influx of British textiles did not immediately destroy the local crafts industry. Rather the interior textiles industry declined slowly until the railroad completed the destruction (p. 91). Further, both Halperín-Donghi, pp. 8-22, and John Lynch, *The Spanish-American Revolutions, 1808-1826* (New York: W. W. Norton, 1973), pp. 58-59, recognize that Argentina in the nineteenth century must be analyzed in terms of four regional economies—northwest, far west, midwest, Buenos Aires and other littoral provinces.

2. BA/HC 4.1.3.5, B.A., 21 January 1825, W. P. Robertson to Swinton E. Hollard, emphasizes the advantages the treaty brought. *Handbook of Commercial Treaties* (London: Majesty's Stationery Office, 1931), pp. 15-17.

3. PRO/F.O. 354/8, 1824-1831, Woodbine Parish, Report on British Committee.

4. UM/HR Letter Book, B.A., 14 November 1833, 19 November 1833, Hodgson and Robinson to Owens. The bibliography of the Rosas period is quite

extensive. The Argentine historians are themselves in the process of reexamining the Rosas period, although it appears at this date that the new interpretations may more nearly coincide with the general opinions of the nineteenth-century British merchants.

5. For information on privateers: AMB/HD, 16 February 1821, Dallas protest against privateers. AGN/DC 1818-1845 IC-31-2-7. PRO/F.O. 6/20, 10 November 1827, public declaration of protest by Stewart Seite. PRO/F.O. 6/25, B.A., 11 March 1828, Christopher Claxton to committee managing affairs of Lloyds. PRO/F.O. 354/4, B.A., 19 December 1827, PRO/F.O. 6/25, facts referred to in the accompanying memorial, signed B.A., 7 January 1828. AMB/HD, 30 December 1817, Colonia, Juan Wilson to Dallas.

6. PRO/F.O. 6/25, B.A., 11 March 1828, Christopher Claxton to committee managing the affairs of Lloyds.

7. See Benjamin Keen, *David Curtis De Forest and the Revolution of Buenos Aires* (New Haven: Yale University Press, 1947), and also PRO/F.O. 6/25, B.A., 11 March 1828, Christopher Claxton to committee managing the affairs of Lloyds. AMB/HD, London, 3 December 1917, Colleman and Lambert to Dallas; B.A., 22 April 1818, Mr. Robert Hym to D. Gowland.

8. UM/OO, B.A., 21 December 1841, Hodgson and Robinson to Owens.

9. PRO/F.O. 6/66, 14 May 1838, Griffiths to Palmerston.

10. AMB/HD, Havana, 27 September 1829, Hernández and Chavitau to Dallas; B.A., *British Packet and Argentine News*, 9 July 1831; *Espíritu de Buenos Aires*, 9 February 1832, pp. 48-51.

11. AMB/HD, Santa Fe, 21 May 1819, Philip Parkins to Dallas; Corrientes, 4 March 1817, Parkins to Dallas. AGN/TC 6-4-6-5, 1830.

12. PRO/F.O. 97/48, General Correspondence, 4 April 1853, dispatch.

13. KW, B.A., 4 June 1853, Krabbé to Darbyshire. BA/HC 4.1.24.4, 1852, memoranda prepared by George White.

14. AMB/HD, 15 February 1820, Miller to Dallas.

15. UM/HR, B.A., 16 November 1840, Hodgson and Robinson to Owens.

16. GP, General Correspondence, September 1927-1934, memoir Sir Herbert Gibson. BA/HC 4.1.13.3, B.A., 6 October 1829, Forbes to Joshua Bates, London.

17. 7 July 1864, p. 341.

18 Brazilian blockade, *British Packet and Argentine News*, 3 August 1833, p. 2. French blockade, *British Packet and Argentine News*, 7 November 1840; 31 March 1838. French-British blockade, *British Packet and Argentine News*, 27 September 1845; 24 June 1848.

19. *Brazil and River Plate Mail*, 22 July 1880. Ferns, *Britain and Argentina*, pp. 164-165. UM/HR, B.A., 23 December 1825, Green and Hodgson to Joseph Green, Liverpool. AMB/HD, B.A., 12 February 1821, Joseph Hierta to Dallas. UM/HR Letter Book, B.A., 13 January 1826, Green and Hodgson to Joseph Green, Liverpool; UM/OO, Liverpool, 4 December 1829, Wildes, Pickersgill to Hodgson and Robinson.

20. AMB/HD, Rio, September 1829, Miller to Dallas; Corrientes, 27 January 1817, Philip Parkins to Dallas and Baxada, 28 September 1819, to Dallas. T. H. Baines, *Observations on the Present State of Affairs of the River Plate* (Liv-

erpool: Liverpool Times Office, 1845), pp. 10-11. PRO/F.O. 72/157, 22 June 1822, Staples to Viscount Castlereagh. *Brazil and River Plate Journal,* 23 February 1864; 21 January 1865. UM/OO, B.A., 1 April 1846, Wilfred Latham and Co. to Owens.

21. PRO/F.O. 6/20, B.A., February 1828, Woodbine Parish to Foreign Office, and F.O. 6/19, B.A., 4 December 1827, Ponsonby to Viscount Dudley; PRO/F.O. 353/4, 31 December 1827, report from British merchants to Parish. *British Packet and Argentine News,* 31 August 1833; 13 November 1847; 22 January 1848; 16 June 1838, p. 1; 21 April 1838, p. 1; 28 May 1838.

22. PRO/F.O. 97/48, General Correspondence, 12 April 1844, letter of Duncan Stewart. Ferns, *Britain and Argentina,* pp. 167-168, 242-243.

23. UM/HR, Liverpool, 31 January 1826, Green and Hodgson to Joseph Green; UM/HR Letter Book, B.A., 20 July 1840, 12 May 1828, and 8 June 1838, Hodgson and Robinson to Fielden Brothers. UM/HR, Liverpool, 23 June 1838, Pickersgill and Co. to Hodgson and Robinson, B.A. James Hodgson Outgoing Letters, 3 July 1828, Hodgson to Robinson. *British Packet and Argentine News,* 24 June 1848, AGN/MH Doc. 921.

24. PRO/F.O. 97/48, General Correspondence, 12 April 1844, letter of Duncan Stewart.

25. UM/OO, B.A., 18 September 1841, Hodgson and Robinson to Owens.

26. PRO/F.O. 6/227, General Correspondence.

27. The best secondary work which makes an attempt at dealing with epidemics is Nicolás Besio Moreno, *Buenos Aires puerto del Río de la Plata, capital de la Argentina: estudio crítico de su población 1536-1936* (Buenos Aires: Talleres Gráficos Tuduri, 1939), esp. pp. 136-175. The cholera epidemic of 1867-1868 is discussed in *The Brazil and River Plate Mail,* 7 February 1868, p. 4; 22 February 1868, p. 7; 7 March 1868, p. 7.

28. The material on the yellow fever epidemic is from AGN/BN lego. 686, exp. 11.282, 23 June 1871, Villegas to Felix Frias; lego. 686, exp. 11.277-11.289, from 24 April 1871 to 26 May 1871, Villegas to Felix Frias; and lego. 687, exp. 11.475, B.A., 24 June 1871, Luis L. Dominguez to Felix Frias. The government's handling of the yellow fever epidemic is discussed in *Registro oficial del Gobierno de Buenos Aires, [Buenos Aires, 1871], pp. 157, 186, 194, 199, 296. Manual Bilbao, Tradiciones y recuerdos de Buenos Aires* (Buenos Aires: Gráf Ferrari Hnos., 1934), pp. 242-247. *Brazil and River Plate Mail* 22 April 1871, p. 4; 8 May 1871, p. 4; 20 May 1871, p. 4; 8 June 1871, p. 2; 22 March 1872, p. 4; 7 November 1872, p. 4; 22 June 1871, p. 4.

29. Burgin, *Economic Aspects,* p. 277. Ferns, *Britain and Argentina,* p. 492.

30. Clifton B. Kroeber, *The Growth of the Shipping Industry in the Río de la Plata Region* (Madison: University of Wisconsin Press, 1957), p. 122. Burgin, *Economic Aspects,* p. 276.

31. BA/unpublished, list of loans issued from 1824.

32. H. S. Ferns, "Investment and Trade between Britain and Argentina in the Nineteenth Century," *Economic History Review,* 2nd ser. 3, no. 2 (1950), 210. For a general discussion of markets, trade, imports, and exports see D. C. M. Platt, *Latin America and British Trade, 1806-1914* (New York: Barnes and Noble, 1973).

33. PRO/F.O. 354/8, Woodbine Parish, report on British Committee on Trade; UM/HR, B.A., 9 March 1833, Fred K. Kalman to Hodgson Robinson. *Brazil and River Plate Mail*, 22 May 1872, pp. 7-8. "Exports and Imports of Montevideo and Buenos Aires from 1838-1842," *Merchant's Magazine*, July-December 1843, p. 9.

34. The figures for 1825 came from Burgin, *Economic Aspects*, p. 36; the *Buenos Aires Standard*, Diamond Jubilee edition, 1861-May 1, 1920, p. 55; PRO/Customs 4/20-1825 and were calculated on the basis of value of a gold ounce so that the percentage can be figured for 1880. Latzina, *Estadística retrospectiva*, pp. 220-223.

35. Latzina, *Estadística retrospectiva*, pp. 220-223.

36. Ibid.

37. PRO/F.O. 6/336, extract of letter to the editor in the *Buenos Aires Standard* included in a letter of the consul to the Earl of Derby, 5 February 1876.

38. Burgin, *Economic Aspects*, pp. 49, 167, 196. *Registro estadístico del estado de Buenos Aires*, vol. 2 (Buenos Aires: Imprenta de la Tribuna, 1861), p. 145. Great Britain, House of Commons, *Sessional Papers*, 1872, vol. 57, p. 10.

39. *Brazil and River Plate Mail*, 7 September 1871, pp. 5-6. PRO/F.O. 6/285, General Correspondence, B.A., 15 July 1867, MacDonnell to Stuart.

40. For percentage of revenue raised from customs receipts see Aldo Ferrer, *The Argentine Economy: An Economic History of Argentina* (Berkeley: University of California, 1967), pp. 59; *Brazil and River Plate Mail*, 2 March 1867, p. 14; PRO/F.O. 6/285, General Correspondence, B.A., 15 July 1867, MacDonnell to Stuart.

41. AGN/DA, Petición de comerciantes. UM/HR Letter Book, 5 March 1836, Hodgson and Robinson to Geo. Faulkner and Co.; 8 June 1838, Hodgson and Robinson to Owens. *Brazil and River Plate Mail*, 7 February 1868, p. 5; 23 August 1869, p. 7. One of the most interesting articles on the tariff problem is by José Mariluz Urquijo, "Aspectos de la política proteccionista durante la década 1810-1820," *Boletín de la Academia Nacional de la Historia*, 37 (1965), 115-154; he emphasizes the protectionist policy of the tariff for the early period. See also *Mayo Documental*, vol. 12, 23 July 1810, Oficio de Lord Strangford al Marques de Wellesley, Rio de Janeiro.

42. BA/HC 4.1.24.4, 1852, memoranda prepared by George White. Alfredo Estévez, "La contribución directa, 1821-1852," *Revista de Ciencias Económicas*, 4th ser. 48, no. 4 (April-June 1960), pp. 123-211, for a very well documented and comprehensive article on the tax.

43. *British Packet and Argentine News*, September 6, 1834, p. 2.

44. Provincia de Buenos Aires, *Impuesto de patentes: registro de los contribuyentes de ciudad de Buenos Aires* (Buenos Aires, 1870); Great Britain, House of Commons, *Sessional Papers*, "License required by Commercial Travellers," 1897, vol. 88, p. 89.

45. Halperín-Donghi, *Politics, Economics*, p. 369, also emphasizes that landowners and merchants agreed on the economic policy of government and disagreed only on distribution of financial benefits, rather than on the financial policy per se.

46. Banco de la Nación Argentina, *El Banco de la nacion en su cincuentario, 1891-1941* (Buenos Aires: Banco de la Nación Argentina, 1940), pp. 14-16. Norberto Piñero, *La moneda, el crédito y los bancos en la Argentina* (Buenos Aires: James Menendez, 1921), pp. 49-50. German O. E. Tjarks, *El consulado de Buenos Aires y su protecciones en la historia del Río de la Plata* (Buenos Aires: Universidad de Buenos Aires, Facultad de Filosofia y Letras, 1962), vol. 2, pp. 237-255. PRO/F.O. 6/19, B.A., 19 September 1827, Ponsonly to Viscount Dudley; *Brazil and River Plate Mail*, 22 July 1865, p. 419; 6 June 1866, p. 250; 22 February 1866, p. 73; 22 February 1867, p. 5. Ferns, *Britain and Argentina*, pp. 83-84. Ferrer, *Argentine Economy*, pp. 60-61.

47. PRO/F.O. 6/341, B.A., 14 January 1877, commercial no. 5, West to Derby, "Report on the Silver Currency of the Argentine Republic." Juan Alvarez, *Temas de historia económica Argentina* (Buenos Aires: El Atenco, 1929), pp. 88-106.

48. PRO/F.O. 6/341, B.A., 14 January 1877, commercial no. 5, West to Derby, "Report on the Silver Currency of the Argentine Republic." *Brazil and River Plate Mail*, 23 November 1875, p. 14. Alvarez, *Temas*, pp. 88-106. A. G. Ford, *The Gold Standard, 1880-1914: Britain and Argentina* (Oxford: Clarendon Press, 1962), pp. 90-93.

49. *Brazil and River Plate Mail*, 23 February 1864, p. 126; 22 September 1864, p. 460.

50. *Brazil and River Plate Mail*, 7 September 1864, pp. 444-445.

51. BA/HC 4.1.24.4, B.A., 1852, George White to Barings.

52. BA/HC 4.1.24.4, B.A., 1852, George White to Barings. *Brazil and River Plate Mail*, 7 September 1864, pp. 444-445.

53. *Brazil and River Plate Mail*, 22 February 1865, p. 173; 8 August 1873, p. 3.

54. BA/HC 4.1.34, B.A., 3 April 1857, George White to Barings; same, 3 April 1857, 1 May 1857, 29 June 1857. PRO/F.O. 6/262, B.A., 24 March 1866, Francis Clare Ford to the Earl of Clarendon. UM/HR Letter Book, B.A., 9 May 1838, Hodgson and Robinson to Fielden Brothers. UM/OO, B.A., 18 December 1843, Hodgson and Robinson to Owens. *The British Packet and Argentine News*, 21 March 1820, p. 3; 3 December 1836, p. 1. *Brazil and River Plate Mail*, 6 October 1864, p. 485; 22 February 1865, p. 173; 6 May 1865, p. 295; 23 January 1866, p. 30; 7 April 1866, p. 152.

55. UM/HR Letter Book, December 1843, Hodgson and Robinson to Owens.

56. Statistics for 1880 and 1908 were cited in Arthur P. Whitaker, *Argentina* (Englewood Cliffs, N. J.: Prentice Hall, 1964), pp. 51-52. Railroad mileage is given by Scobie, *Revolution on the Pampas*, p. 171. Investments for 1910 and 1913 are given in J. Fred Rippy, *British Investments in Latin America: A Case Study in the Operations of Private Enterprise in Retarded Regions* (Hamden, Conn.: Archon Books, 1966), p. 159.

57. E. J. Hobsbawm, *Industry and Empire: An Economic History of Britain since 1750* (London: Weidenfeld and Nicolson, 1968), pp. 146-147.

58. James R. Scobie, *Argentina: A City and a Nation* (New York: Oxford University Press, 1964), p. 176.

59. UM/HR Letter Book, B.A., 29 August 1833, Hodgson and Robinson to Owens.

60. UM/HR, 5 April 1837, Wilder and Pickersgill to Hodgson and Robinson.

61. H. S. Ferns, "Investment and Trade," p. 210.

62. The discussion of the financial crisis is based on the *Brazil and River Plate Mail* for the years 1875 to 1877; for 1839 to 1842 see R. W. Hidy, *The House of Baring in American Trade and Finance: English Merchant Bankers at Work, 1763-1861* (Cambridge: Harvard University Press, 1949), pp. 295-296.

63. GH, James, Thomas, and Thomas Powell, London Hide Brokers, *Trade Circulars.*

64. For the influence of the Napoleonic Wars see Ferns, "Investment and Trade," pp. 213-214; for the Franco-Prussian War, *Brazil and River Plate Mail*, 8 October 1870, p. 4, and 8 December 1870, p. 4.

65. PRO/F.O. 6/153 General Remarks, 2 March 1850, Hood to Palmerston, pp. 93-94.

66. H. Hallam Hipwell, "Trade Rivalries in Argentina," *Foreign Affairs*, 8 (October 1929), 150-154; Sanford Mosk, "Latin America and the World Economy, 1850-1914," *Inter-American Economic Affairs*, 2 (1948), 53-82.

67. See James R. Scobie, "Buenos Aires as a Commercial-Bureaucratic City, 1880-1910: Characteristics of a City's Orientation," *American Historical Review*, 77, no. 4 (October 1972), 1035-1073.

3. Politics and Society in Buenos Aires

1. Henry Marie Brackenridge, *Voyage to Buenos Ayres Performed in the Years 1817 and 1818 by Order of the American Government* (London: Sir Richard Phillips and Co., 1820), pp. 57, 59, 65.

2. For a description of the social and cultural life of Buenos Aires see the following: E. E. Vidal, *Picturesque Illustrations of Buenos Ayres and Montevideo* (London: R. Ackermann, 1943), pp. 5-51; Brackenridge, *Voyage to Buenos Ayres*, pp. 89-94; Samuel Haigh, *Sketches of Buenos Ayres, Chile and Peru* (London: Effingham, Wilson, Royal Exchange, 1831), pp. 13-26; George Thomas Love, *A Five Years' Residence in Buenos Ayres during the Years 1820-1825 Containing Remarks on the Country and Inhabitants; a Visit to Colonia del Sacramento by an Englishman* (London: G. Herbert, 1825), pp. 55-81.

3. BA/HC 4.1.14, B.A., 12 July 1842, Francis Falconnet to Baring Brothers; BA/HC 4.1.23, B.A., 8 May 1845, I. W. C. Moore to Joshua Bates, New York.

4. PRO/F.O. 6/304, MacDonnell Commercial January-December 1871, "Report on the Condition of the Industrial Classes and Immigration in the Argentine Republic," pp. 131-132, calculates mortality rates.

5. *Brazil and River Plate Mail*, 22 December 1869, p. 5.

6. Gino Germani, *Política y sociedad en una época de transición de la sociedad tradicional a la sociedad de masas* (Buenos Aires: Editorial Paidos, 1963), p. 188, for figures of population over age 20; p. 184, population leaving Argentina. For an excellent discussion of the various censuses of Buenos Aires see An-

tonio Zinny, "Censo de la ciudad de Buenos Aires," *Revista Argentina*, 13 (1872), 479-495.

7. *Brazil and River Plate Mail*, 7 June 1864, p. 193. "Irish Influence in Argentina," *Buenos Aires Herald*, Diamond Jubilee Ed., 15 September 1876-September 1936, pp. 60-63. Horace Rumbold, *The Great Silver River: Notes of a Residence in Buenos Ayres, 1880-1881* (London: John Murray, 1890), pp. 111-115. PRO/F.O. 6/304, MacDonnell Commercial, January-December 1871, pp. 67-70.

8. The quotation is from José M. Salaverria, *Paisajes Argentinos* (Barcelona: Gustavo Gili, 1918), p. 128, but the whole chapter, pp. 123-131, illustrates the point. The original quotation in Spanish reads as follows: "Vamos al país ancho y luminoso; al país que no tiene límites, a la patria de la inconsciencia; a la tierra que no cuenta, ni mide, ni ahorra, ni racela; al país que no tiene miedo del mañana, sino que ama al mañana, con la clara y confiada alegría del niño. Vamos a la tierra de promisión, donde existe todavía el azar, y lo fortunito, y lo imprevisto, y las locas sorpresas."

9. For comments on Sarmiento see Roberto Tamagno, *Sarmiento, los liberales y el imperialismo Inglés* (Buenos Aires: A Peña Lillo, 1963), pp. 133-134. See also D. F. Sarmiento, *Life in the Argentine Republic in the Days of the Tyrants* (New York: Collier Books, 1961).

10. The map of the city of Buenos Aires and the locations are based on *Plano comercial y estadístico de la ciudad de Buenos Aires, año 1862* (Buenos Aires: Librería de la Revista, 1862). The locations of the firms in 1830 are described in J. J. M. Blondel, *Almanaque político y de comercio de la ciudad de Buenos Aires* (Buenos Aires: Imprenta del Estado, 1830), pp. 54-58.

11. José Antonio Wilde, *Buenos Aires desde setenta años atrás* (Buenos Aires: Biblioteca de "La Nación," 1908), pp. 107-110.

12. M. G. Mulhall, *The English in South America* (Buenos Aires: Standard, 1878), p. 589 for 1824. Woodbine Parish reported that in 1825, 779 persons were registered at the Buenos Aires Consulate, of which 508 were English, 143 Scotch, 128 Irish. But since not everyone registered and men were not careful in registering their wives and children, the population was larger than that. M. G. Mulhall, *The Handbook of the River Plate* (Buenos Aires: Standard, 1869), p. 14, suggests 8,000. In 1869 the estimated foreign population of the province of Buenos Aires was 250,000, with 30,000 Irish, 10,000 English and Scotch, 79,000 Italians, 40,000 Basques, 30,000 French, and 30,000 Spaniards. Since the English and Scotch tended to settle in the city, it can be assumed that most of that population was in Buenos Aires. Argentine Republic (Comisión Directiva del censo), *Primero censo de la República Argentina*, verificado en los dias 15, 16, 17 de setiembre de 1869 (Buenos Aires, 1892), pp. 26-29, 45, gives a lower number for the city.

13. Figures for later immigration are given in (Argentine Republic, Comisión Directiva del Censo) *Segundo censo de la República*, 10 May 1895 (Buenos Aires: Taller tip, de la Penitenciaria Nacional, 1898), pp. 1, 643-644, for the years 1876-1897.

14. This was noted in the examination of registrations of British subjects held by British Consul in Buenos Aires.

15. Mulhall, *Handbook*, 1869, p. 15. Ferns, *Britain and Argentina*, p. 76, pp. 7-8. A. Stuart Pennington, *The Argentine Republic: Its Physical Features, History, Fauna, Geology, Literature and Commerce.* (London: Stanley Paul and Co., 1910), p. 48, and discussion with E. C. Warr, Secretary of the British Chamber of Commerce, Buenos Aires, August 19, 1968.

16. Love, *A Five Years' Residence*, pp. 37-39. "The Sentiment of British Trade," in *Buenos Aires Herald*, Diamond Jubilee Ed., p. 27.

17. *British Packet and Argentine News*, 6 December 1843, pp. 2-3; 14 January 1832; 21 January 1832.

18. *British Packet and Argentine News*, 11 April 1829, 21 April 1828, p. 2. *El Avisador: guía general de comercio y de forasteros, 1863 y 1864* (Buenos Aires: Imprenta de el Mercurio, 1864), p. 103.

19. J. Monteith Drysdale, *A Hundred Years in Buenos Aires, 1829-1929. Being a Brief Account of St. Andrew's Scots Church and Its Work during the First Century of Its Existence* (Buenos Aires: John A. Geldart, 1929); "First English Church," in *Buenos Aires Herald*, Diamond Jubilee Ed., p. 74. PRO/F.O. 6/20 has accounts of the contributions and support of the British chapel, i.e., 6 November 1828, F.O. 6/25, 1863, F.O. 6/197, 1856, to list a few.

20. C. M. Fleming and J. W. Colguhoun, eds., *Book of the Bazaar* (Buenos Aires: Kidd's Printing, 1927), pp. 7-11. *British Packet and Argentine News*, 10 February 1838, p. 1. *Buenos Aires Herald*, Sunday Supplement, 1 September 1868.

21. Woodbine Parish, *Buenos Ayres and the Provinces of the Río de la Plata* (London: John Murray, 1852), p. 421, for a discussion of foreign education; Thomas J. Hutchinson, *Buenos Ayres and Argentine Gleanings: With Extractions from a Diary of Salado Exploration in 1862-1863.* (London: Edward Stanford, 1865), pp. 24-26; Emilio Delpech, *Una vida en la gran Argentina, relatos desde 1869 hasta 1944* (Buenos Aires: Peuser, 1944), p. 18, for a discussion of Argentine education.

22. Newspapers such as the *British Packet and Argentine News*, *Buenos Aires Standard*, and *Buenos Aires Herald* reported the social activities of the British community. See for general articles the *Buenos Aires Herald*, Diamond Jubilee Ed., "Scottish Brotherhood," p. 73; "Argentina's National Game: How Soccer Grew in Its Early Days," p. 271; "Strutting the Boards—English Amateur Theatricals," p. 31; "Sixty Years of Argentine Cricket," pp. 54-57.

23. JRL 1217/1, 1217/2, Walter Heald diary. The records of Walter Heald from 1866 to 1870 give a good picture of the life of a British merchant clerk. The diary of Gibson (GP) indicates a similar picture of Buenos Aires in the period after 1880.

24. JRL 1217/1, Walter Heald diary, 16 April 1866.

25. The material on the Foreign Club is based on Jorge Navarro Viola, *El club de residentes extranjeros: breve reseña histórica homenaje a sus fundadores* (Buenos Aires: Imprenta y Casa Editora, 1941), pp. 10-16, 20, 34-38, 41-47, 58-60, 80-90.

26. AGN/DA Acta de Fundación de Bolsa de comercio. *El Avisador: Guía general de comercio y de forasteros*, third edition, 1866, 1867 (Buenos Aires: Imprenta de el Mercurio, 1866), pp. 122-123. Antonio Pillado, *Diccionario de Bue-*

nos Aires o sea guía de forasteros (Buenos Aires: Imprenta del Porvenir, 1864), pp. 77-81. Mulhall, *Handbook*, 1869, pp. 69-70. *La Bolsa de Comercio de Buenos Aires en su Centenario, 1854/10 de Julio/1954* (Buenos Aires: Impreso en la Argentina, 1954), pp. 31, 55, 58, 62-69.

27. Horatio Juan Cuccorese, "Historia sobre los orígenes de la sociedad Rural Argentina," *Humanidades* (La Plata), 35 (1960), 45-52. Mulhall, *Handbook*, 1869, pp. 78-80.

28. *Anuario general del comercio de la industria de la magistratura y de la administración de Buenos Aires, 1854 and 1855* (Buenos Aires: Imprenta del British Packet, 1854), pp. 83-86; Pillado, *Diccionario*, p. 120; *Avisador*, 1870, p. 8. Mulhall, *Handbook*, 1885, pp. 249-250.

29. AGN/DC, Sección Gobierno, Tribunales, Cartas de Ciudadanía, Legajo, no. 19. *Brazil and River Plate Mail*, 7 July 1866, p. 297.

30. PRO/F.O. 354/3, 26 September 1824, Parish to George Canning, p. 166.

31. José Maria Mariluz Urquijo, "Los matrimonios entre personas de diferente religión ante el derecho patrio Argentina," *Instituto de Historia del Derecho Conferencias y comunicaciones* (Buenos Aires), 22 (1948), 17-46.

32. The statistical material is based on the information included on the members who first organized the club; Navarro, *El Club*, pp. 109-187.

33. *Brazil and River Plate Mail*, 21 June 1872, p. 5.

34. *British Packet and Argentine News*, 22 November 1834, p. 1.

35. The details of the resolution are as follows: "First, that when bills are drawn on foreign places and are returned under protest for non-payment, the sterling amount on the face of the same, shall be repaid to the holder, with 15% additional in lieu of interest and damages, and with the actual expense incurred in postages, protest, charges and commission. Second, that when two or more merchants are called in to survey damaged goods, the charges for such survey shall be 2½% on the gross sales, to be divided between them. Third, that 2½% commission shall be charged by the consignees of vessels entering this port, on the amount of freight inwards, whether paid at the port of loading, or payable in Buenos Aires, as a remuneration for transacting the business of the vessel, independent of the usual commission on disbursements and for procuring freight." *British Packet and Argentine News*, 23 July 1836.

36. The freight rates were to be 2.5 percent on the total amount of freight earned by the ship on the outward voyage, 5 percent on the homeward voyage including ship brokerage, and 2.5 percent on disbursement. In cases where vessels had paid full commission on their inward freight at Montevideo before proceeding to Buenos Aires with the balance of the cargo, consigned to the same establishment, no further charges were to be made. The compensation of merchants called in to survey damaged goods was to be 1.5 percent on their value. City of Buenos Ayres, *Report of the Committee of British Merchants Elected at the General Meeting Held 27th May 1852* (Buenos Aires: Imprenta del Comercio, 1853).

37. PRO/F.O. 6/104, Montevideo, 27 August 1845, W. Ouseley to Earl of Aberdeen.

38. To ascertain English names in government, I examined the almanacs for

various years. *Anuario general del comercio*, 1855, lists names of Gowland and Linch, pp. 45-46. From time to time a less well-known English name would appear among government officials. The number of English names found were quite few.

39. PRO/F.O. 6/330, London, 7 July 1875, Cowper to Derby; F.O. 6/4, 17 February 1823, B.A. to Sir Thomas Hardy; F.O. 6/91, B.A., 16 October 1843, Griffiths to Aberdeen; F.O. 6/316, B.A., 13 August 1873, Bridgett to Granville. *British Packet and Argentine News*, 2 May 1835, p. 1. "The Story of the British Hospital," *Buenos Aires Herald*, Diamond Jubilee Ed., pp. 24-26.

40. City of Buenos Ayres, *Report of the Committee of British Merchants*. *British Packet and Argentine News*, 23 July 1836.

41. PRO/F.O. 354, Woodbine Parish papers, 21 December 1830, Parish to Thomas Duguid; PRO/F.O. 6/202, B.A., 1 October 1857, petition of British residents to Clarendon.

42. "On the Trail of Diplomats—the British Representation," *Buenos Aires Herald*, Diamond Jubilee Ed., p. 20, lists consuls from 1823-1880; UM/HR Letter Book, B.A., 14 February 1818, James Hodgson to Mess. Rhodes and Briggs, Halifax. AHP Tribunal de Cuentas, Reclamaciónes de súbditos ingleses, Legajo 1038, B.A., 29 February 1844, Mendeville to Felipe Arana. PRO/F.O. 6/330, 25 November 1875, Bridgett to Earl of Derby; PRO/F.O. 6/5, B.A., 4 November 1824, Woodbine Parish to George Canning.

43. There is extensive material on this subject in the Archivo Histórico de la Provincia de Buenos Aires, Legajo 38, and PRO/F.O. 97/48, 97/49, 97/56.

44. PRO/F.O. 354/9, B.A., 22 January 1832, James Breton to Woodbine Parish. PRO/F.O. 354/4, 31 December 1827. PRO/F.O. 6/19, B.A., 1 December 1827, Ponsonby to Robert Gordon. PRO/F.O. 354/4, 4 December 1826, Parish to Hood. PRO/F.O. 6/1, B.A., 24 August 1823, British Merchants to Captain G. W. Willes of H. M. S. *Brazen*.

45. Kroeber, *Growth of Shipping*, p. 71; H. S. Ferns, "British Informal Empire in Argentina, 1806-1914," *Past and Present*, no. 4 (November 1953), 69. Arthur Redford, *Manchester Merchants and Foreign Trade, 1794-1858* (Manchester: Manchester University Press, 1934), pp. 100-105. PRO/F.O. 72/282, July 1822, petition to the House of Commons for the recognition of independence of South American Countries from merchants of Liverpool; F.O. 71/282, December 1822, petition from merchants of Glasgow; 6 August 1823, petition from merchants of Manchester.

46. AGN/DA, Petición de Comerciantes Ingleses, 1810. *Gaceta de Buenos Aires*, 19 July 1810, pp. 191-192.

47. City of Buenos Ayres, *Report of the Committee of British Merchants*; Kroeber, *Growth of Shipping*, p. 105.

48. UM/OO, Hodgson and Robinson to Owens, 7 May 1841, 14 May 1841, 31 March 1842.

49. *Registro nacional de la República Argentina* (Buenos Aires: Imprenta del Comercio del Plata, 1858), vol. 2, p. 168. *Almanaque nacional de la confederación Argentina para los años de 1855 y 1856* (Montevideo: Imprenta del Uruguay, 1856), p. 66. PRO/F.O. 6/104, Montevideo, 27 August 1845, W. Ouseley to Earl of Aberdeen.

50. AGN/GN Gran Bretaña, Hullett Hermanos y Cía Correspondencia, Hullet to Rivadavia, no. 674, 24 September 1816; no. 675, October 1816; no 658, 5 July 1816.

51. *Gaceta Ministerial*, 18 September 1812, p. 187; BL/MSS 37292, Ellesly papers, R. Elliot to British merchants at Buenos Aires, 3 March 1811, ff. 310; 4 March 1811, ff. 308-309, 304-305. PRO/F.O. 6/20, British Consul, B.A., 21 July 1827, Woodbine Parish to John Bidwell; F.O. 6/60, B.A., 2 September 1837, Charles Griffiths to Palmerston.

52. *British Packet and Argentine News*, 3 October 1829, 7 June 1832; 26 September 1829; 22 March 1834, p. 1; 19 March 1836, p. 1. PRO/F.O. 6/66, British Consul, B.A., 5 May 1838, Charles Griffiths to Palmerston.

53. John Alex Hammerton, *The Real Argentina: Notes and Impressions of a Year in the Argentine and Uruguay* (New York: Dodd, Mead and Co. 1915), pp. 228; PRO/F.O. 6/336, British Consul, B.A., 14 September 1876, Ronald Bridgett to Earl of Derby, commercial no. 4.

54. AGN/DC, Actas del Consulado, vol. 7, 1814-1816, pp. 6-21. Tjarks, *El consulado*, pp. 91-92, 356-357, examination of the catalog of court cases, AGN/TC.

55. For this expression of antiforeign feeling see Julio Mafud, *El desarrollo Argentino: clave Argentina para un estudio social americano*, 2nd ed. (Buenos Aires: Editorial Americalee, 1966), pp. 73-91, and Leopoldo Lugones, *La Grande Argentina*, 2nd ed. (Buenos Aires: Editorial Huemul, 1962), pp. 36-41, for two examples of feelings of a large number of Argentine writers in the twentieth century. Also see Carl Solberg, *Immigration and Nationalism: Argentina and Chile, 1890-1914* (Austin: University of Texas Press, 1970), pp. 80-92.

4. The Organization and Operation of the British Mercantile House

1. UM/HR Green and Hodgson Outgoing Letter Book, November 1818, James Hodgson to Sam.

2. Analysis is based on comparison of table 4 with information in chapter 2.

3. PRO/F.O. 6/153, B.A., 2 March 1850, Hood to Parlmerston.

4. For a description of the A. Rivolta Co., see SAI, Buenos Aires, Montevideo Rosario Notebook, 1865-1874, p. 3, and PRO/F.O. 6/153, B.A., 2 March 1850.

5. For a discussion of Daniel Gowland see *Diccionario Histórico Argentino* (Buenos Aires: Ediciones Históricas Argentinas, 1955), vol. 4, p. 94; BA/HC 16, 1857, report by George White on houses in Buenos Aires and Montevideo; and BA/HC 16, 1836-1849, report by Francis de Palesieux Falconnet in 1844 on Buenos Aires houses.

6. *Brazil and River Plate Mail*, 21 January 1864, p. 85.

7. JRL 1221/1, Manchester, 12 September 1872, Heald to Krabbé; 1221/1, Bowden, 14 September 1872, Heald to Milroy; 1221/1, Bowden, 18 September 1872, Heald to Milroy.

8. UM/HR Green and Hodgson Outgoing Letter Book, B.A., 14 February 1818, James Hodgson to Joshua Rawdon, Liverpool. AMB/HD, Rio, 12 April

1818, Henry Miller to Hugh Dallas.

9. In 1818 James Hodgson wrote to some young relatives that they should not count on receiving partial payments earlier than eight months from the time of shipping the goods or count on obtaining returns before eighteen months. UM/HR Underbank, 30 August 1817, James Hodgson to a friend; B.A., 17 February 1818, James Hodgson to James and Thomas Hodgson.

10. UM/HR Sheffield, February 1831, McNam, Roberts, and Company to Joseph Green.

11. JRL 1221/1, Manchester, 12 September 1872, Heald to Krabbé; UM/HR, B.A., 22 December 1834 and 10 April 1835, Hodgson and Robinson to George Faulkner, Manchester.

12. David Joslin, *A Century of Banking in Latin America* (London: Oxford University Press, 1963), pp. 20, 30, 33-37.

13. Mulhall, *Handbook*, 1875, pp. 77-78.

14. UL/LB D1, no. 10, London, 3 April 1875, to B.A.

15. See UL/LB for many examples of credit arrangements.

16. Hidy, *House of Baring*, particularly pp. 141-163 and pp. 141-142. However, Baring Brothers did not always maintain their "double account" policy. Zimmermann, Frazier, and Company, operating in the Río de la Plata, maintained an account with Baring Brothers and with Frederick Huth, and Company.

17. WP, B.A., April 1827, Duncan Wright to Hugh Wright.

18. See BA/HC 16, 1836-1849, B.A., June 1844, report by Francis de P. Falconnet on the houses in Buenos Aires and Montevideo.

19. For information on Thomas Armstrong see Navarro Viola, *El Club*, pp. 109-111; BA/HC 16, report by Francis Falconnet, 1844, and George White, 1857; Belgium, *Recueil consulaire publié en exécution de l'arrêté royal*, vol. 4, (Brussels, H. Tarlier, 1863), p. 247.

20. See PRO/F.O. 6/150, 1850.

21. For Barbour Barclay see PRO/F.O. 6/153, 1850; UL/LB, D1, no. 9, London, 23 February 1874, to B.A.; KB, *Confidential Report on Firm Standing*, United Kingdom, vol. 1, p. 8; Belgium, *Recueil consulaire*, vol. 9, p. 248;

22. JRL 1217/2, 22 January 1869; JRL 1221/1, Liverpool, 19 August 1876, Heald to his brothers; 17 April 1875, Heald to Milroy. JRL 1221/1, 31 October 1876, Walter Heald to William Barbour, Liverpool.

23. UM/HR Green and Hodgson Outgoing Letter Book, B.A., 7 October 1818, James Hodgson to Joseph Green. For references to the partnerships of Green, Hodgson, and Robinson, see UM/HR Green and Hodgson Outgoing Letter Book, the following letters: London, 22 November 1828, James Hodgson to Green and Hodgson; Liverpool, 1 June 1829, Joseph Green to John Robinson, and the agreement between James Hodgson and Mary Green.

24. Karl Wilhelm Körner, "El Consul Zimmermann, su actuación en Buenos Aires, 1815-1847," *Boletín del Instituto de Historia Argentina, "Dr. Emilio Ravignani,"* 2nd ser. 7-8, no. 5 11-13 (1966), 19; *British Packet and Argentine News*, 2 December 1833, p. 4; BA/HC 16, June 1844 report by Francis Falconnet.

25. For a discussion of De Forest see Keen, *David Curtis De Forest*, pp.

15-31, and Körner, "El Consul Zimmermann," pp. 14-19.

26. H. S. Ferns, "The Establishment of British Investment in Argentina," *Inter-American Economic Affairs*, 5, no. 2 (Autumn 1951), 74.

27. JRL 1221/1, 7 July 1875, Walter Heald to Archie; 31 October 1876, Walter Heald to William Barbour.

28. JRL 1221/1, 18 October 1876, Heald to C. A. Milligan, Archibald Williamson; Belgium, *Recueil consulaire*, vol. 9, 248; for Hughes Brothers see BA/-HC 15, 1844 Francis Falconnet.

29. JRL 1221/1, Bowden, 15 September 1872, Heald to Kerr; Bowden, 18 September 1872, Heald to Milroy; Liverpool, 15 January 1875, Heald to Milroy; 17 April 1875, Heald to Milroy; 20 April 1875, Heald to Wilson; 7 July 1875, Heald to Archie; 2 April 1876, Heald to Charlie. For further reference on the death of a partner dissolving the partnership see AGN/TC Lego. J., 136, "Jump Contra Nutall."

30. The failure of the Darbyshire houses is dealt with quite extensively in the Bank of London and South America papers (UL/LB). See particularly the following letters: D1, no. 12, London, 12 April 1878, George Warden to manager, B.A. branch; D49, no. 11, Montevideo, 31 January 1876 to B.A.; D49, Montevideo, 24 April 1878, to B.A.; D49, Montevideo, 3 May 1878, to B.A.

31. W. P. Robertson and J. P. Robertson, *Letters on South America* (London: John Murray, 1843), vol. 3, p. 151; UM/HR Outgoing Letter Book, B.A., 7 October 1818.

32. *Brazil and River Plate Mail*, 22 August 1865, p. 462; UM/HR Letter Book, B.A., 21 March 1863, James Hodgson to Joseph Green; AMB/HD, Guernsey, 21 July 1817, Henry Miller to Hugh Dallas; JRL 1217, diary of Walter Heald, particularly 10 and 11 July 1866, 1 April 1867, 14 January 1869; KW, B.A., 1 August 1853, Krabbé to Darbyshire; 2 April 1853, Krabbé to Darbyshire.

33. See UM/HR account books for 1818-1844.

34. The amounts are given in Argentine dollars (pesos) and British pounds. UM/H.R. Letter Book, B.A., 7 October 1818, 21 March 1823, James Hodgson to Joseph Green. KW, B.A., 1 August 1853, 2 April 1853, Krabbé to Darbyshire. BA/HC 4.1.24.4., B.A., 1852, George White to Barings. Aldo Ferrer, *Argentine Economy*, p. 60.

35. JRL 1217/1, diary of Walter Heald, 13 April 1866; 1217/2, 3 February 1868. *Brazil and River Plate Mail*, 23 July 1868, p. 4; PRO/F.O. 6/30, 15 July 1871, "Report on the Conditions of the Industrial Class," pp. 132-133.

36. Kroeber, *The Growth of Shipping*, p. 151.

37. For problems in shipping and payment see UM/HR, B.A., 16 April 1836, Hodgson and Robinson to Owens; also AMB/HD, various receipts to Dallas.

38. Pillado, *Diccionario*, pp. 21-28, discusses in detail what is involved in exporting or transshipping produce and goods.

39. UM/OO, 1 May 1841, Hodgson and Robinson to Owens; UM/HR Letter Book, 19 September 1833, Hodgson and Robinson to Owens.

40. GP notebook 1, 1899-1903, "The International Trade and the Present Market and Argentine Industry," pp. 6-8.

41. UM/OO, 10 June 1841, Hodgson and Robinson to Owens.

42. See UM/HR Letter Book, B.A., 16 April 1836, Hodgson and Robinson to Owens; 1 December 1840, Hodgson and Robinson to Whitaker and Company, Santos; AMB/HD, charter party of brig *Tarah*, 21 March 1820. For 1874 and 1875 freight rates see BA/HC 4.1.64, part 1, B.A., 14 December 1875, Nicolas Bouwer to Bansyo; H. S. Ferns, *The Argentine Republic, 1516-1971* (New York: Barnes and Noble, 1973), p. 57.

43. For indication of shipwrecks, see the *British Packet and Argentine News*, e.g. 18 October 1828; for early development of marine insurance in Buenos Aires see Gotardo C. Pedemonte, *Estado económico y financiero de las compañías Argentinas de seguros: informaciónes, notas, financieras, reseñas, retrospectivas, balances* (Buenos Aires: Talleres Gráficos A. Pedemonte, 1929), pp. 163-164, and *The Brazil and River Plate Mail*, 23 April 1877, pp. 8-9. For types of policies see AMB/HD, London, 12 October 1820, McIntosh and Miller to Dallas; UM/HR Letter Book, B.A., 15 July 1836, to Wilder, Pickersgill, and Company; Liverpool, 19 September 1833, to Owen Owens.

44. AMB/HD, Guernsey, 1 October 1819, and R. W. Isemonger to Dallas; UM/HR Letter Book, B.A., 19 August 1833, to Captain Corkholl; 2 September 1833, to Thomas Walker, Manchester.

45. UM/HR Letter Book, 7 December 1833, Hodgson and Robinson to Paul Campbell, Liverpool; Liverpool, 18 November 1836, Wilder, Pickersgill, and company to Hodgson and Robinson.

46. SAI, Owens' report, 1885, p. 85. "Commerce and General Industry of the Argentine Republic," *Brazil and River Plate Mail*, 23 April 1877, pp. 8-9.

47. SAI, Owens' report, 1885, pp. 88-90, 100.

48. SAI Buenos Ayres, Montevideo, Rosario Notebook, pp. 3-9, 12-15, 59, 71, 103, 120.

49. For specialized consignments see UM/HR, 3 September 1829, Turner, Brade, and Company to Green, Hodgson, and Robinson, B.A.; Rio, 3 September 1833, James Dutton to James Hodgson.

50. The number of introductions included in the house correspondence was numerous. Generally letters of introduction presented a clerk seeking employment, a captain of a ship desiring a cargo, a traveling merchant looking the market over, or a merchant planning to set up business; occasionally a professional person was introduced.

51. BA/HC 4.1.24.4, B.A., 31 August 1852, George White to Barings.

52. AGN/TC, Lego. 189, Thomas Mendenhall resident in Philadelphia gives power of attorney to Zimmermann Frazier y cía. (Zimmermann Frazier contra Banco Nacional).

53. Calculated from shipping data of *British Packet and Argentine News* for the year 1831.

54. *Brazil and River Plate Mail*, 18 July 1876, "Argentine Progress," pp. 6-7.

55. Great Britain, House of Commons, *Sessional Papers*, "Report by Acting Consul Bridgett on the Trade 1894," vol. 72, for Buenos Aires during year 1872; and James R. Scobie, *Buenos Aires: Plaza to Suburb, 1870-1910* (New York: Oxford University Press, 1974), p. 71.

56. BA/HC 4.1.14, B.A., 12 July 1842, Francis Falconnet to Baring Brothers.

57. See the following sources for a discussion of the expansion of port

facilities: Love, *A Five Years' Residence*, pp. 1-5; BA/HC 4.1.24.4, memoranda prepared by George White, "Notes on the State of Buenos Aires, 1852"; BA/HC 4.1.14, B.A., 12 July 1842, Francis Falconnet to Baring Brothers; *Brazil and River Plate Mail*, 8 March 1871, p. 5; PRO/F.O. 6/269, B.A., 23 February 1867, Mathews, Commercial 1867, pp. 7-9; Kroeber, *Growth of Shipping*, pp. 34-35; *British Packet and Argentine News*, 4 October 1834, p. 3. Scobie, *Buenos Aires: Plaza to Suburb*, pp. 70-91, gives a detailed account of the debate and problems in the improvement of port facilities in Buenos Aires.

58. BN/Mss., Treaty between the United Kingdom and the Argentine Confederation for the Free Navigation of the Rivers Paraná and Uruguay, July 10, 1853. Discussion with radio and telegraph operator on a trip down Paraná to Buenos Aires in July 1968. Kroeber, *Growth of Shipping*, pp. 49-52, and Jonathan C. Brown, "Dynamics and Autonomy of a Traditional Marketing System: Buenos Aires, 1810-1860," *Hispanic American Historical Review*, 56, no. 4 (November 1976), 613.

59. BA/HC 4.1.24.4, Notes on the State of Buenos Aires, 1852, on roads. For number of carts entering Buenos Aires, *Brazil and River Plate Mail*, 21 January 1864, pp. 84. For cost of transportation, Burgin, *Economic Aspects*, pp. 116-118, and UM/OO, B.A., 1 April 1846, Wilfred Latham and Company to Owen Owens. Ferns, *Argentine Republic*, p. 33, calculates that in the 1830s and 1840s it was cheaper to send produce from Buenos Aires to Liverpool than from Córdoba to Buenos Aires.

60. Calculation is based on information given in Herbert Gibson, *The History and Present State of the Sheep-Breeding Industry in the Argentine Republic* (Buenos Aires: Ravenscroft and Mills, 1893), p. 185.

61. GPO Packet Report Book 1, no. 66A, 29 June 1808, pp. 81-84; no. 159, 12 April 1810; no. 159A, 12 April 1810.

62. UM/HR, Rio, 29 November 1833, Rostron and Dutton to Hodgson and Robinson, B.A.; UM/OO, B.A., 12 May 1841, Hodgson and Robinson to Owen Owens and Sons, Manchester. UM/HR Letter Book, B.A., 13 October 1838, Hodgson and Robinson to Wildes, Pickersgill, Liverpool.

63. Arthur Wardle, "The Post Office Packets," in *Trade Winds*, ed. C. Northcote Parkinson (London: George Allen and Unwin, 1948), pp. 283-284.

64. GPO Packet Report Book 4, no. 257, 7 November 1823, pp. 658-659; no. 264D, 17 December 1823, pp. 675-676; GPO Packet Report Book 5, no. 37E, 16 August 1824, pp. 69-72.

65. GPO Public Notices and Instructions, no. 48, August 1854; no. 20, April 1873; 22 May 1876, no. 19; 14 November 1878. Also packet 801, 1863, contract signed with Royal Mail Steam Packet, 13 July 1863; Public Notices and Instructions to Postmaster, no. 14, 8 March 1859, concerning contract with Liverpool, Brazil and River Plate Steam Navigation Company; post 29, packet 177, 1872, contract for carrying mails to River Plate; Notices and Instructions to Postmasters, no. 34, 25 July 1870. For a discussion of Royal Mail Steam Packet Company, Liverpool River Plate Steam Navigation Company, and Brazil and River Plate Mail, Post 29 contract packet 209, 1875.

66. See GPO Public Notices and Instructions to Postmasters, for February 1825.

67. GPO Public Notices and Instructions to Postmasters, February 1852, no. 3.

68. PRO/F.O. 6/318, B.A., 14 February 1873, Frank Parish to Carl Granville; PRO/F.O. 6/315, London, 21 August 1873, Commercial General Post Office to Edmund Hammond; GPO post 29, packet 257C, 1877, on the United Kingdom postal convention with Argentina. Also GPO packet 553D, 1878, B.A. 15 January 1878, from Dirección General de Correos y Telégrafos de la República Argentina; PRO/F.O. 6/349, B.A., 8 April 1878, J. P. Harris Gastrell to Marques of Salisbury. *Brazil and River Plate Mail*, 8 June 1876, p. 19.

69. UM/HR Letter Book, B.A., 29 October 1825, Hodgson to C. F. Kalkman, Baltimore.

70. UM/OO, B.A., 28 October 1841, Hodgson and Robinson to Owen Owens; B.A., 22 October 1841, Hodgson and Robinson to Owen Owens.

71. AMB/HD, London, 13 November 1819, MacIntosh, Miller, and Company to Dallas; Santiago, 6 January 1819, Joshua Waddington to Dallas; Rio, 7 May 1819, Gil Fielding and Brander to Dallas; London, 22 August 1829, MacIntosh, Miller, and Company to Dallas; UM/HR Outgoing Letter Book, 26 June 1841, Hodgson to John Jackson and Company, Manchester.

72. PRO/F.O. 354/1, Woodbine Parish papers, 11 December 1823, General Post Office to Parish, B.A., pp. 93-96. GPO post 29, packet 144G 1856, "Particulars of Information Relative to Postal Improvements in the Argentine Confederation as Requested in the Earl of Clarendon's Letter of August 15, 1853."

73. *Brazil and River Plate Mail*, 8 July 1874, p. 3; 22 August 1874, p. 5; 8 July 1876, "Argentine Progress." JRL 1221/1, Liverpool, 26 September 1872, Heald to Milroy.

5. Operating in Argentina

1. Kroeber, *Growth of Shipping*, p. 116, and PRO/F.O. 6/11, Gross Returns of British and Foreign Trade at the Port of Buenos Aires during the Half Year Ending 31 December 1825, Enclosed with a Letter of 5 April 1825.

2. PRO/F.O. 6/153, 2 March 1850, Martin F. Hood to Palmerston.

3. PRO/F.O. 6/153, 2 March 1850, Martin F. Hood to Palmerston. Correspondence of British houses further indicates the inclination of the British to carry on French business: AMB/HD, 31 March 1818, Francis Martin and Company, Havre, to Hugh Dallas, B.A.

4. PRO/F.O. 6/153, B.A., 2 March 1850, Martin Hood to Palmerston.

5. R. A. Humphreys, *Tradition and Revolt in Latin America and Other Essays* (London: Weidenfeld and Nicolson, 1969), p. 143. Humphreys argues that the Anglo-American commercial rivalries in the early years did not exist. However, the examination of the number of United States versus British ships entering the port of Buenos Aires tends to undercut this thesis. In 1825, 99 British ships and 102 United States ships entered Buenos Aires (*British Packet and Argentine news*, 3 August 1833). In 1830, 73 British ships and 83 United States ships entered; and in 1835, 54 British and 51 United States ships entered Buenos Aires.

6. Keen, *David Curtis De Forest*, pp. 40-58, 121-128.

7. Belgium, *Recueil consulaire*, vol. 9, 1863. Italy, *Bollettino Consolare* (Turin: Dalla Tipografia Di G. B. Paravia E. Comp. 1863), vol. 2, p. 880.

8. BA/HC, 16 June 1844, Falconnet; Belgium, *Recueil consulaire*, vol. 9, p. 248. Armstrong papers, Liverpool, 14 July 1835, Middleton to Armstrong; *SAI* Notebook, B.A., pp. 3, 4.

9. UM/HR Letter Book, B.A., 15 April 1836, Hodgson and Robinson to Thomas Broadbent. For further support as to the importance of the political and economic environment in determining decision making, see the general correspondence of James Hodgson or the papers of Baring Brothers.

10. N. L. Watson, *The Argentine as a Market: A Report to the Electors to the Gartside Scholarship on the Results of a Tour in Argentina in 1906-1907* (Manchester: Manchester University Press, 1908), pp. 37-39. Importing and exporting in the later part of the century: Great Britain, House of Commons, *Sessional Papers*, "Conditions and Prospects of British Trade in Certain South American Countries: The Argentine Republic," report by T. Worthington, 1899, vol. 96, p. 487. Early part of the century AMB/HD and UM/HR.

11. For reference to Green, Hodgson, and Robinson partnerships are UM/HR Outgoing Letter Book, the following letters: London, 22 November 1828, James Hodgson to Green and Hodgson; 1 June 1824, Joseph Green to John Robinson, Liverpool; and the agreement between James Hodgson and Mary Green.

12. For the trip of Hodgson to England see the correspondence of James Hodgson, UM/HR Private Letter Book, 2 August 1828-14 October 1829. UM/HR Green and Hodgson Outgoing Letter Book, London, 8 September 1817, James Hodgson to James Rawdon; UM/HR Outgoing Letter Book, Manchester, 8 June 1829, James Hodgson to Green, Hodgson, and Robinson; Hamburg, 19 May 1829, Hodgson to C. G. Becker, Leipzig; Underbank, 30 August 1817, James Hodgson to Joshua Rawdon; London, 7 August 1833, Hodgson to James Redman.

13. UM/HR Outgoing Letter Book, Hamburg, 19 May 1829, Hodgson to C. G. Barker; 15 January 1818, Hodgson to Joshua Rawdon; 30 August 1817, James Hodgson to Joshua Rawdon.

14. UM/OO, B.A., 13 January 1844 and 23 December 1841, Hodgson and Robinson to Owen Owens. See also AMB/HD, particularly the following letters: London, 13 February 1819, Frederic Thiessen to Dallas; Glasgow, 19 March 1819, R. F. Alexander to Dallas.

15. Manchester Central Library 89/1, C1827, James Hodgson to Owen Owens; UM/OO, 29 June 1841, Hodgson and Robinson to Owen Owens; UM/HR Green and Hodgson Outgoing Letter Book, 17 February 1818, James Hodgson to James and Thomas Hodgson; 30 September 1841, Hodgson and Robinson to Owen Owens.

16. UM/OO, B.A., 3 February 1845, Wilfred Latham and Company to Owen Owens. UM/HR Letter Book, B.A., 30 December 1833, Hodgson and Robinson to George Faulkner.

17. UM/HR Letter Book, B.A., 8 June 1841, Hodgson and Robinson to Captain Phillips; 3 July 1841, to Fielden Brothers; AMB/HD, London, 15 February 1819, Thomas Coates to Dallas. Antonio Pillado, *Diccionario*, pp. 10-21, goes into details on exact form of registration of the cargo and the conditions

under which the cargo could be stored.

18. UM/HR Letter Book, 22 November 1828, James Hodgson to Green and Hodgson, B.A.

19. AMB/HD, London, 17 December 1819, Henry Miller to Dallas; London, 24 March 1829, Blanc, Khagen, and Gothen to Dallas gives one example of the problems of the market, while UM/HR, Letter Book, 23 October 1833, Hodgson and Robinson to Daniel Campbell, Liverpool, and 3 July 1841, to Fielden Brothers, give another.

20. UM/HR Letter Book, B.A., 7 July 1838; UM/OO, B.A., 2 December 1841, Hodgson and Robinson to Owens; 30 January 1841, to Owens; UM/HR Letter Book, 7 July 1838, to Fielden Brothers; 22 May 1838, Hodgson and Robinson to Stanley Black and Company, Montevideo; 22 May 1838, to same.

21. Extract from the *Buenos Aires Standard*, 5 February 1876, included in Consul Report PRO/F.O. 6/336; see also Blondel, *Almanaque Político*, 1825, pp. 84-85, for earlier peroid.

22. UM/HR Letter Book, London, 22 November 1828, James Hodgson to Juan; James Hodgson, Private Letter Book, B.A., 22 November 1828, James Hodgson to J. Black and Company, Montevideo, and UM/HR Letter Book, B. A., 27 October 1834, Green and Hodgson to George Faulkner and Company, Manchester; Rio, 11 October 1839, to George Faulkner.

23. UM/HR Letter Book, 28 January 1834, to George Faulkner. Hodgson's underlining.

24. For the discussion of fancy rugs see the following: UM/HR Letter Book, 28 January 1834, to George Faulkner. Also see Letter Book, B.A., 2 December 1834, 23 December 1834, 5 January 1835, 10 April 1835, 19 May 1835, 25 June 1835, 18 July 1835, 17 August 1835, 23 August 1835, 9 September 1835, 16 October 1835, 8 November 1835, 19 December 1835, 19 March 1836, and 22 June 1836, James Hodgson to George Faulkner.

25. UM/HR Letter Book, November 1826, to Green, Hartly, and Tully.

26. See letters in UM/OO pertaining to the *D'Arcy* venture, Santos, 8 December 1840, 7 September 1841, 21 September 1841; 21 September 1841, William Whitaker to James Hodgson, and B.A., 10 June 1841, 16 August 1841; 17 August 1841; 2 September 1841; 21 December 1841, Hodgson and Robsinson to Owen Owens. UM/HR Letter Book, 15 December 1838, 21 June 1841, Hodgson and Robinson to Fielden Brothers.

27. UM/HR, 21 September 1822, James Hodgson to Alexander Brown.

28. For the establishment of commercial relations in Buenos Aires and Europe see Robertson and Robertson, *Letters on South America*, vol. 3, pp. 40-41, 98-101; see also Humphreys, *Tradition and Revolt*, pp. 113-117. An examination of the account sales of Hodgson and Robinson indicates less than half a dozen of the buyers were foreigners. UM/OO, 8 June 1842, 21 December 1841, Hodgson and Robinson to Owen Owens.

29. AMB/HD, Colonia, 17 December 1817, Juan Wilson to Hugh Dallas; for reference to political problems see Maldonado, 10 October 1818, Colin Mackenzie to Dallas.

30. Robertson and Robertson, *Letters on South America*, vol. 1, pp. 174-176, 181-186, 238-239, 251-252, 259-265, 267-268; Michael G. Mulhall, *The En-*

glish in South America (Buenos Aires: Standard, 1878), pp. 58-59.

31. Brown, "Dynamics and Autonomy," pp. 624-629, argues convincingly that Creoles dominated the overland and river trade and operated the warehouses and saladeros.

32. UM/HR, Córdoba, 7 March 1836, John King to Hodgson and Robinson, Yesúa; 15 December 1831, H. L. Jones to James Hodgson. UM/OO, B.A., 1 April 1846, Wilfrid Lathan to Owens.

33. For a discussion of where the merchants procured their produce see AMB/HD, B.A., 23 May 1818, Francisco Delgado receipt for $2,000; B.A., 8 March 1818, Roque del Sar to Dallas; 6 February 1818, McCall to Dallas; 13 August 1819, Saladero to Dallas; JRL 1221/1, Liverpool, 24 February 1874, Heald to Krabbé; *Brazil and River Plate Mail*, 23 April 1877, p. 9; UM/HR Letter Book, 2 August 1828, James Hodgson to Hodgson and Robinson.

34. Blondel, *Almanaque Político*, pp. 83-84. For wool GP 1, 1899-1903, International Trade and the Present Market of Argentina Trade, pp. 8-12.

35. See specifically KW, B.A., 26 September 1853, 27 September 1853, 1 October 1853, 2 November 1853, Krabbé to Darbyshire; UM/OO, B.A., 2 October 1841, Hodgson and Robinson to Owens.

36. AMB/HD, London, 31 January 1818, Thomas and William March to Dallas.

37. AMB/HD, London, 10 April 1818 and 16 March 1818, March to Dallas; AMB/HD, 5 April 1821, Dallas to Collins Brothers, Guernsey; London, 5 May 1818, Henry Miller to Hugh Dallas.

38. AMB/HD, Havre, 31 July 1818, 13 March 1818, Emanuel Bingham to Dallas.

39. See AMB/HD, 18 February 1820, 26 February 1820, Henry Miller to Dallas; UM/HR, Rio, 12 March 1833, 18 April 1833, Rostron and Dutton to Hodgson and Robinson.

40. AMB/HD, 2 April 1818, Henry Miller to Dallas.

41. For further discussion of the speculation see AMB/HD, 7 April 1818, 8 June 1818, 22 July 1818, Henry Miller to Dallas; London, 8 January 1819, MacIntosh, Miller, and Company to Dallas; 7 January 1818, 8 August 1818, 24 November 1818, 15 October 1819, 17 November 1819, Gill, Fielding, and Brandes to Dallas.

42. See the following letters AMB/HD, Rio, 27 April 1817; 13 September 1818; 17 April 1819; 5 May 1819; 2 June 1820, Henry Miller to Dallas; London, 12 October 1820, MacIntosh, Miller, and Company to Dallas; London, 18 November 1818; 21 December 1818, John Symonds to Dallas; UM/HR particularly the Invoice Book and Letter Book, B.A., 2 August 1831, Hodgson and Robinson to Thomas Ellen and Company, Sheffield.

43. UM/HR Green and Hodgson Letter Book, 23 December 1826; Rio, 2 November 1842, Rostron, Dutton, and Company to Hodgson and Robinson.

44. UM/OO, 13 January 1844, Hodgson and Robinson to Owen Owens; BA/HC 4.1.11.1, Manchester, 14 April 1829, Charles Holland to Baring Brothers, London.

45. UM/HR Letter Book, B.A. 17 February 1818, James Hodgson to

Thomas Hodgson; and B.A., 9 May 1838, Hodgson and Robinson to Fielden Brothers.

46. UM/HR Letter Book, 5 May 1838, to Fielden Brothers; 8 August 1831, agreement between Joseph Green and Yates and Company, Liverpool.

47. BA/HC 16, report by Falconnet, June 1844. AMB/HD, London, 3 April 1820, Thomas Coates to H. Dallas.

48. For various types of coastal trade see AMB/HD, Rio, 13 February 1819, Henry Miller to Hugh Dallas; Rio, 23 June 1821, Miller to Dallas; Bahia, 27 June 1820, Miller and Nicholson to Dallas; B.A., 7 November 1819, Dallas to Miller and Nicholson.

49. There was a large amount of correspondence dealing with this type of transaction. For a few examples, see AMB/HD, Rio, 27 August 1817, 5 August 1817, 22 August 1817, 7 July 1817, 7 February 1818, 25 April 1820, Henry Miller to Hugh Dallas.

50. For examples of this type of transaction see AMB/HD, Montevideo, 5 March 1818, Stewart, McCall, and Company to Dallas, Montevideo, 16 May 1818, William Robinson to Dallas; Montevideo, 29 May 1818, William Robinson to Dallas; 1 September 1818, Colin McKenzie to Dallas. *Brazil and River Plate Mail*, 23 April 1877, "Commercial and General Industry in the Argentine Republic."

51. For a discussion of this speculation see the following correspondence: AMB/HD, Santiago, Chile, 26 April 1819, 5 May 1819, 19 May 1819, 30 June 1819, 9 August 1819, 31 August 1819, 4 October 1819, 14 October 1819, 29 October 1819, 12 November 1819, 9 December 1819, 30 December 1819, 31 December 1819, Joshua Waddington of Winter, Brittain, and Company to Dallas; 15 January 1829, Henry Miller to Dallas; 31 July 1819, 26 August 1819, Gil, Fielding, and Brandes to Hugh Dallas.

52. AMB/HD, Rio, 25 March 1820; 7 April 1820; 19 May 1820; Henry Miller and Company to Dallas; Havana, 20 May 1820, Disdier Morphy to MacIntosh, Miller, and Company; London, 2 June 1820, Henry Miller to Dallas; Havana, 24 June 1820, Disdier Morphy to Dallas.

53. See PRO/F.O. 6/153, 1842, 1850; JRL 1221/1, B.A., 18 May 1874, Heald to Milroy; BA/HC, 16, report of White, 1857; AGN/TC Lego. 392, 1847, Expediente que manda formar de oficio sobre las cuentas que presentan los síndicos de todos los concursos.

54. *British Packet and Argentine News*, 26 September 1835, pp. 1-2; 3 October 1835, p. 1; 17 October 1835, p. 2; 12 March 1836, p. 1; AGN/TC Lego. 302, Don M. Langenhein síndico por la fallido de Sebastian Lezica Hermanos & Frederico Hornung 12 September 1837.

55. UL/LB D1, no. 13, 4 December 1878, 15 May 1879, 7 August 1879, 14 August 1879, 21 August 1879, George Warden to B.A. Manager. BA/HC 4.1.65 part 1, B.A., 11 March 1877, Nicolas Bouwer to Baring Brothers.

56. AGN/TC Lego. 57, Concurso acredores a casa fallido Davison & Milner.

57. For examples of court cases see AGN/TC. For the quote from Armstrong see *British Packet and Argentine News*, 28 January 1834, p. 4.

58. For liquidation of Green and Hodgson see UM/HR Letter Book, 13 October 1830, to Robinson; agreement between James Hodgson and Mary Green; Liverpool, 14 December 1831, Green to Hodgson and Robinson. For further discussion of length of liquidations see *British Packet*, 7 May 1831, liquidation of James Noble; for Bates and Stokes, UL/LB, B.A., 25 April 1867, to London.

59. For further information on Bates and Stokes see UL/LB D1, no. 8, London, 12 July 1872, to B.A.; D1, no. 10, 7 May 1875; D1, no. 11, 3 January 1875; D1, no. 12, 3 May 1878; D6, B.A., 26 October 1872, to Montevideo; D35, B.A., 31 August 1878, to London. For Darbyshire and McKinnel see UL/LB D1, no. 12, London, 12 April 1878, 1 May 1878, to B.A. For Black see AGN/TC Lego. 14, Concurso de Guillermo y Juan Black. For Pereira see UM/HR, 7 March 1844, to Owens; UL/LB D35, B.A., 2 March 1874, to London.

60. For Holland see BA/HC 4.1.11.5, Liverpool, 15 August 1831, Charles Holland to Baring Brothers; for Nicholson and Green see UL/LB, B.A., 25 April 1867, 24 April, to London; for Black see AGN/TC Lego. 14, Concurso.

61. For Pereira see UM/OO, 7 March 1844, Hodgson and Robinson to Owens; for Davison Milner see AGN/TC, Lego. 57, 1834-1836, Concurso acreedores a casa fallido Davison Milner.

62. For Black see AGN/TC, Lego. 14, 1837, Concurso.

6. Merchants, British Investment, and the Economic Development of Argentina

1. Rippy, *British Investment*, p. 5.

2. Mulhall, *English in South America*, p. 529.

3. Rippy, *British Investments*, p. 159.

4. Mulhall, *Handbook*, p. 23. Great Britain, House of Commons, *Sessional Papers*, "Argentine Republic," report by Francis Clare Ford, 1867 (3791), vol. 69, p. 320.

5. See particularly Robertson and Robertson, *Letters on South America*; Humphreys, *Tradition and Revolt*, pp. 113-127; James Dodds, *Records of the Scottish Settlers in the River Plate and Their Churches* (Buenos Aires: Grant and Sylvester, 1897), pp. 3-4; Alberto S. J. de Paula, "El arquitecto Richard Adams y la colonia escocesa de Santa Catalina," *Anales del instituto de Arte Americano e Investigaciones Estéticas*, no. 21 (1968), pp. 14-21. Also see BA/H.C. 4.1.3.3, 30 December 1824, Robertson to Baring Brothers; HC 4.1.3.2, ibid; HC 4.1.3.11, 14 December 1827, John Robertson to Baring Brothers, and *Brazil and River Plate Mail*, 22 September 1864, p. 472.

6. BA/HC 4.1.14, Falconnet to Barings, 1844. PRO/F.O. 6/153, report on mercantile houses, 1842, 1850. Navarro Viola, *El Club*, pp. 109-111. Mulhall, *English in South America*, pp. 417-420. *British Packet and Argentine News*, 9 April 1831, p. 1; 9 February 1833, p. 1. *Brazil and River Plate Mail*, 7 June 1864, p. 343; 23 July 1875, p. 4; 8 July 1875, p. 14; 8 March 1876, p. 17. BA/HC 4.1.29, part 3, B.A., 25 August 1863, Thomas Armstrong to David Robertson. AGN/TS 3679, Sucesión de Thomas Armstrong, Thomas Armstrong papers.

7. Navarro Viola, *El Club*, pp. 141-143. AGN/TS, Lego. 6087, Testamentaria de Thomas Gowland, 1876. For Daniel Gowland, *Bolsa de Comercio de Buenos Aires*, p. 70; BA/HC 4.1.14, Falconnet to Barings, 1844. AGN/TS, Lego.

6129, Daniel Gowland.

8. Leland Hamilton Jenks, *The Migration of British Capital to 1875* (New York: Alfred A. Knopf, 1927), pp. 276-278. Rippy, *British Investments*, pp. 17, 20, 224.

9. Marvin D. Bernstein, ed., *Foreign Investment in Latin America: Cases and Attitudes* (New York: Alfred A. Knopf, 1966), pp. 31-33. H. S. Ferns, "Beginnings of British Investment in Argentina," *Economic History Review*, 2nd ser. 4, no. 3 (1952), 342-349. Humphreys, *Tradition and Revolt*, pp. 123-126. BA/HC 4.1.20 part 3, 7 December 1863, David Robertson to John Fair. Barings archives in London and the Barings papers in Ottawa both have extensive material on the loan of 1824. Hugo Raúl Galmarini, *Negocios y política en la época de Rivadavia: Braulio Costa y la burguesia comercial porteña, 1820-1830*. (Buenos Aires: Libreria y Editorial Platero, 1974).

10. AMB Libro de Acuerdos para la Junta de Directores del Banco de Buenos Aires, 15 January 1822, pp. 1-2; Piñero, *La moneda, el crédito*, p. 65.

11. Banco de la Nación Argentina, *El Banco de la Nación Argentina*, pp. 21, 28. AMB Libro de Acuerdos, 18 March 1822, p. 8.

12. Piñero, *La moneda, el crédito*, p. 63.

13. AMB Libro de Acuerdos, 3 September 1824, p. 179; 10 September 1823, p. 49; 9 January 1826.

14. AMB Libro de Acuerdos, 10 September 1824, p. 177.

15. Banco de la Nación Argentina, *El Banco de la nación Argentina*, p.31. PRO/F.O. 6/11, B.A., 26 January 1826, Woodbine Parish to George Canning.

16. Nicolás Casarino, *El Banco de la Provincia de Buenos Aires en su primer centenario, 1822-1922* (Buenos Aires: Peuser, 1922), p. 19.

17. Luis Roque Gondra, *Historia económica de la República Argentina* (Buenos Aires, Editorial Sudamericana, 1943), pp. 334-335. BA/HC 4.1.4.1, B.A., 30 December 1827.

18. AMB Carpeta de Cartas, no. 2, 13 June 1826, p. 35, Banco Nacional to the Ministro de Hacienda. AMB Libro de Correspondencia 24 May 1826, Sebastian Lezica to the bank.

19. AMB Libro de Correspondencia, 24 May 1826, Sebastian Lezica to the bank; ibid., 16 July 1826, p. 45; ibid., 30 March 1826, p. 12.

20. The statutes of the bank are given in Banco de la Nación Argentina, *El Banco de la Nación Argentina*, pp. 46-52, 52-62.

21. AMB Libro de Acuerdos, no. 2, 25 August 1828, p. 239.

22. AMB Libro de Acuerdos, no. 2, 10 December 1827, pp. 159-160; ibid., 9 February 1827, pp. 88-89; ibid., 13 February 1829, p. 413.

23. AMB Libro de Acuerdos, 1826-1830, p. 466.

24. *British Packet and Argentine News*, 24 September 1831.

25. AMB Gran Libro de Accionistas del Banco Nacional, p. 1, 295.

26. Casarino, *El Banco de la Provincia*, pp. 48-49, 52.

27. AMB Archivo 396, B.A., 14 March 1827.

28. *Anuario general comercio*, 1855, p. 59. *Almanaque para el año de Nuestro Señor, 1861* (Buenos Aires: Imprenta de la "Reforma," 1861), p. 22.

29. Joslin, *A Century of Banking*, pp. 19, 20, 30, 33-37.

30. UL/LB D1, no. 12, London, George Warden to manager B. A. branch,

23 February 1878, *Brazil and River Plate Mail*, 7 May 1867, p. 13.

31. Archives of the Bank of London and South America, Buenos Aires, Memorandum and Articles of Association of the London and Buenos Ayres˝and River Plate Bank Limited, 27 September 1862. Ibid, Archives Ledger, Current Accounts, no. 1, 1863-1864.

32. UL/LB D1, no. 6, 8 April 1871, Smithers to B.A. manager.

33. UL/LB D1, no. 9, 8 February 1871, Smithers to B.A. branch.

34. *El Avisador*, 1870, p. 33.

35. Ferns, *Britain and Argentina*, pp. 358-360. Joslin, *Century of Banking*, BA/HC 4.1.29 part 3 section 1858-1862, Ladykirk, Eng., 29 September 1862, John Fair, B.A., to David Robertson.

36. PRO/F.O. 6/293, B.A., 20 June 1870, MacDonell to Earl of Clarendon, dispatch no 27, pp. 196-201.

37. AGN/TS 8739, Federico Wanklyn, 1877; AGN/TC Lego. 170, Eduardo Lumb y Don Federico Wanklyn pidiendo una contrata de sociedad.

38. UL/LB D1, no. 6, 8 April 1871, Smithers to B.A. manager.

39. AGN/TS 8739, Federico Wanklyn, 1877.

40. PRO/B.T. 31/1736-6406 Commercial Bank of the River Plate. UL/LB D1, no. 8, 22 June 1872, 28 June 1872, Smithers to manager of B.A. branch.

41. Pedemonte, *Estado económico y financiero*, pp. 163-164.

42. Ibid., pp. 163-167.

43. Kroeber, *Growth of Shipping*, pp. 3-4, 46, 52, 59-60, 63. *Brazil and River Plate Mail*, no. 7, 1863, p. 8.

44. C. R. Fayle, "Shipping and Marine Insurance," in *Trade Winds*, ed. C. N. Parkinson, pp. 27-28.

45. Herbert Gibson, "British Interests in Argentina," *United Empire*, n.s. 5 (1914), 218.

46. For import-export operations of Carlos and Edward Lumb and their investments in Argentine railroads: Great Britain, House of Commons, *Sessional Papers*, 1878 (1888), vol. 72, p. 15; Octávio C. Battolla, *Los primeros Ingleses en Buenos Aires, 1780-1830* (Buenos Aires: Editorial Muro, 1928), p. 169.

47. Thomas A. Turner, *Argentina and the Argentines: Notes and Impressions of a Five Years' Sojourn in the Argentine Republic, 1885-1890* (London: S. Sonnenschein and Co., 1892), pp. 69-88.

48. I am indebted to Dr. Horacio Juan Cuccorese, who directed me to the correct legajo at the Archivo Histórico de la Provincia de Buenos Aires for material on the Western Railroad. AHP Cámara de Representes, 1854, exp. 144, 48-5-71, decrees and petitions dated 17 September 1853, 19 December 1853, 9 January 1854.

49. Horacio Juan Cuccorese, *Historia de los ferrocarriles en la Argentina* (Buenos Aires: Ediciones Macchi, 1969), p. 12.

50. AMB Libro de Comprobante, Lista de Accionistas del Ferrocarril del Oeste, B.A., 19 February 1863 to 17 November 1863. The personnel at the Archivo y Museo Histórico de Banco de la Provincia de Buenos Aires compiled the list. I am indebted to Alberto S. J. de Paula for sending me a copy.

51. Cuccorese, *Historia de los ferrocarriles*, pp. 9-15. Dr. Cuccorese contends that the Western Railroad was sold because the government desired the

sterling to improve the exchange rate of the paper dollar. However, Cuccorese does not distinguish between the reason the government sought to sell the railroad, and the reasons the shareholders sold the railroad to the government. The 6 percent annual interest in dividends was a low return of capital invested, and this was the highest received. Thus, while Cuccorese's explanation is satisfactory for the government's reasons for selling the railroad, it does not serve to explain the shareholders' reasons. The unprofitable nature of the railroad would have been a factor in their desire to sell it. And the shareholders did hold a majority interest in 1862.

52. *El Avisador*, 1866-1867. *Buenos Aires Standard*, Diamond Jubilee Ed., 1 May 1920, "Great Southern Railway," pp. 101-103. Colin Lewis allowed me access to his notes dealing with the directorates of the Great Southern Railway. His information was based on *Bradshaw's Guide*, 1863, vol. 15, p. 379; 1868, vol. 20, p. 403; 1875, vol. 27, p. 419; 1880, vol. 30, p. 464. *Brazil and River Plate Mail*, 6 March 1866, p. 191; 23 February 1864, p. 143; 22 April 1864, p. 221. BA/HC 4.1.29 part 3, B.A., 26 August 1863, Armstrong to David Robertson.

53. "The River Plate," in *Brazil and River Plate Mail*, 13 December 1870, p. 3. Raúl Scalabrini Ortiz, *Historia de los ferocarriles, Argentinos*, 2nd ed. (Buenos Aires: Editorial Devenir, 1968), pp. 99-101. *Bradshaw's Guide*, 1876, vol. 28, p. 464; 1865, vol. 22, p. 407.

54. PRO/B.T. 31/2781 Northern Railway of Buenos Aires; *Bradshaw's Guide*, 1864, vol. 16, p. 387. Ferns, *Britain and Argentina*, p. 347. Discussion with Colin Lewis. Also see Winthrop R. Wright, *British-Owned Railways in Argentina: Their Effect on the Growth of Economic Nationalism, 1854-1948* (Austin: University of Texas, 1974), pp. 469.

55. "Billinghurst, Mariaño," in *Diccionario Histórico Argentino, 1955*, vol. 2, p. 584. *Registro Oficial del Provincia de Buenos Aires, 1871* (Buenos Aires: Imprenta del Estado, 1871), pp. 766-768.

56. *Brazil and River Plate Mail*, 8 April 1870, p. 15; 22 March 1871, p. 22. "Anglo-Argentine Tramway Companies" *Buenos Aires Standard*, Diamond Jubilee, Ed., 1 May 1929, p. 83. Also see Scobie, *Buenos Aires*, pp. 160-168.

57. Mariluz Urquijo, "Las Sociedades Anónimas," pp. 54-55. *El Avisador*, 1866-1867, p. 111; *Anuario Pillado de la deudo pública y sociedades anónimas establecidas en la República Argentina para 1899*, comp. Ricardo Pillado (Buenos Aires: Imprenta de la Nación, 1899), pp. 188-189, and Irving Stone, "The Composition and Distribution of British Investments in Latin America, 1865 to 1913" (Ph.D. diss., Columbia University, 1962), pp. 81, 277.

58. Grosvenor Bunster *Observations on Captain F. B. Head's Reports relating to the Failure of the Río de la Plata Mining Association, with Additional Remarks, and an Appendix of Original Documents* (London: E. Wilson, 1827), p. 1. Henry English, *A Complete View of the Joint Stock Companies Formed during the Years 1824-1825* (London: Boosey and Sons, 1827), pp. 56-58. Stone, "Composition and Distribution," pp. 41-44.

59. English, *Complete View*, pp. 27-28. Adolfo Dorfman, *Historia de la industria Argentina* (Buenos Aires: Escuela de Estudios Argentinos, 1942), p. 55. Galmarini, *Negocios*, pp. 160-162, lists shareholders in the Famatina Mining Company.

60. José María Mariluz Urquijo, "La industria molinera porteña," pp. 143-151, discusses major steam-operated flour mills in the period 1846-1868.

61. Dorfman, *Historia de la industria*, p. 47. Rippy, *British Investments*, p. 160.

62. Stone, "Composition and Distribution," pp. 116, 135. Belgium, *Recueil consulaire*, vol. 4 (1858), 22 March 1858, report of George Fernau, pp. 356-357. Ferns, *Argentine Republic*, pp. 34-35, argues that the expansion of exports was a stimulus to the increase of local industry. However, his suggestion of 106 factories and 746 workshops employing 2,000 workers in the early 1850s does not prove large investments in industry.

63. Halperín-Donghi, "La expansión ganadera en la campaña de Buenos Aires, 1810-1852," *Desarrollo Económico*, 3 nos. 1-2 (April-September 1963), 68. UM/HR, B.A., 26 October 1832, circular. PRO/F.O. 6/153, list of British Mercantile houses established in Buenos Aires in 1850.

64. Halperín-Donghi, "La expansión ganadera," p. 68. Simon G. Hanson, *Argentine Meat and the British Market: Chapters in the History of the Argentine Meat Industry* (Stanford: Stanford University Press, 1938), pp. 18, 24, 29-31, 53-58, 64, 143-144.

65. Dorfman, *Historia de la industria*, p. 71. Juan E. Richelet, La ganadería *Argentina y su comercio de carnes* (Buenos Aires: J. Lajouane and Co., 1928), pp. 34-46; page 46 gives a list of the directorates of the meat-packing companies.

66. AGN/TS 3679, Thomas Armstrong papers.

67. Mulhall, *English in South America*, pp. 403-406. Drysdale, *Hundred Years*, p. 6. De Paula, "El arquitecto," pp. 13-21.

68. UM/HR, copy of deed to Estancia Río Cuatro in the province of Córdoba.

69. GP1, 1899-1903, International Trade and the Present Market of Argentine Trade. GP Herbert Gibson private letters, vol. 1, 14 January 1904, to A. R. Halme, pp. 279-282.

70. Mulhall, *Handbook*, 1885, pp. 34-35.

71. GP Herbert Gibson private letters, vol. 1, 25 February 1902, to father and brother Thomas, p. 178.

72. Herbert Gibson, *The History and Present State of the Sheep-Breeding Industry in the Argentine Republic* (Buenos Aires: Ravenscroft and Mills, 1893), pp. 7-39. Dorfman, *Historia de la industria*, pp. 49-50.

73. UM/HR, Liverpool, 16 April 1829, Yates and Cox to Green, Hodgson, and Robinson, B.A.

74. GP General Correspondence, September 1927-1934, memoir Sir Herbert Gibson and letter, Herbert Gibson to Thomas Gibson, 25 September 1901.

75. WP letters of 1869-1880 and Yerúa Estancia Company report for year ending 30 April 1880.

76. Rippy, *British Investments*, p. 34.

77. WP Yerúa Estancia Company report for year ending 30 April 1880.

78. According to Wilfrid Latham, *The States of the River Plate, Their Industries and Commerce* (London: Longmans, Green and Co, 1866), pp. 177-185, my estimates on the profits in sheep farming would be conservative.

79. The number of merchants returning to England in the period 1841-1880 is based on information given in Navarro Viola, *El Club*, pp. 107-187. The as-

sumption that a large amont of capital was left in Argentina is based on the observation that those merchants on whom I have specific information tended to leave capital in Argentina in *estancias*, railroads, and mercantile firms.

80. BA/HC, 16 B.A., 1857.

7. British Merchants as Entrepreneurs

1. GP 1, 1899-1903, "International Trade and the Present Market of Argentine Trade," pp. 8-12.

2. Great Britain, House of Commons, *Sessional Papers* "Conditions and Prospects of British Trade," 1899, vol. 96, p. 447.

3. Roland T. Ely, *Comerciantes cubanos del siglo XIX* (La Habana: Editorial Librería Marti, 1960), pp. 21-29, 51-52, 56-58.

4. "Commerce of Cuba," *Hunt's Merchant's Magazine*, 8 (October 1842), pp. 321-322, 330.

5. Richard Pares, *A West India Fortune* (London: Longmans, Green and Co., 1950), p. 179.

6. Ibid., pp. 253-258.

7. Wallis Hunt, *Heirs of Great Adventure: The History of Balfour Williamson and Company Limited* (Norwich, Eng.: Jarrold and Sons, 1951), vol. 1, pp. 25-57. Jay Kinsbruner, *Chile: A Historical Interpretation* (New York: Harper and Row, 1973), pp. 73-111, provides background to British mercantile operations and explains the lack of interest of Chileans in commerce and mining.

8. Hunt, *Heirs of Great Adventure*, pp. 34, 37-38, 45, 56, 77-78, 81-91.

9. Ibid., pp. 131-134.

10. Frank Safford, "Foreign and National Enterprise in Nineteenth Century Colombia" *Business History Review*, 39, no. 4 (1965), 525, provides interest rates for Colombia. PRO/F.O. 6/153, B.A., 2 March 1850, Hood to Palmerston, relates rates for Buenos Aires. Ely, *Comerciantes cubanos*, p. 56, gives interest rates for Europe and Cuba.

11. One of the more interesting recent studies of Argentineans involved in the development of their nation is Hugo Galmarini's *Negocios y política en la época de Rivadavia*. This well documented study proves the influence of Braulio Costa and thirteen other Argentines such as Félix Castro and Miguel de Riglos in the development of Argentine banking, industry, commerce, mining, and land improvement.

12. Burton Benedict, "Family Firms and Economic Development," *Southwestern Journal of Anthropology*, 24, no. 1 (1968), 1-19; Robert Aubey, John Kyle, and Arnold Strickon, "Investment Behavior and Elite Social Structures in Latin America," *Journal of Inter-American Studies and World Affairs*, 16, no. 1 (February 1974), 73-93, emphasize the social relationships of family and friends as offering both constraints and rewards that influence decision making.

Bibliography

Archival Sources

Argentina

The Krabbé and Williamson papers, held by John Lough of Argentina, include both family and business correspondence for the years 1834 to 1872. Of particular relevance for this book was the business correspondence between B. Darbyshire of Liverpool and Charles B. Krabbé of Buenos Aires during the years 1848 to 1853. Señora Justo Dose de Zemborain owns a small collection of accounts, bills, and letters of the merchant Thomas Armstrong. Clement Gibson of Gibson Brothers possesses an extensive collection of papers relating to the family estancia business and mercantile house. Unfortunately, most of the papers for the pre-1880 period have been lost or destroyed. St. John's Pro-Cathedral holds burial records for members of the British community beginning in April 1821, baptism records beginning in September 1825, and marriage records from June 6, 1824. The Office of the British Consul maintains the registers of British subjects in Argentina since 1824. The Bank of London and South America holds the first account books and ledgers of the bank. The Archivo y Museo Histórico del Banco de la Provincia de Buenos Aires retains the commercial correspondence of the British merchant Hugh Dallas. In addition, the archives' material on banking history is abundant and little of it has been adequately used. In the Archivo General de la Nación, material of particular interest includes the Commercial Court records (Tribunales Comerciales), Customhouse records, and tax records. The archives also include other interesting small collections, such as the correspondence of Hullet Brothers, a British merchant bank that carried on business for the Argentine government. The Archivo General de los Tribunales possesses a few collections of will settlements of British merchants. The Archivo Público de Geodesia de la Provincia de Buenos Aires in La Plata has the records of land ownership in the provinces. Each property is carefully measured and mapped. The Archivo Histórico de la Provincia de Buenos Aires, also in La Plata, holds some material on British claims against the Buenos Aires government.

Great Britain

The Wright papers, held by Hugh MacIntyre of Alticry, Port Williams, document interesting descriptions of clerk speculations. The Baring Brothers' archives contain material on credit ratings of mercantile houses and on the political and economic situation in Argentina from 1810 to 1880. The Sun Alliance and London Insurance Group archives provided the material that documented the link between import-export houses and merchant promotion of insurance companies. The Kleinwort, Benson Ltd. archives in Newbury, Berks, retained material on firm credit ratings.

The University of London library holds the extensive collection of the merchant bankers Frederick Huth and Company Ltd., as well as the London and River Plate Bank papers. The University of Manchester has the collection of Hodgson and Robinson firm from 1817 through 1844 and also the papers of the Manchester house of Owen Owens. Both sets include the account currents, day books, and ledgers.

The John Rylands Library in Manchester inherited the diaries and business correspondence of Walter Heald, who served as a clerk in Buenos Aires and later became a partner in a mercantile house. The Guild Hall Library of London has trade circulars and some collections of commerical papers for South America for the post-1880 period. The Bank of England ledgers indicate that a number of British merchants in Buenos Aires held accounts with the bank.

Of the record offices, the Public Record Office of London provides much political and economic information on nineteenth-century British and Argentine relations. Of particular importance are the custom records and the consular reports in the Foreign Office papers. The Liverpool Record Office maintains correspondence of the merchant Henry Eld Symonds, who traded with South America. The Dorset Record Office has the letters that Thomas and Charles Carter wrote from Rio de Janeiro and Buenos Aires in 1809 and 1810.

The Manchester Central Reference Library possesses some business correspondence of the merchant John Owens. The British Library manuscript collection contains a few papers pertaining to the nineteenth-century South American political situation. The H. M. Customs and Excise Library possesses useful volumes on the import and export trade. The General Post Office archives provide material on communications problems in the nineteenth century. The Probate Registry holds the wills on various British merchants who resided in Buenos Aires, such as Thomas Barton and Samuel Puddicombe.

Canada

The Canadian Public Archives in Ottawa owns a small collection of papers from the Baring Brothers archives.

Travel Accounts

Baines, T. H. *Observations on the Present State of Affairs of the River Plate.* Liverpool: Liverpool Times Office, 1845.

Balcarce, M. *Buenos-Ayres: sa situation présente, ses lois liberales, sa population immigrante, ses progrès commerciaux et industriels,* 2nd ed. Paris: A. Blondeau, 1857.

Bateman, John Frederic La Trobe. *Port of Buenos Ayres: Supplemental Report to Señor Don P. Agote, the Minister of Finance of the Province of Buenos Aires on Improved Harbour Accommodation, 8 April 1871.* London: Kell Brothers, 1871.

Beaumont, J. A. B. *Travels in Buenos Ayres, and the Adjacent Provinces of the Río de la Plata. With Observations Intended for the Use of Persons Who Contemplate Emigrating to the Country; or Embarking Capital in Its Affairs.* London: J. Ridgway, 1828.

Brackenridge, Henry Marie. *A Letter on the Present State of That Country to James Monroe, President of the United States.* Washington: Office of National Register, October 15, 1817.

——————·*Voyage to Buenos Ayres Performed in the Years 1817 and 1818 by Order of the American Government.* London: Sir Richard Phillips and Co., 1820.

Bunster, Grosvenor. *Observations on Captain F. B. Head's Reports Relating to the Failure of the Río de la Plata Mining Association, with Additional Remarks and an Appendix of Original Documents.* London: E. Wilson, 1827.

Bustamente, José Luis. *Los cinco errores capitales de la intervención Anglo-Francesa en La Plata.* Buenos Aires: Solar, 1942.

Campbell, Allan. *Introductory Remarks on the Provinces of La Plata, and the Cultivation of Cotton; Paraná and Córdoba Railway, Report of Allan Campbell, esq; Proposal for an Interoceanic Railway between the Río de la Plata and Pacific: Being a Paper Read at a Meeting of the Royal Geographic Society, 23 January 1860.* London: W. M. Watts, 1861.

——————. *Memoire sur l'étude d'une ligne de chemin de fer entre la ville de Córdoba et un point a determiner sur la rivière de Paraná dans la confederation Argentine.* Paris: Imprimerie et Libraires Centrales des Chemins de Fer, 1856.

Darbyshire, Charles. *My Life in the Argentine Republic.* London: Frederick Warne and Co., 1917.

Davie, John Constance. *Letters from Buenos Ayres and Chile.* London: R. Ackermann, 1819.

——————. *Letters from Paraguay: Describing the Settlement of Montevideo and Buenos Aires.* London: G. Robinson, 1805.

Delpech, Emilio. *Una vida en la gran Argentina, relatos desde 1869 hasta 1944.* Buenos Aires: Peuser, 1944.

Dillon, L. A. *Twelve Months Tour in Brazil and in the River Plate with Notes on Sheep Farming.* Manchester: A. Ireland and Co., 1867.

Dodds, James. *Records of the Scottish Settlers in the River Plate and Their Churches.* Buenos Aires: Grant and Sylvester, 1897.

Eastwick, R. W. *The Master Mariner, Being the Life and Adventures of Captain Robert William Eastwick.* London: Fisher, Uneven, 1891.

English, Henry. *A Complete View of the Joint Stock Companies Formed during the Years 1824-1825.* London: Boosey and Sons, 1827.

——————. *A General Guide to the Companies Formed for Working Foreign Mines with Their Prospectuses, Amount of Capital, Number of Shares, Names of Directors.* London: Boosey and Sons, 1825.

Femin, M. César. *Chile, Paraguay, Uruguay, Buenos Ayres.* Paris: Imprimeur-Libraires de l'Institute de France, 1840.

Gerstäcker, Frederick. *Gerstacker's Travels.* London: T. Nelson & Sons, 1854.

Gibson, Herbert. *The History and Present State of the Sheep-Breeding Industry in the Argentine Republic.* Buenos Aires: Ravenscroft and Mills, 1893.

Gillespie, Alexander. *Gleanings and Remarks Collected during Many Months of Residence at Buenos Ayres and within the Upper Country*. Leeds: B. Dewhirst, 1818.

Goodwin, William. *Wheat Growing in the Argentine Republic*. Liverpool: Northern Publishing Company, 1895.

Granada, Nicolas. *Narración del viaje de la comisión Uruguaya*. Montevideo: Imprenta a vapor de la nación, 1886.

Hadfield, William. *Brazil, the River Plate and the Falkland Islands*. London: Longman, Brown, Green, and Longhams, 1854.

———. *Brazil and the River Plate, 1870-76 with Supplement*. London: Edward Stanford, 1877.

Haigh, Samuel. *Sketches of Buenos Ayres, Chile and Peru*. London: Effingham Wilson, Royal Exchange, 1831.

Hammerton, John Alex. *The Real Argentina: Notes and Impressions of a Year in the Argentine and Uruguay*. New York: Dodd, Mead, and Co., 1915.

Head, Sir Francis B. *Rough Notes Taken during Some Rapid Journeys across the Pampas and among the Andes*, 4th ed. London: John Murray, 1846.

Hopkins, Edward A. *Historico-Political Memorial upon the Regions of the Río de la Plata and Conterminous Countries to James Buchanan, President of the United States*. New York: Pudney and Russell Printers, 1858.

Humphreys, R. A., ed. *British Consular Reports on the Trade and Politics of Latin America, 1824-1826*. Camden 3rd Series, vol. 63. London: Royal Historical Society, 1940.

Hutchinson, Thomas J. *Buenos Ayres and Argentine Gleanings: With Extractions from a Diary of Salado Exploration in 1862-1863*. London: Edward Stanford, 1865.

———. *The Paraná; with Incidents of the Paraguayan War, and South American Recollections from 1861 to 1868*. London: Edward Stanford, 1868.

Isabelle, Arsenio. *Viaje a Buenos Aires, Montevideo y Brazil en 1830*. Trans. Pablo Palant. Buenos Aires: Editorial America, 1943.

Johnson, H. C. Ross. *A Long Vacation in the Argentine Alps, or Where To Settle in the River Plate States*. London: Richard Bentley, 1868.

King, John Anthony. *Tales and Adventures in the Argentine Republic with the History of the Country and an Account of Its Conditions, before and during the Administration of Governor Rosas*. London: Longman, Brown, Green, and Longmans, 1852.

Latham, Wilfrid. *The States of the River Plate, Their Industries and Commerce*. London: Longmans, Green and Co., 1866.

Love, George Thomas. *A Five Years' Residence in Buenos Ayres during the Years 1820-1825 Containing Remarks on the Country and Inhabitants; a Visit to Colonial del Sacramento by an Englishman*. London: G. Herbert, 1825.

McCann, William. *Two Thousand Mile Ride through Argentine Provinces: Being an Account of the Natural Products of the Country, and Habits of the People, with a Historical Retrospect of the Río de la Plata, Montevideo and Corrientes*. 2 vols. London: Smith, Elder and Co., 1853.

Mansfield, Charles B. *Paraguay, Brazil and the Plate: Letters Written in 1852-1853*. Cambridge, England: Macmillan and Co., 1856.

Martínez, Carlos. *Buenos Aires: su naturaleza, sus costumbres, sus hombres, observaciones de un viajero desocupado.* Mexico: Tipografía de Augilar e hijos, 1890.

Mayer, Arnold. *Del Plata a los Andes: viaje histórico-pintoresco a través de la República Argentina (en la época de Rosas).* Buenos Aires: Editorial Huarpes, 1944.

Miers, John. *Travels in Chile and La Plata, Including Accounts Respecting the Geography, Geology, Statistics, Government, Finances, Agriculture, Manners and Customs and Mining Operations in Chile Collected during a Residence of Several Years in These Countries.* 2 vols. London: Baldwin, Cradock and Joy, 1826.

Nolte, Vincent. *Fifty Years in Both Hemispheres or Reminiscences of the Life of a Former Merchant.* Trans. from German. New York: Redfield, 1854.

Nuñez, Ignacio. *An Account Historical, Political and Statistical of the United Provinces of the Río de la Plata with an Appendix Concerning the Usurpation of Montevideo by the Portuguese and Brazilian Governments.* Trans. from Spanish. London: Ackermann, 1825.

Ogilvie, Campbell P., ed. *Argentina from a British Point of View and Notes on Argentine Life.* London: Wartheimer Lea and Co., 1910.

Ouseley, William Gore. *Description of Views in South America from Original Drawings Made in Brazil, the River Plate, the Paraná.* London: Thomas McLean, 1852.

Parish, Woodbine. *Buenos Ayres and the Provinces of the Río de la Plata.* London: John Murray, 1852.

Pennington, A. Stuart. *The Argentine Republic: Its Physical Features, History, Fauna, Flora, Geology, Literature, and Commerce.* London: Stanley Paul and Co., 1910.

Robertson, W. P., and J. P. Robertson. *Letters on South America.* 3 vols. London: John Murray, 1843.

Rodney, Caesar Augustus, and John Graham. *The Reports on the Present State of the United Provinces of South America.* London: Baldwin, Cradock, and Joy, 1819.

Rumbold, Horace. *The Great Silver River: Notes of a Residence in Buenos Ayres, 1880-1881.* London: John Murray, 1890.

Shaw, Arthur E. *Forty Years in the Argentine Republic.* London: Elkin, Matthews, 1907.

Turner, Thomas A. *Argentina and the Argentines: Notes and Impressions of a Five Years' Sojourn in the Argentine Republic, 1885-1890.* London: S. Sonnenschein and Co., 1892.

Vidal, E. E. *Picturesque Illustrations of Buenos Ayres and Montevideo.* London: R. Ackermann, 1943.

Webster, Stephen. *Emigration to the River Plate: Success of British Subjects in Buenos Ayres.* London: Bates and Hendy, 1871.

Wilde, José Antonio. *Buenos Aires desde setenta años atrás.* Buenos Aires: Biblioteca de "La Nación," 1908.

Woodgate, C. Frederick. *Sheep and Cattle Farming in Buenos Ayres: With*

Sketch of the Financial and Commercial Position of the Argentine Republic, 2nd ed. London, 1876.

Almanacs, Guides, and Documents

Almanak mercantil o guía de comerciantes para el año de 1802. Madrid: Imprenta de Vega y compañía, 1802.

Almanaque: agrícola, pastoril e industrial de la República Argentina y de Buenos Aires. Buenos Aires: P. Morta, 1865.

Almanaque comerical y guía de forasteros para el estado de Buenos Aires año de 1855. Buenos Aires: Imprenta de la Tribuna, 1855.

Almanaque comercial y guía de los forasteros para 1877. Buenos Aires: Courrier de la Plata, 1876.

Almanaque nacional de la confederación Argentina para los años de 1855 y 1856. Montevideo: Imprenta del Uruguay, 1856.

Almanaque nacional para 1869. Buenos Aires: Imprenta del Siglo, 1868.

Almanaque nacional para 1871. Buenos Aires: Imprenta del Siglo, 1870.

Almanaque para el año de Nuestro Señor 1861. Buenos Aires: Imprenta de la "Reforma," 1861.

Almanaque popular doble, 1864. Buenos Aires: Imprenta de Conl, 1864.

Alvarez, Francisco M. *Tratados de comercio.* Buenos Aires: Casa Editora de Jésus Menéndez, 1922.

Anuario general del comercio de la industria de la magistratura y de la administración de Buenos Aires, 1854 and 1855. Buenos Aires: Imprenta del British Packet, 1854.

Anuario Pillado de la deuda publica y sociedades anónimas establicidas en la República Argentina para 1899. Comp. Ricardo Pillado. Buenos Aires: Imprenta de la Nation, 1899.

Argentine Republic, Comisión Directiva del Censo. *Primero censo de la República Argentina, verificado en los dias 15, 16, 17 de setiembre de 1869.* Buenos Aires: Imprenta del Estado, 1892.

Argentine Republic, Congreso Cámara de Senadores. *Biblioteca de Mayo: colección de obras y documentos para la historia Argentina,* Vols. 1-18. Buenos Aires: Senado de la Nación, 1960-1963.

Argentine Republic, Ministerio de Hacienda. *Cuestión monetaria.* Buenos Aires: Compañía Sud-América de Billetes de Banco, 1905.

Avisador General: La guía de los ferrocarriles, vapores, diligencias, etc. Buenos Aires: Imprenta Buenos Aires, 1870.

El Avisador: guía general de comercio y de forasteros. Buenos Aires: Wenceslao R. Solveyra, 1862, 1863, and 1864, 1866 and 1867.

Beck-Bernard, Charles. *La République Argentine: manuel de L'émigrant et du Cultivateur.* Bern: J. Allemann, 1872.

Blondel, J. J. M. *Almanaque político y de comercio de la ciudad de Buenos Aires para años 1826, 1829, 1830.* Buenos Aires: Imprenta del Estado, 1826, 1829, 1830. Buenos Aires: Imprenta del Estado, 1826, 1829, 1830.

————. *Guía de la ciudad y almanaque de comercio de Buenos Aires para el años*

1833, 1834. Buenos Aires: Imprenta de la Independencia, 1833-1834.

———. *Guía de la ciudad y almanaque de comercio de Buenos Aires para el año de 1836.* Buenos Aires: Imprenta de la Libertad, 1836.

Bollettino Consolare. Ministero per Gli Affari Esteri Di S. M. II Turin: Dalla Tipografia Di G. B. Paravia E. Comp. Vols. 1-16, 1861-1880.

Buenos Aires, Provincia de. *Registro gráfico de la terrenos de propiedad pública y particular de la Provincia de Buenos Aires.* Provincia de Buenos Aires: Departmento Topográfico, 1830.

———. *Impuesto de patentes: registro de los contribuyentes de ciudad de Buenos Aires.* Buenos Aires, 1870.

———. *Registro gráfico, mapa de terrenos de propiedad del Provincia de Buenos Aires.* Provincia de Buenos Aires: Departmento Topografico, 1865.

Buenos Ayres, City of. *Report of the Committee of British Merchants Elected at the General Meeting Held 27th May, 1852.* Buenos Aires: Imprenta del comercio, 1853.

De Angelis, Pedro. *Colección de obras y documentos relativos a la historia antigua y moderna de las provincias del Río de la Plata.* 6 vols. Buenos Aires: Imprenta del Estado, 1837.

Gran guía general comercial de la República Argentina: estadística, agricultura, administración, 1878-1879. Buenos Aires, 1879.

Gran guía general de la República de Argentina, 1873. Buenos Aires: Imp. Litografía y Fundición a vapor de la Sociedad Anónima, 1873.

Great Britain, House of Commons, *Sessional Papers,* 1863-1899.

Guía del comercio y de la industria de la ciudad y Provincia de Buenos Aires. Buenos Aires: Aug de Missolz, 1881.

Handbook of Commercial Treaties. London: Majesty's Stationery Office, 1931.

Mayo documental: documentos para la historia Argentina. Vols. 1-12. Buenos Aires: Universidad de Buenos Aires, Facultad de Filosofia y Letras, 1964.

Mulhall, M. G. and E. T. *The Handbook of the River Plate Republics.* Buenos Aires: M.G. & E. T. Mulhall, 1869, 1875, 1885, 1892.

Pillado, Antonio. *Diccionario de Buenos Aires o sea guía de forasteros.* Buenos Aires: Imprenta del Porvenir, 1864.

Plano comercial y estadístico de la ciudad de Buenos Aires, año 1862. Buenos Aires: Librería de la Revista, 1862.

Plano de la ciudad de Buenos Aires con sus juzgado de paz y parroquias y sus estaciones 1878. Brussels: L. P. Compañía, 1878.

Prado y Rojas, Aurelio. *Leyes y decretos promulgados en la Provincia de Buenos Aires desde 1810 a 1876.* Buenos Aires: Imprenta del Mercurio, 1877.

Recueil consulaire contenant les rapports commerciaux des agents belges à l'étranger. Publíe en exécution de l'arrêté royal du 13 novembre 1855, 1839-1880, vols. 1-35. Brussels: H. Tarlier, 1856-1880.

Registro estadístico del estado de Buenos Aires, 1858-1868. Buenos Aires: Imprenta de la Tribuna, 1858-1872.

Registro gráfico de las propiedades rurales de la Provincia de Buenos Aires construido por el Departmento Topográfico y publicado con autorización del Superior Gobierno de la Provincia, 1864.

Registro nacional de la República Argentina. Buenos Aires: Imprenta del Comercio del Plata, 1851-1880.

Registro oficial de la República Argentina. Vol. 1, *1810-1821.* Vol. 2, *1822-1852.* Buenos Aires: Imprenta de Orale, *1878 and 1880.*

Registro oficial del Gobierno de Buenos Aires. Vols. 1-20 (1821-1840). Buenos Aires: Imprenta del Estado, 1821-1840.

Registro oficial del Provincia de Buenos Aires. Buenos Aires: Imprenta del Estado, 1871-1879.

Ruiz, Francisco. *Gran guía general de comercio de la República Argentina, 1874.* Buenos Aires: Imprenta Lit. y fund de typos de la sociedad anónima, Belgrano, 1874.

Taullard, A. *Los planos más antiguos de Buenos Aires, 1580-1880.* Buenos Aires: Peuser, Editores, 1940.

Torres Gigena, Carolos. *Tratos de comercio de la República Argentina, 1812-1943.* Buenos Aires: Imprenta de la Universidad, 1945.

Newspapers and Magazines

Banker's Magazine (London), 1-30 (1844-1880).

Brazil and River Plate Mail. 7 November 1863 to 23 December 1880.

The British Packet and Argentine News, 1-11 (1828-1848).

Buenos Aires Herald, September 1876-1936.

Buenos Aires Standard, 1 May 1861-1880.

Gaceta de Buenos Aires, 1810-1821.

Merchants' Magazine and Commercial Review, 1-63 (1839-1870).

Revista del Río de la Plata, 1-13 (1871-1877).

Secondary Materials

Acevedo, Carlos Alberto. *Ensayo historíco sobre la legislación comercial Argentina.* Buenos Aires: Alsina, 1914.

Albion, Robert G. "British Shipping in Latin America, 1806-1914." *Journal of Economic History,* 11 (Fall 1951), 361-374.

Alvarez, Juan. *Estudio sobre las guerras civiles Argentinas y el problema de Buenos Aires en la República.* 3rd ed. Buenos Aires: Editorial Universitaria de Buenos Aires, 1936.

————. *Temas de historia económica Argentina.* Buenos Aires: El Atenco, 1929.

Anchorena, Juan José Cristobal de. *Dictamen sobre el establecimiento de una compañía general del comercio en las Provincias Unidas de la Plata.* Buenos Aires: Imprenta de la Independencia, 1818.

Antología histórica de Británicos vistos por ojos Argentinos. Buenos Aires: Nucleo Argentino de estudios históricos, impreso en las Talleres Gráficos de la editorial "Multi-Revista," 1941.

Aubey, Robert, John Kyle, and Arnold Strickon. "Investment Behavior and Elite Social Structures in Latin America." *Journal of Inter-American Studies and World Affairs,* 16, no. 1 (February 1974), 73-93.

Banco de la Nación Argentina. *El Banco de la Nación Argentina en su cincuentenario, 1891-1941.* Buenos Aires: Banco de la Nacion Argentina, 1940.

Banco de la Provincia de Buenos Aires. *Alhensión al sesquicentenario de Revolunción de Mayo 1810 de Mayo 1860.* Buenos Aires: Impreso en las Talleres

Gráficos del Banco de la Provincia de Buenos Aires, 1960.

Barres, Francisco. *Reseña de los ferrocarriles argentinos: principales antecedentes legales y estadísticos, 1857-1944.* Buenos Aires, 1945.

Battolla, Octávio C. *Los primeros Ingleses en Buenos Aires, 1780-1830.* Buenos Aires: Editorial Muro, 1928.

Bealer, Lewis Winkler. *Los corsarios de Buenos Aires: sus actividades en las guerras hispano-Americanas de la Independencia, 1815-1821.* Buenos Aires: Imprenta y Casa Editora, 1937.

Benedict, Burton. "Family Firms and Economic Development." *Southwestern Journal of Anthropology,* 24 (1968), 1-19.

Bernstein, Marvin D., ed. *Foreign Investment in Latin America: Cases and Attitudes.* New York: Alfred A. Knopf, 1966.

Berthold, Victor M. *History of the Telephone and Telegraph in the Argentine Republic, 1857-1921.* New York, 1921.

Besio Moreno, Nicolás. *Buenos Aires: puerto del Río de la Plata, capital de la Argentina: estudio crítico de su población 1536-1936.* Buenos Aires: Talleres Gráficos Tuduri, 1939.

Beverina, Juan. *Las invasiones Inglesas al Río de la Plata, 1806-1807.* Buenos Aires: República Argentina, Taller Gráfico de L. Bernard, 1939.

Bidabehere, Fernando A. *Bolsas y mercados de comercio en La República Argentina.* Buenos Aires: Talleres Gráficos Argentinos, 1930.

Bilbao, Manuel. *Tradiciones y recuerdos de Buenos Aires.* Buenos Aires: Gráf Ferrari Hnos., 1934.

La Bolsa de Comercio de Buenos Aires en su centenario, 1854/ 10 de Julio/ 1954. Buenos Aires: Impreso en la Argentina, 1954.

Bourne, Henry Richard. *English Merchants: Memoirs in Illustration of the Progress of British Commerce.* London: Chatto and Windus, Piccadilly, 1886.

Brady, George S. *Railways of South America.* Part 1, *Argentina.* Washington, D.C.: Government Printing Office, 1926.

Brandenburg, Frank Ralph. *The Development of Latin American Private Enterprise.* Washington, D.C.: National Planning Association, 1964.

Brown, Jonathan C. "Dynamics and Autonomy of a Traditional Marketing System: Buenos Aires, 1810-1860." *Hispanic American Historical Review,* 56, no. 4 (November 1976), 605-629.

Bruce, James. *Those Perplexing Argentines.* New York: Longmans, Green and Co., 1953.

Burgin, Miron. *The Economic Aspects of Argentine Federalism, 1820-1852.* Cambridge: Harvard University Press. 1946.

Bushell, T. A. *Royal Mail: A Centenary History of the Royal Mail Line, 1839-1939.* London: Trade and Travel Publications, 1939.

Cady, John Frank. *Foreign Intervention in the Río de la Plata, 1838-1850.* Philadelphia: University of Pennsylvania Press, 1929.

Cameron, Rondo Emmett. *Banking in the Early Stages of Industrialization: A Study in Comparative Economic History.* New York: Oxford University Press, 1967.

Cárcaño, Ramón J. *Historia de los medios de comunicación y transportes en la República Argentina.* Buenos Aires: Lajouane, 1893.

Casarino, Nicolás. *El Banco de la Provincia de Buenos Aires en su primer centenario, 1822-1922*. Buenos Aires: Peuser, 1922.

Ceppi, José. *Cuadros Sud-Americanos*. Buenos Aires: Librería Universal de Alejandro Miroli, 1888.

Chandler, Charles Lyon. "United States Merchant Ships in the Río de la Plata, 1801-1808, as shown by early newspapers." *Hispanic American Historical Review*, 2 (1919), 26-54.

Cheyney, Edward Potts. *European Background of American History, 1300-1600*. New York: Harper and Brothers, 1904.

Christolow, A. "Great Britain and the Trades from Cádiz and Lisbon to Spanish America and Brazil." *Hispanic American Historical Review*, 27 (1947), 1-29.

————. "Contraband Trade between Jamaica and the Spanish Main, and the Free Port Act of 1766." *American Historical Review*, 22 (1942), 309-343.

Clapp, Brian William. *John Owen: Manchester Merchant*. Manchester: Manchester University Press, 1945.

Cortés Conde, Roberto. *The First Stages of Modernization in Spanish America*. New York: Harper and Row, 1974.

————. "Problemas del crecimiento industriel de la Argentina, 1870-1914." *Desarrollo Económico*, 3, nos. 1-2 (April-September 1963), 143-171.

Cortés Conde, Roberto, and Ezequiel Gallo. "El crecimiento económico de la Argentina: notas para un análisis histórico." *Anuario del Instituto de Investigaciones Históricas* (Univ. Nacional del Litoral, Facultad de Filosofía, Letras y Ciencias de la Educatión, Rosario), 6 (1962-1963), 267-335.

Cuccorese, Horace Juan. *Historia de los ferrocarriles en la Argentina*. Buenos Aires: Ediciones Macchi, 1969.

————. "Historia sobre los orígenes de la sociedad Rural Argentina." *Humanidades* (La Plata) 35 (1960), 23-53.

Cuneo, James A. "Argentina's Banking Structure." *Bulletin of Pan American Union*, 62 (1928), 885-894.

Cuneo, Niccolo. *Storia dell' emigrazione Italiana in Argentina, 1810-1870*. Milan: Garzanti Editore, 1940.

Daireaux, Emile. *La vie et les moeurs a la Plata*. Vol. 1, *La société des villes*. Vol. 2, *Industries et productions*. Paris: Librairie Hachette, 1889.

Díaz Alejandro, Carlos F. *Essays on the Economic History of the Argentine Republic*. New Haven, Conn.: Yale University Press, 1970.

Dickson, P. G. M. *The Sun Insurance Office, 1710-1960: The History of Two and a Half Centuries of British Insurance*. London: Oxford University Press, 1960.

Diffie, Bailey W. *Latin American Civilization: Colonial Period*. Harrisburg, Pa.: Stackpole Sons, 1945.

Dorfman, Adolfo. *Historia de la industria Argentina*. Buenos Aires: Escuela de Estudios Argentinos, 1942.

Drysdale, J. Monteith. *A Hundred Years in Buenos Aires, 1829-1929. Being a Brief Account of St. Andrew's Scots Church and Its Work during the First Century of Its Existence*. Buenos Aires: John A. Geldart, 1929.

Ellis, Aytoun. *Heir of Adventure: The Story of Brown, Shipley & Co., Merchant Bankers, 1810-1960*. London: Burrup, Mathieson and Co., 1960.

Ely, Roland T. *Comerciantes cubanos del siglo XIX.* La Habana: Editorial Librería Marti, 1960.

English Commerce in South America: The Argentine Confederation. London: J. Moore, 1858.

Estévez, Alfredo. "La contribución directa, 1821-1852." *Revista de Ciencias Económicas,* 4th ser. 48, no. 4 (April-June 1960), 123-345.

Fayle, C. R. "Shipping and Marine Insurance." In *Trade Winds,* ed. C. N Parkinson. London: George Allen and Unwin, 1948.

Ferns, Henry Stanley. *The Argentine Republic, 1516-1971.* New York: Barnes and Noble, 1973.

―――. "Beginnings of British Investment in Argentina." *Economic History Review,* 2nd ser. 4, no. 3 (1952), 341-352.

―――. *Britain and Argentina in the Nineteenth Century.* Oxford: Clarendon Press, 1960.

―――. "British Informal Empire in Argentina, 1806-1914." *Past and Present,* no. 4 (November 1953), 66-75.

―――. "The Establishment of British Investment in Argentina." *Inter-American Economic Affairs,* 5, no. 2 (Autumn 1951), 67-90.

―――. "Investment and Trade between Britain and Argentina in the Nineteenth Century." *Economic History Review,* 2nd ser. 3, no. 2 (1950), 203-218.

Ferrer, Aldo. *The Argentine Economy.* Trans. Marjory M. Urquidi. Berkeley, Calif.: University of California, 1967.

Fillol, Tomás Roberto. *Social Factors in Economic Development: The Argentine Case.* Cambridge: M.I.T. Press, 1961.

Fitte, Ernesto. *Historia de un empresito: la emisión de Baring Brothers en 1824.* Buenos Aires: Emece Editores, 1962.

Fleming, C. M., and J. W. Colguhoun, eds. *Book of the Bazaar.* Buenos Aires: Kidd's Printing, 1927.

Ford, A. G. *The Gold Standard, 1880-1914: Britain and Argentina.* Oxford: Clarendon Press, 1962.

―――. "British Investment and Argentine Economic Development, 1880-1914." In *Argentina in the Twentieth Century,* ed. David Rock. Pittsburgh: University of Pittsburgh Press, 1975.

Galmarini, Hugo Raúl. *Negocios y política en la época de Rivadavia: Braulio Costa y la burguesia comercial porteña, 1820-1830.* Buenos Aires: Librería y Editorial Platero, 1974.

Garrigos, O. *El Banco de la Provincia.* Buenos Aires: Imprenta de Pablo, 1873.

Germani, Gino. *Política y sociedad en una época de transición de la sociedad tradicional a la sociedad de masas.* Buenos Aires: Editorial Paidos, 1963.

Gibbs, John Arthur. *The History of Antony and Dorothea Gibbs and of Their Contemporary Relatives, Including the History of the Origin and Early Years of the House of Antony Gibbs and Sons.* London: St. Catherine Press, 1922.

Giberti, Horacio C. E. *Historia económica de la ganadería Argentina.* Buenos Aires: Editorial Raigal, 1954.

Gibson, Herbert. "British Interests in Argentina." *United Empire,* n.s. 5 (1914), 211-229.

Glade, William P. *The Latin American Economies: A Study of Their Institutional Evolution*. New York: Van Nostrand, 1969.

Goebel, Dorothy Burne. "British Trade to the Spanish Colonies, 1796-1823." *American Historical Review*, 43 (June 1938), 288-320.

Gori, Gastón. *Immigración y colonización en la Argentina*. Buenos Aires: Eudeba Editorial Universitaria, 1964.

Graham, G. S., and R. A. Humphreys, eds. *The Navy and South America, 1807-1823: Correspondence of the Commanders-in-chief in the South American Station*. London: Navy Records Society, 1962.

Graham, Richard. "Sepoys and Imperialists: Techniques of British Power in Nineteenth Century Brazil." *Inter-American Economic Affairs*, 23, no. 2 (Autumn 1969), 23-37.

Halls Kay-Shuttleworth, Nina L. *A Life of Sir Woodbine Parish*. London: Smith, Elder and Co., 1910.

Halperín-Donghi, Tulio. "La expansión ganadera en la campaña de Buenos Aires, 1810-1852." *Desarrollo Económico*, 3 nos. 1-2 (April-September, 1963), 57-111.

————. *Politics, Economics and Society in Argentina in the Revolutionary Period*. Trans. Richard Southern. Latin America Studies, no. 18. New York: Cambridge University Press, 1975.

————. "La Revolución y la crisis de la estructura mercantil colonial en el Río de la Plata." *Estudios de historia social* (Buenos Aires: Universidad de Buenos Aires, Facultad de Filosofia y Letras, Centro de Estudios de Historia Social), 2 no. 2 (April 1966), 78-125.

Halsey, Frederic M. *Investments in Latin America and the British West Indies*. Special Agents Series, no. 169. Washington, D.C.: Department of Commerce, Government Printing Office, 1918.

Hanson, Simon G. *Argentine Meat and the British Market: Chapters in the History of the Argentine Meat Industry*. Stanford: Stanford University Press, 1938.

Harratt, Juan. *Estudios prácticos sobre la cría y refinamiento del ganado lanar*. Buenos Aires: Tipográfico de la Pampa, 1885.

Harris, J. R., ed. *Liverpool and Merseyside: Essays in the Economic and Social History of the Port and Its Hinderland*. London: Frank Cass and Co., 1969.

Heaton, Herbert. "A Merchant Adventurer in Brazil, 1808-1818." *Journal of Economic History*, 6 (May 1946), 1-23.

Heras, Carlos. "Notas sobre los porteños y la libre navegación despúes de Caseros." *Humanidades* (La Plata), 2nd ser. 25 (1936), 5-39.

Hernando, Diana. "Casa y Familia: Spatial Biographies in Nineteenth Century Buenos Aires." Ph.D. diss., University of California, Los Angeles, 1973.

Hidy R. W. *The House of Baring in American Trade and Finance: English Merchant Bankers at Work, 1763-1861*. Cambridge: Harvard University Press, 1949.

Hipwell, H. Hallam. "Trade Rivalries in Argentina." *Foreign Affairs* (October 1929), 150-154.

Hobsbawm, E. J. *Industry and Empire: An Economic History of Britain since*

1870. London: Weidenfeld and Nicolson, 1968.

Humphreys, R. A. *Liberation in South America, 1806-1827: The Career of James Paroissien.* London: Athlone Press, 1952.

————. *Tradition and Revolt in Latin America and Other Essays.* London: Weidenfeld and Nicolson, 1969.

Hunt, Wallis. *Heirs of Great Adventure: The History of Balfour Williamson and Company Limited.* Vol. 1, *1851-1901.* Vol. 2, *1901-1951.* Norwich, Eng.: Jarrold and Sons, 1951, 1960.

Imaz, José Luis De. *Los que mandan.* Buenos Aires: Eudeba, 1964.

Ingenieros, José. *Sociología Argentina.* Buenos Aires: Editorial Lasada, 1946.

Irazusta, Julio. *Balance de siglo y medio, 1810-1960.* Buenos Aires: Ediciones Theoría, 1966.

————. *Influencia económica Británica en el Río de la Plata.* Buenos Aires: Editorial Universitaria de Buenos Aires, 1963.

Irazusta, Rodolfo, and Julio Irazusta. *La Argentina y el imperialismo Británico: los eslabones de una cadena, 1806-1833.* Buenos Aires: Editorial Tor, 1934.

Jenks, Leland Hamilton. *The Migration of British Capital to 1875.* New York: Alfred A. Knopf, 1927.

John, Arthur Henry. *A Liverpool Merchant House: Being the History of Alfred Booth and Company, 1863-1958.* London: George Allen, Unwin, 1959.

Joslin, David. *A Century of Banking in Latin America.* London: Oxford University Press, 1963.

Keen, Benjamin. *David Curtis De Forest and the Revolution of Buenos Aires.* New Haven: Yale University Press, 1947.

Kinsbruner, Jay. *Chile: A Historical Interpretation.* New York: Harper and Row, 1973.

Knight, Franklin W. "Origins of Wealth and Sugar Revolution in Cuba, 1750-1850." *Hispanic American Historical Review,* 57, no. 2 (May 1977), 231-253.

Koebel, William Henry. *British Exploits in South America: A History of British Activities in Exploration, Military Adventure, Diplomacy, Science, and Trade in Latin America.* New York: Century Co., 1917.

————. *South America: An Industrial and Commercial Field.* London: T. Fisher Unwin, 1918.

Körner, Karl Wilhelm. "El Consul Zimmermann, su actuación en Buenos Aires, 1815-1847." *Boletín del Instituto de Historia Argentina, "Dr. Emilio Ravignani,"* 2nd ser. 7-8, nos. 11-13 (1966), 3-166.

Kroeber, Clifton B. *The Growth of the Shipping Industry in the Río de la Plata Region, 1794-1860.* Madison: University of Wisconsin Press, 1957.

Kuczynski, Robert R. "Freight Rates on Argentine and North American Wheat." *Journal of Political Economy,* 10, no. 3 (June 1902), 333-360.

Lamas, Andrés. *Estudio histórico y científico del Banco de la Provincia de Buenos Aires.* Buenos Aires: El Nacional, 1886.

————. "La Primera iniciativa para la creación de un banco de descuentos y una compañía de seguros marítimos en Buenos Aires." *Revista del Río de la Plata,* 5 (1873), 651-656.

Latzina, Francisco. *The Argentine Republic as a Field for European Emigration.* Buenos Aires: Lithographic and Printing Establishment, 1883.

————. *Estadística retrospectiva del comercio exterior Argentino 1875-1904.* Buenos Aires: Compañía Sud-América de Billetes de Banco, 1905.

————. *Sinopsis estadística Argentina.* Buenos Aires: Compañía Sud-América de Billetes de Banco, 1914.

Levene, Ricardo. *Historia de la nación Argentina: desde los orígenes hasta la organización definitiva en 1862,* 3rd ed., 11 vols. Buenos Aires: El Ateno, 1963.

————. *Investigaciones acerca de la historia económica del Virreinato del Plata.* Buenos Aires: El Ateneo, 1952.

Levin, Jonathan V. *The Export Economies: Their Pattern of Development in Historical Perspective.* Cambridge: Harvard University Press, 1960.

Lewis, Colin. "Problems of Railway Development in Argentina, 1857-1890." *Inter-American Economic Affairs,* 22, no. 2 (Autumn 1968), 55-75.

Lugones, Leopoldo. *La Grande Argentina,* 2nd ed. Buenos Aires: Editorial Huemul, 1962.

Lynch John. *Spain under the Hapsburgs.* Vol. 1, *Empire and Absolutism, 1516-1598.* Oxford: Basil Blackwell, 1964.

————. *Spain under the Hapsburgs.* Vol. 2, *Spain and America, 1598-1700.* New York: Oxford University Press, 1969.

————. *The Spanish-American Revolutions, 1808-1826.* New York: W. W. Norton and Co., 1973.

Mafud, Julio. *Èl desarrollo Argentino: clave Argentina para un estudio social americano,* 2nd ed. Buenos Aires: Editorial Americalee, 1966.

Mariluz Urquijo, José María. "Aspectos de la política proteccionista durante la década 1810-1820." *Boletín de la Academia Nacional de la Historia,* 37 (1965), 115-154.

————. "El capital y la técnica en la industria porteña 1810-1835." *Boletín de la Academia Nacional de la Historia,* 36 (1965), 69-93.

————. *Estado e industria, 1810-1862.* Buenos Aires: Ediciones Mucchi, 1969.

————. "La industria molinera porteña a mediedo del siglo XIX." *Boletín de la Academia Nacional de la Historia,* 39 (1966), 143-151.

————. "Los matrimonias entre personas de differente religión ante el derecho patrio Argentina." *Instituto de Historia del Derecho Conferencias y Comunicaciones,* 22 (1948), 17-46.

————. "El plan y bases del código de comerochileno expuestos en cuadro sinóptico de Juan B. Alberdi." *Revista del Instituto de Historia del Derecho* (Buenos Aires Universidad Facultad de Derecho y Ciencias Sociales), no. 6 (1954), 107-111.

————. "Protección y librecambio durante el period 1820-1835." *Boletín de la Academia Nacional de la Historia,* 34, no. 2 (1963), 699-717.

————. "La regulación del aprendizaje industrial en Buenos Aires, 1810-1835." *Revista del Instituto de Historia Derecho, "Dr. Ricardo Levene"* (Buenos Aires Universidad Facultad de Derecho y Sciencias Sociales), no. 14 (1963), 59-86.

————. "Las sociedades anónimas en Buenos Aires antes del código de comercio." *Revista del Instituto de Historia del Derecho, "Dr. Ricardo Levene"* (Buenos Aires Universidad Facultad de Derecho y Ciencias Sociales), no. 16

(1965), 31-74.

Marriner, Sheila. *Rathbones of Liverpool, 1845-1873.* Liverpool: Liverpool University Press, 1961.

Mosk, Sanford. "Latin America and the World Economy, 1850-1914." *Inter-American Economic Affairs,* 2 (1948), 53-82.

Mulhall, Michael G. *The English in South America.* Buenos Aires: Standard, 1878.

Navarro Viola, Jorge. *El Club de residentes extranjeros: breve reseña histórica homenaje a sus fundadores.* Buenos Aires: Imprenta y Casa Editora, 1941.

Naylor, Bernard. *Accounts of Nineteenth Century South America: An Annotated Checklist of Works by British and United States Observers.* London: Athlone Press, 1969.

Nicolau Juan Carlos. *Antecedentes para la historia de la industria Argentina: la industria durante la colonial: la industria Argentina de 1810 a 1835.* Buenos Aires, 1968.

Ochoa, Pedro. "La Política comercial durante la organización nacional, 1862-1880." *Revista de Ciencias Económicas,* 2nd ser. 15 (1927), 305-325.

Oddone, Jacinto. *El factor económico en nuestras luchas civiles.* Buenos Aires: Imprenta y Editorial, "La Vanguardia," 1937.

Oritz, Ricardo M. *Historia económica de la Argentina, 1850-1930.* 2 vols. Buenos Aires: Editorial Raigal, 1955.

Pares, Richard. *A West India Fortune.* London: Longmans, Green and Co., 1950.

Parish, George. "Great Britain's Capital Investments in Individual Colonial and Foreign Countires." *Journal of the Royal Statistical Society,* 74, no. 2 (January 1911), 1867-1920.

Parkinson, C. Northcote, ed. *The Trade Winds: A Study of British Overseas Trade during the French Wars 1793-1815.* London: George Allen and Unwin, 1948.

Paula, Alberto S. J. de. "El arquitecto Richard Adams y la colonia escocesa de Santa Catalina." *Anales del Instituto de Arts Americano e investigaciones estética,* no. 21 (1968), 5-32.

Payne, Peter F. *British Commercial Institutions.* London: George G. Harrap & Co., 1961.

Pedemonte, Gotardo C. *Estado económico y financiero de las compañías Argentinas de seguros: informaciones, notas, financieras, reseñas retrospectivas, balances. Recopilación comentada destinada a la exposición ibero americana de Sevilla.* Buenos Aires: Talleres gráficos A. Pedemonte, 1929.

Pinedo, Federico. *Siglo y media de economía Argentina.* Mexico: Centro de Estudios Monetarios Latinoamericanos, 1961.

Piñero, Norberto. *La moneda, el crédito y los bancos en la Argentina.* Buenos Aires: James Menendez, 1921.

Platt, D. C. M. "British Diplomacy in Latin America since Emancipation." *Inter-American Economic Affairs,* 21 (1967), 21-41.

―――. *Finance, Trade, and Politics in British Foreign Policy, 1815-1914.* London: Oxford University Press, 1968.

―――. *Latin America and British Trade 1806-1914.* New York: Barnes & Noble, 1973.

Pratt, E. J. "Anglo-American Commercial and Political Rivalry on the Plata, 1820-1830." *Hispanic American Historical Review*, 11, no. 3 (August 1931), 302-335.

Puentes, Gabriel A. *La intervención francesa en el Río de la Plata*. Buenos Aires: Ediciones Theoría, 1958.

Puigbó, Raúl. *Historia social y económica Argentina*. Part 1, *De la colonia a la immigración*. Buenos Aires: Ediciones Esnaola, 1964.

Puiggros, Rodolfo. *Historia económica el Río de la Plata*. Buenos Aires: A Peña Lillo, 1946.

Ramm Doman, Roberto A. *Política monetaria y bancaria en la Argentine*. Buenos Aires: Imprenta Guillermo Kraft, 1914.

Ramsay, G. D. *English Overseas Trade during the Centuries of Emergence: Studies in Some Modern Origins of the English Speaking World*. London: Macmillan Co., 1957.

Razori, Amilcar. *Historia de la ciudad Argentina*. Buenos Aires: Imprenta Lopez, 1945.

Rebora, Juan Carlos. *Desenvolvemiento de la economía general*. La Plata: Talleres la Popular, 1911.

———. "La finanzas de Buenos Aires." Ph.D. diss., Universidad de Buenos Aires, 1911.

Redford, Arthur. *Manchester Merchants and Foreign Trade, 1794-1858*. Manchester: Manchester University Press, 1934.

Rennie, Ysabel. F. *Argentine Republic*. New York: Macmillan Co., 1945.

Richelet, Juan E. *La ganadería Argentina y su comercio de carnes*. Buenos Aires: J. Lajouane and Co., 1928.

Rippy, J. Fred. *British Investments in Latin America: A Case Study in the Operations of Private Enterprise in Retarded Regions*. Hamden, Conn.: Archon Books, 1966.

———. "French Investments in Argentina and Brazil." *Political Science Quarterly*, 64 (December 1949), 560-578.

———. "German Investments in Argentina." *Journal of Business of the University of Chicago*, 21 (1948), 50-54.

———. "Investments of Citizens of the United States in Latin America." *Journal of Business of the University of Chicago*, 22 (1949), 17-29.

———. *Latin America and the Industrial Revolution*. New York: G. P. Putnam's Sons, 1944.

———. *Rivalry of the United States and Great Britain over Latin America, 1808-1830*. Baltimore: Johns Hopkins Press, 1929.

Roberts, Carlos. *Las invasiones inglesas del Río de la Plata 1806-1807 y la influencia inglesa en la independencia y organización de la provincias del Río de la Plata*. Buenos Aires: Talleres Gráficos, 1938.

Robinson, Howard. *Carrying British Mails Overseas*. London: George Allen and Unwin, 1964.

Rogind, Williams. *Historia del Ferrocarril Sud*. Buenos Aires: Gráfico Argentino, 1937.

Roque Gondra, Luis. *Historia económica de la República Argentine*. Buenos Aires: Editorial Sudamericana, 1943.

Rosa, José María. *Defensa y pérdida de nuestra independencia económica.* Buenos Aires: Librería Huemul, 1943.

Safford, Frank R. "Foreign and National Enterprise in Nineteenth Century Colombia." *Business History Review,* 39, no. 4 (1965), 503-526.

Salaverria, José M. *Paisajes Argentinos.* Barcelona: Gustavo Gili, 1918.

Sanchez Viamonte, Carlos. *El pensamiento liberal Argentino en el siglo XIX: tres generaciones históricas.* Buenos Aires: Ediciones Gure S. R. L., 1957.

Sarmiento, D. F. *Life in the Argentine Republic in the Days of the Tyrants.* Trans. from Spanish. New York: Collier Books, 1961.

Scalabrini Ortiz, Raúl. *Historia de los ferrocarriles Argentinos,* 2nd. ed. Buenos Aires: Editorial Devenir, 1958.

————. *Política Británica en el Río de la Plata.* Buenos Aires: Editorial plus Ultra, 1965.

Scobie, James R. *Argentina: A City and a Nation.* New York: Oxford University Press, 1964.

————. "Buenos Aires as a Commercial-Bureaucratic City, 1880-1910: Characteristics of a City's Orientation." *American Historical Review,* 77, no. 4 (October 1972), 1035-1073.

————. *Buenos Aires: Plaza to Suburb, 1870-1910.* New York: Oxford University Press, 1974.

————. "Monetary Developments in Argentina, 1852-1865." *Inter-American Economic Affairs,* 8 no. 2 (Autumn 1954), 54-83.

————. *Revolution on the Pampas: A Social History of Argentine Wheat, 1860-1910.* Austin: University of Texas Press, 1964.

Sergio Villalobos, R. *Comercio y contrabando en el Río de la Plata y Chile, 1700-1811.* Buenos Aires: Eudeba, Editorial Universitaria, 1965.

Simpson, J. Dyer. *The Liverpool and London and Globe—Our Centenary Year.* Liverpool, 1963.

Smith, Peter H. *Politics and Beef in Argentina: Patterns of Conflict and Change.* New York: Columbia University Press, 1969.

Soares, Ernesto E. *Ferrocarriles Argentinos: sus orígines, antecedentes legales, leyes, que los rigen y reseñas estadísticas.* Buenos Aires: Compañía Impresora Argentina, 1937.

Socolow, Susan Migden. "Economic Activities of the Porteño Merchants: The Viceregal Period." *Hispanic American Historical Review,* 55, no. 1 (February 1975), 1-24.

Solberg, Carl. *Immigration and Nationalism: Argentina and Chile, 1890-1914.* Austin: University of Texas Press, 1970.

Stone, Irving. "The Composition and Distribution of British Investment in Latin America, 1865 to 1913." Ph.D. diss., Columbia University, 1962.

Tamagno, Roberto. *Sarmiento, los liberales y el imperialismo inglés.* Buenos Aires: A Peña Lillo, 1963.

Terry, José Antonio. *Contribución a la historia financiera de la República Argentina.* Buenos Aires: La Nación, 1910.

Tjarks, German O. E. *El consulado de Buenos Aires y sus protecciones en la historia del Río de la Plata.* 2 vols. Buenos Aires: Universidad de Buenos Aires, Facultad de Filosofia y Letras, 1962.

Tjarks, German O. E., and Alicia Vidaurreta. *El comercio inglés y el contrabando: nuevos aspectos en el estudio de la política económica en el Río de la Plata, 1807-1810.* Buenos Aires, 1962.

Tornquist, Ernesto, and Co. *The Economic Development of the Argentine Republic in the Last Fifty Years.* Buenos Aires: Tornquist and Co., 1919.

Trifilo, Samuel Samuel. *La Argentina vista por viajeros ingleses: 1810-1860.* Buenos Aires: Ediciones Gure, 1959.

United Nations, Economic Commission for Latin America. *The Economic Development of Latin America and Its Principal Problems.* Lake Success, N.Y.: United Nations, Department of Economic Affairs, 1950.

Vedia, Agustin de. *El banco nacional: historia financiera de la República Argentina, 1811-1854.* Buenos Aires: Félix Lajouane, 1890.

Wardle, Arthur C. "The Post Office Packets." In *Trade Winds,* ed. C. Northcote Parkinson. London: George Allen and Unwin, 1948.

Watson, N. L. *The Argentine as a Market: A Report to the Electors to the Gartside Scholarship on the Results of a Tour in Argentina in 1906-1907.* Manchester: Manchester University Press, 1908.

Wedovoy, Enrique. *Manuel José de Lavarden: nuevo aspecto del comercio en el Río de la Plata.* Buenos Aires: Editorial Raigal, 1955.

Williams, David M. "Merchanting in the First Half of the Nineteenth Century: The Liverpool Timber Trade." *Business History,* 8, no. 2 (July 1966), 103-121.

Williams, John H. *Argentine International Trade under Inconvertible Paper Money, 1880-1890.* Cambridge: Harvard University Press, 1920.

Williams, Judith Blow. "The Establishment of British Commerce with Argentina." *Hispanic American Historical Review,* 15, no. 1 (February 1935), 43-64.

Whitaker, Arthur P. *Argentina.* Englewood Cliffs, N.J.: Prentice Hall, 1964.

Wright, Winthrop R. *British-Owned Railways in Argentina: Their Effect on the Growth of Economic Nationalism, 1854-1948.* Institute of Latin American Studies, Latin American Monographs, no. 34. Austin: University of Texas Press, 1974.

Young, G. K. *Merchant Banking Practice and Prospects.* London: Weidenfeld and Nicholson, 1966.

Zinny, Antonio. "Censo de la ciudad de Buenos Aires." *Revista Argentina,* 13 (1872), 479-495.

Index

HARVARD STUDIES IN BUSINESS HISTORY

*Out of print.